Critical Reflexive Research Methodologies

Studies in Critical Social Sciences Book Series

Haymarket Books is proud to be working with Brill Academic Publishers (www.brill.nl) to republish the *Studies in Critical Social Sciences* book series in paperback editions. This peer-reviewed book series offers insights into our current reality by exploring the content and consequences of power relationships under capitalism, and by considering the spaces of opposition and resistance to these changes that have been defining our new age. Our full catalog of *SCSS* volumes can be viewed at https://www.haymarketbooks.org/series_collections/4-studies-in-critical-social-sciences.

Series Editor
David Fasenfest (York University, Canada)

Editorial Board
Eduardo Bonilla-Silva (Duke University)
Chris Chase-Dunn (University of California–Riverside)
William Carroll (University of Victoria)
Raewyn Connell (University of Sydney)
Kimberlé W. Crenshaw (University of California–LA and Columbia University)
Heidi Gottfried (Wayne State University)
Alfredo Saad-Filho (King's College London)
Chizuko Ueno (University of Tokyo)
Sylvia Walby (Lancaster University)
Raju Das (York University)

CRITICAL REFLEXIVE RESEARCH METHODOLOGIES

Interdisciplinary Approaches

EDITED BY
DAWN ONISHENKO
NOB DORAN
ROSE ANN TORRES
DIONISIO NYAGA

Haymarket Books
Chicago, IL

First published in 2023 by Brill Academic Publishers, The Netherlands
© 2023 Koninklijke Brill NV, Leiden, The Netherlands

Published in paperback in 2024 by
Haymarket Books
P.O. Box 180165
Chicago, IL 60618
773-583-7884
www.haymarketbooks.org

ISBN: 979-8-88890-346-9

Distributed to the trade in the US through Consortium Book Sales and Distribution (www.cbsd.com) and internationally through Ingram Publisher Services International (www.ingramcontent.com).

This book was published with the generous support of Lannan Foundation, Wallace Action Fund, and the Marguerite Casey Foundation.

Special discounts are available for bulk purchases by organizations and institutions. Please call 773-583-7884 or email info@haymarketbooks.org for more information.

Cover design by Jamie Kerry and Ragina Johnson.

Printed in the United States.

Library of Congress Cataloging-in-Publication data is available.

Contents

Acknowledgements IX
List of Figures X
Notes on Contributors XI

Introduction 1
 Dawn Onishenko, Nob Doran, Rose Ann Torres and Dionisio Nyaga

PART 1
Critical Review of Qualitative Research Approaches

1 Making Research Black and Strange
  Why History Matters in the Current Disappearing World 9
  Dionisio Nyaga

2 Grounded Theory: Effects of COVID-19 on Homeless Youth
  Methodological Reflections 22
  Dionisio Nyaga, Dawn Onishenko and Rose Ann Torres

3 Reflexivity, Recursion and Re-evaluation
  Some Reflections On 'Institutional Ethnography' 34
  Nob Doran

PART 2
Overview of Critical Reflexive Research Methodologies

4 Resisting through Research
  Developing a Qualitative "Mixed Methods" Approach in Research with Sex Workers 71
  Laura Winters

5 Beyond Codified Logics of Ethics
  Jungle and the Ethics of Non-violence 87
  Dionisio Nyaga

6   Africa beyond Africa
Afro-pessimism as an Ethical Demand   98
       Waywaya Nyaga and Dionisio Nyaga

7   Markets Logics in Research Process and the Denigration of Black Bodies   121
       Dionisio Nyaga

PART 3
Critical Reflexive Research Methods

8   Teaching to the Tensions
Pushing the Boundaries of Qualitative Social Work Research   135
       Susan Preston, Susan Silver and Purnima George

9   Qualitative Research as Resistance
The Use of Vignettes to Support Situated Knowledge and the Deconstruction of Colonial Policies   160
       Laura Wyper

10   Remembering in Research
Doing Research in Asian Communities   174
       Rose Ann Torres

11   Application of Research to Africa's Peace and Security Conundrum
The Ethical and Moral Divide between the Ideal and Real   190
       Michael Sitawa

PART 4
Reflexivity and Ethics

12   Ethics of Doing Research in the Indigenous Community   213
       Rose Ann Torres

13   A Reflexive Gaze on Qualitative Policy Research
Deconstructing Traditional Policy Research with the Interface of Youth-Voice and Arts-Based Focus Groups   223
       Dawn Onishenko and Julie Erbland

14 A Co-constructed Critical Autoethnographical Conversation with Social Work Students regarding Reflexive Research Engagement   240
    Marco Giuliani, Michelle Brochu, Albina Magomedova, Michelle Boehm and Dawn Onishenko

15 Arendtian Phenomenology of Politics   267
    Lawrence Ofunja Kangei

    Index   283

Acknowledgements

Dawn Onishenko: I would like to acknowledge the various communities and individuals who have facilitated my personal reflexive engagement with the research process. I would also like to acknowledge my co-editors and book contributors for their critical engagement with research methods and willingness to go on a reflexive journey in the development of this book.

Nob Doran: First, I wish to thank Paul Drew for his initial inspiration with regard to taking 'reflexivity' seriously. His undergraduate lectures were truly amazing in this regard. Also, I would like to thank Rose, Dionisio and Dawn for their tremendous enthusiasm and collegiality throughout the production of this text. The Maritime Inter-Disciplinary Arts Seminar (MIDAS) also needs to be thanked for providing us with a forum in which to discuss some of the issues being raised in this volume. As always, the unwavering support of Dayle, Pat, Carm, Gez, Shaz and Bren is truly appreciated. Finally, an enormous debt of gratitude is owed to the late Dorothy E. Smith. Her writings provided an unsurpassed moral and intellectual compass for so many scholars, while her intellectual activism blazed a trail for all of us to follow.

Rose Ann Torres: I would like to thank my co-editors and all the contributors for all the work that you contributed to this book. I would also like to acknowledge my family for their unwavering love and support. For my wonderful children Waywaya, Samuel, and Simon for your understanding and patient during the making of this book. *Kenni nanang ko ken tatang ko agyamanak unay ti amin nga ayat nga impaay yo kaniak-ayayaten kayo unay nanang ko ken tatang ko. Agyamanak met kenni Apo Dios tayo iti amin nga impaay na nga ayat kadatayo amin!*

Dionisio Nyaga: I would love to acknowledge that I am in the land of Indigenous peoples of Turtle Island. This work would not have been possible without the support and engagement of all editors and contributors. I would also like to remember our ancestors and those who have gone before us. We owe you a lot for setting the pace of decolonization. Personally, I would love to thank my family for being patient during the writing of my chapters. I would also like to remember my grandmother for being present in the writing of my chapters. You are physically gone but spiritually present. Thank you.

Figures

11.1　Africa Peace and Security Architecture (APSA)　192
11.2　U.S. aid to Africa, top recipients, recent allocations vs. FY2021 request　201
13.1a　Policy research as a tool for youth resistance　223
13.1b　Deconstructing traditional focus group research and the use of youth voice　232
13.2　Youth as policy experts　235
13.3　Policy is intersectional and layered　236

Notes on Contributors

Michelle Boehm
has recently completed a BSW at Toronto Metropolitan University. With social work training at both the college and university levels, Boehm has dedicated many years of her life to understanding the social world we live in, as well as the best practices needed to engage with current social issues. Going forward, Boehm is open to continuing her education, but is otherwise hopeful to work at an agency that values human dignity and social justice.

Michelle Brochu
is a fourth-year part-time BSW student at Toronto Metropolitan University. She completed her Hon. B. Sc. (University of Toronto), Social Service Worker Diploma and Addiction Certificate (George Brown College). A Registered Social Service Worker (RSSW), employed in the Homeless Sector, Brochu values anti-oppressive approaches which facilitate raising the voices of people who access the Sector's services. She is deeply grateful to her late parents, who emigrated to Toronto to secure a future for their children. They instilled in her their love of learning and sense of hope.

Nob Doran (né[e] Chris)
is a Professor in the Department of Social Science at the University of New Brunswick. Their publications can be found in the following peer-reviewed journals: *Social Studies of Science, Canadian Journal of Political and Social Theory, Canadian Journal of Sociology, Women and Criminal Justice, Journal of Historical Sociology, Canadian Review of Sociology and Anthropology, Social and Legal Studies, International Journal of the Humanities, Theoretical Criminology*, as well as in other edited collections. Currently, they are finishing up a manuscript for Routledge, tentatively entitled *The Birth of Panoptic Liberalism: A Genealogy from Below*.

Julie Erbland
is the Manager at the Ontario Office of the Chief Coroner for the Child and Youth Death Review and Analysis team. Her work supports death investigation related to children and youth who had child welfare involvement and other youth-serving systems. Erbland holds an interdisciplinary PhD in Policy Studies with a specialization in Social Policy from Toronto Metropolitan University. She has a strong belief in the connection between research and practice, which stems from her Master's in Social Work, with a specialization

in working with children and their families. Areas of research interest include the criminalization of youth, social inclusion/exclusion, youth rights and citizenship. She has extensive experience working in the Ontario government on issues related to criminalization and victimization, including youth justice issues, violence against women and children, and larger issues of criminalization. She is a proud member of the queer community and has engaged in research aimed at supporting 2SLGBTIQ + youth. She is passionate about the role of qualitative research and in finding ways for lived experience to inform policy.

Purnima George
is an Associate Professor in School of Social Work at the Toronto Metropolitan University, which she joined in 2001. Prior to her immigration to Canada, she was a faculty member at the College of Social Work, Mumbai, India, and also managed community projects with slum and pavement dwellers in Maharashtra, India. In Toronto, George has been teaching research courses at the undergraduate and the graduate level along with supervising graduate students doing their Major Research Paper. George's current scholarship is situated at the intersection of social work and law, with a focus on domestic violence experiences of racialized immigrant women and children in Ontario. Her teaching and scholarship are informed by Critical Race Feminism, Intersectionality, Anti-colonial, and Dehegemonization frameworks.

Marco Giuliani
completed his BSW at Toronto Metropolitan University. Giuliani has developed a strong interest in anti-oppressive approaches to research and is beginning an MSW where he will explore community-based research methodology and the Rainbow community. Giuliani is passionate about advancing the rights of 2SLGBTIQ + persons, with a particular interest in identifying and addressing the shifting needs and perspectives of different generations within the community.

Lawrence Ofunja Kangei
holds Diploma in Religious Studies (Dip/RS), from Consolata Institute of Philosophy, Kenya, Bachelor of Philosophy (B-PHL), from Pontifical University Urbaniana, Rome, Italy, both Master of Arts in Philosophy (MA-PHL) and Doctor of Philosophy in Philosophy (PhD-PHL), from the Catholic University of Eastern Africa, Nairobi, Kenya. He is currently pursuing Bachelor of Laws (LLB) at this latter institution.

Albina Magomedova

completed her Social Service Work Diploma before transferring to Toronto Metropolitan University to complete her BSW. She has worked in the nonprofit sector for six years in the field of disability where she has worked with all kinds of disabled folks and has been a strong advocate for accessibility. She will continue to pursue her passions of supporting disabled folks as she pursues a Masters of Public Policy, where she will merge the two worlds of disability and policy and continue supporting this community from a macro level.

Dionisio Nyaga

is an Assistant Professor at Algoma University, School of Social Work, Ontario Canada. Nyaga has a PhD from Social Justice Education-SESE/University of Toronto. He holds master's and bachelor's degrees from Toronto Metropolitan University (TMU), Department of Social Work. Nyaga previously taught both undergraduate and graduate courses at TMU's School of Social Work. His Doctoral research focussed on uncoupling Black masculinity through the narratives of Kenyan men in Toronto. His areas of teaching, research and practice interest are: Critical Anti-oppression, ethical duties and responsibility, post-colonial/structural, community development and engagement, Anti-Blackness, Black masculinity studies, diaspora and transnational studies, cultural studies, men and masculinities, social justice, Indigenous and spirituality studies. Nyaga's recent co-edited book (with Rose Ann Torres) *Critical Research Methodologies: Ethics and Responsibilities* (Brill, 2021) focusses a keen and critical interest on issues of ethics and knowledge production.

Waywaya Nyaga

graduated as a Valedictorian and is currently enrolled in an International Baccalaureate School at Korah Collegiate & Vocational School in Sault Ste. Marie, Ontario, Canada. Her focus is on African and Asian studies that look at race along the intersection of diaspora and ethnic diversity. She is currently working on looking at how elementary schools in Canada can open spaces for critical imagination of mathematics from African and Asian perspectives.

Dawn Onishenko

is an Associate Professor in the School of Social Work at Toronto Metropolitan University. She has been a social justice activist in the areas of gender, women in conflict with the law, anti-poverty, housing and homelessness, HIV/AIDS and queer rights. Onishenko's research interests include 2SLGBTIQ+ rights, identity and liberation and anti-oppressive social work practice. She has engaged in research, and published in the area of social movements and social change, citizenship, equality rights, and the role of jurisgenerative politics/praxis in bringing about social change. Her current research projects explore the experiences of sexual minorities seeking refugee status in Canada, the experiences of gender and sexual minority youth in state care, specifically the child welfare and the youth justice systems, and critical human rights and youth policy.

Susan Preston
is an Associate Professor in the School of Social Work at Toronto Metropolitan University (TMU). Prior to becoming a faculty member in the School of Social Work at TMU in 2006, she worked in the social work field for over 20 years, predominantly in the community based criminal justice sector. Preston primarily teaches research-based courses at the undergraduate and graduate level and has taught social work practice courses. She also supervises graduate students completing their Major Research Paper in the MSW program. Preston's scholarship focus is varied, including remote/northern social work practice, activist pedagogy, and the impact of neoliberalism on social work practice, education, and research. Her teaching and scholarship are informed by feminist intersectionality, and the ongoing journey to decolonize herself and her work.

Susan Silver
is an Associate Professor in the School of Social Work at Toronto Metropolitan University (TMU), which she joined in 1994. Prior to joining TMU, Silver worked in the area of youth unemployment and managed and evaluated various community-based programs. Her interest in research continued when she joined TMU, where she teaches research courses in the BSW and MSW programs and supervises graduate students in their Major Research Paper. Silver also teaches courses in Advanced Social Work Practice and Social Welfare Policy. She brings a critical analysis to issues of representation, positionality, and power relations in social work education, research, and practice. Currently, her areas of scholarship include liminality and chronic illness, the critical use of social media in the research process and resisting neoliberalism through critical pedagogies.

Michael Sitawa
is a Senior Researcher in the Peace and Security Research Department of the International Peace Support Training Centre (IPSTC) in Nairobi, Kenya. He also is the Acting Head of Programme of Postgraduate Studies School leading the MA Programme in Crisis Response and Disaster Management of the

National Defence University, Kenya. He holds a PhD in Sociology (Kenyatta University) and Master of Arts degree in Sociology (University of Nairobi). He holds a Bachelor of Arts degree in Social Sciences (major in Sociology, minor in Political Science) (The Catholic University of Eastern Africa). Sitawa has worked with the African Union Mission in Somalia on capacity building for Somalia's Interim government, as well as Youth Leadership. He has also consulted for the National Council of Churches of Kenya, assessing the conflict trends and the effect of the Peace Education Program in the five refugee camps in Dadaab, Northern Kenya. This Program was funded by UNHCR and UNICEF from 2003 to 2014. Sitawa is a chief editor of the *Africa Amani Journal* of the IPSTC.

Rose Ann Torres
is the Director and Assistant Professor in the School of Social Work at Algoma University. She is currently a Visiting Professor at the Polytechnic University of the Philippines. Prior to joining Algoma University, she was an Assistant Professor at the University of New Brunswick. She is the principal investigator of a Social Sciences and Humanities Research Council (SSHRC) Insight Development Grants funded project that focusses on examining the factors that impede mental health and the barriers associated with accessing services and supports among Filipino health care professionals working in Northern Ontario, and a co-principal investigator for a SSHRC Institutional Grants funded project on "Effects of COVID-19 on Teaching, and Learning: Stories of Indigenous and Racialized Faculty Members and Students at Algoma University". She also co-edited (with Kailan Leung and Vania Soepriatna) *Outside and In-between: Theorizing Asian-Canadian Exclusion and the Challenges of Identity Formation* (Brill, 2021).

Laura Winters
received her PhD in Sociology from the University of New Brunswick. She is an Adjunct Professor at the Memorial University of Newfoundland, and a Research Fellow at the Muriel McQueen Ferguson Centre for Family Violence Research in Fredericton, New Brunswick. Winters's research is on stigma resistance, especially in the everyday "talk back" of people who do sex work. She believes there is a need to think critically about research ethics in the context of research as advocacy with marginalized populations. She has been working with community organizations in her home city of St. John's, Newfoundland for over a decade, currently as CEO of Stella's Circle, a social justice organization offering services in the areas of real home, real help and real work.

Laura Wyper is an Assistant Professor at Algoma University. She has a Bachelor of Health Sciences in Midwifery from Laurentian University, a Bachelor of Education from Trent University, a Master of Arts in Adult Education and Community Development from the Ontario Institute for Studies in Education (OISE) at the University of Toronto, and a PhD in Adult Education and Community Development with a specialization in Comparative, International and Development Education from OISE, at the University of Toronto. She is currently the Chair of the Department of Community Economic and Social Development at Algoma University.

Introduction

Dawn Onishenko, Nob Doran, Rose Ann Torres and Dionisio Nyaga

This edited collection attempts to engage with current qualitative research methodologies and approaches from a critically and ethically reflexive standpoint. This work seeks to unravel colonial practices that continue to hide within qualitative approaches in ways that invite a new reimagining of working within and without qualitative method/ologies. For a while, research has been colonial practice people's stories into one universal truth act of reductionism and simplification comes with material and symbolic consequences: in that if we are going to refer to ourselves as stories, and that we act and are acted upon by those stories, then the very process of research takes away emotional part of life in ways that renders us un-storied and consequently form of disappearance that marginalized communities face today results from the ways that policy informed by current research continue to ontologically, epistemologically, cosmologically and axiologically forget participants and their context. This edited collection therefore seeks to bring to the fore the lived experiences of the studied to their storied lives in ways that are ethically and politically congruent. This work therefore seeks to bring forth Foucault's subterranean narratives steeped in contexts and experiences that can critically invert the dominant (colonial, capitalist, state, etc.,) practices in existing research.

The aim of this volume is to address the complex realities and values expressed through the research process. This critically reflexive piece aims to bring forth ethical dilemmas that continue to pervade research process, by unearthing how left out marginalized realties and value in research also leads communities to disappear physically and psychically. The scope of this book is to engage critically with existing qualitative approaches in ways that make visible these hidden practices and thereafter introduce alternative are subterranean approaches as other ways of doing research.

Chapter 1, "Making Research Black and Strange. Why History Matters in the Current Disappearing World" by Dionisio Nyaga, reads corporate market interest and logics in research as one of the many ways through which research produces Black communities (read this as punishment, disciplining and eventual social death) through a reductive neoliberal registration and management of Black emotions, values and histories that subsequently commit Black genocide in the name of truth making. The chapter seeks to look at how such colonial thingification of Black stories is state sanctioned and driven by market and corporate rationalities, commitment, and logics of profit maximization that ignores, and discounts Black ontologies and therefore implicated Anti-Black racism.

Chapter 2, by Dionisio Nyaga, Dawn Onishenko, and Rose Ann Torres, explores "Grounded Theory: Effects of COVID-19 on Homeless Youth". This chapter looks at the effects of the COVID-19 pandemic among homeless Black youth living in Toronto in order to tease out grounded research approach and considerations – our reflexive musings – in undertaking this project. Thus, this research project sets to draw out the lived experiences of marginalized homeless youth in Toronto, Ontario in order to understand the differentiated challenges they face as a result of their identities and the existing policies/practices during the COVID-19 pandemic. This chapter implicates research process since it is the quintessential definition of broken and singularized policies and practices that continue to forget, and discount marginalized homeless youth.

Chapter 3, by Nob Doran, "Reflexivity, Recursion and Re-evaluation: Some Reflections on 'Institutional Ethnography'", highlights the concept of 'recursion' (when researchers go round 'in circles') as an integral concern for all 'reflexivity-inspired' scholars. Specifically, it starts from a student's perspective, and then examines the reflexively-aware writings of the sociologist, Dorothy Smith, to show that she gets caught up in a recursive loop, because of the contradictions between what she says and what she does. However it ends by moving to a meta-level, and suggests that Smith's work, once it is placed in its specific historical context, should be lauded as an exemplification of the Foucauldian notion of the parrhesian; – one who speaks their *embodied* truth to power(/knowledge).

Chapter 4, by Laura Winters, "Resisting through Research: Developing a Qualitative "Mixed Methods" Approach in Research with Sex Workers", states that, despite Community Action Research's potential utility for her research, the actual practical difficulties involved in carrying out research in St. John's meant that such a strategy could not be easily employed. Fortunately, Miller's (2000) theoretical/methodological form of discourse analysis allowed her, as a researcher, to satisfactorily resolve these issues. Collectively, her use of a novel and unique form of qualitative 'mixed methods' produced some very insightful results; this chapter follows the development of this methodological approach which encourages the researcher to examine both what words 'say' and what words 'do'.

Chapter 5, by Dionisio Nyaga, "Beyond Codified Logics of Ethics: Jungle and the Ethics of Non-violence", argues for ethical qualification of knowledge to allow a return of imagination, emotion, values and realities as an ethical requirement in knowledge production. It is a call for the return of subjugated philosophical assumption in knowledge production as a necessary ethical demand that can also help us reimagine the human as a reflexive being.

Chapter 6, by Waywaya Nyaga and Dionisio Nyaga, speaks of "Africa beyond Africa: Afro-pessimism as an Ethical Demand". The authors look at how the white corporate world looks at Africa as a *tabula rasa*, childlike place, buried in emotional and instinctual turmoil (Mbembe, 2001), and that needs the west to save it from its miserable state of nature and war. Through western modern research, Africa is painted as a space of degeneracy and violence, desperately in needs of the western salvation from self-cannibalization (Webhi, 2017). The authors call out research for such misrepresentation and invite us to get lost in the jungle that is Africa as an ethical necessity in knowledge production.

Chapter 7, by Dionisio Nyaga, looks at "Markets Logics in Research Process and the Denigration of Black Bodies". Nyaga argues that such acts of social elimination and death are an ongoing historical act of registration and management of Black life that marks such bodies as social public excesses that needed to be dispensed to purify and clean the city. He implicates research as having participated in such forms of social elimination of Black bodies by justifying such practices and policies as necessary for the existence of a peaceful and neat city. To un-map such practices, knowledge producers need understand that what we attest in north American street in terms of Black death has been an ongoing psychic practice made physical by the everyday practice of Black extinction.

Chapter 8, by Susan Preston, Susan Silver and Purnima George, is focused on "Teaching to the Tensions: Pushing the Boundaries of Qualitative Social Work Research". The chapter engages with the pedagogy of research, as reflected in teaching and learning. The chapter looks at how qualitative research is implicated in the perpetuation of colonial violence.

Chapter 9, by Laura Wyper, looks at "Qualitative Research as Resistance: The Use of Vignettes to Support Situated Knowledge and the Deconstruction of Colonial Policies". The chapter looks at research through an activist perspective. It employs vignettes as a method of decolonization in knowledge production and helps deconstruct colonial policies. It pays attention to issues of intersectionality to implicate globalization including neoliberalism and New Public Management (Wyper, 2018).

Chapter 10, by Rose Ann Torres, explores the how of "Remembering in Research: Doing Research in Asian Communities". The chapter implicates research as an art of forgetting the ontologies of Indigenous and marginalized groups and calls for the remembering of those subjugated knowledges as fundamental in decolonizing research. The chapter focuses on different ways of 'remembering' when we do research in the Asian communities.

Chapter 11, by Michael Sitawa, is about "Application of Research to Africa's Peace and Security Conundrum: The Ethical and Moral Divide between the Ideal and Real". This chapter poses fundamental questions on the ethical aspects regarding how information on Africa's peace and security is handled, either in terms of application or interpretation. It raises fundamental research questions surrounding the rates, as well as cases to which to respond. It also raises questions on the use of conflict as a tool of convenience for some actors on the global arena whereby deliberate destabilisation opens doors to increased profiteering.

Chapter 12, by Rose Ann Torres, discusses "Ethics of Doing Research in the Indigenous Community". The author shares major conceptual frames of the *how* of research as fundamental ethical necessity in doing research with Indigenous communities. The chapter pays attention to the research process and the art of inclusion and equity in doing research. The plan is to implicate the self in ways that are critically nuanced.

Chapter 13, by Dawn Onishenko and Julie Erbland, explores "A Reflexive Gaze on Qualitative Policy Research: Deconstructing Traditional Policy Research with the Interface of Youth-Voice and Arts-Based Focus Groups". This chapter speaks to the structure and the nuances of the research methodology and the ways in which peer researchers, facilitating focus groups in 'messy spaces' – with food, circuitous discussion, construction paper, glitter, and magazines – contribute to deep understandings of the realities of the migration of youth in relation to youth rights and how those rights are situated within a Canadian social policy context. What surfaced from the research process that upended traditional policy research and its linear approach to question formation, data collection and analysis, was a deep and critical analysis of policy as stories of lived experience.

Chapter 14, by Marco Giuliani, Michelle Brochu, Albina Magomedova, Michelle Boehm and Dawn Onishenko, explores "A Co-constructed Critical Autoethnographical Conversation with Social Work Students regarding Reflexive Research Engagement". This co-constructed autoethnography seeks to bring to the foreground the lived experiences of four undergraduate social work students engaged in grounded theory research on marginalized youth homelessness in a time of COVID-19 as part of our fourth-year placements. This chapter explores the tensions and congruences between our theoretical understandings as social work students at a critical anti-oppressive institution and the concrete realities of conducting qualitative research.

Chapter 15, by Lawrence Ofunja Kangei, is focused on "Arendtian Phenomenology of Politics". The author says that, from the outset era of Edmund Husserl, who is reputed to be the proponent of the philosophical movement known as phenomenology, there has been a heightened utilization of this approach in varied fields coupled with its hailing amidst other Philosophical methodologies. Phenomenology utilises a sort of conscientiousness termed as intentionality. Johanna Hannah Cohn Arendt who is deemed to fall under this scholarly tradition uses this approach in her discourse and presentation of political thought from a research stance. Owing to the erstwhile, this disquisition contends that phenomenology guides the quintessence of politics as regards determining who ought to rule, how ought the resources be distributed and how ought the society be organized for the rationale of actualizing the mutual good. Moreover, phenomenology, coupled with hermeneutics, is able to decipher the foregoing in an apposite mode, as far as history, text, context and mode of conveying the message are oriented to a sole aim of attaining proper meaning through well-delineated research mode, hence, apt construal. Research being the canon of human transactions, it becomes pertinent for the varied societies to pursue an apropos approach to decipher its working for its profound comprehension and applicability. Human life would not gather connotation if a fitting method was not utilized in the realm of politics. Our experiences could only attain meaning upon phenomenology usage in the interpretation and since people are historical-political beings as far as knowledge is concerned, this becomes requisite. The political nature of human beings makes them to be intentional through their actions, such as voting, thus, a dearth of phenomenology sires a desolate political universe.

PART 1

Critical Review of Qualitative Research Approaches

CHAPTER 1

Making Research Black and Strange
Why History Matters in the Current Disappearing World

Dionisio Nyaga

> Given his philosophical heroes (Socrates, Descartes, and David Hume), it is of little surprise that life, for Huxley, "leaves no doubt that [we ought to place a higher value] upon the advancement of knowledge and the promotion of that freedom of thought which is at once the cause and the consequence of intellectual progress (Huxley, 1910, pp. 134–35)".
>
> GLAUDE, 2011, p. 300

∴

For while research has simplified (Creswell, 2013; Creswell & Poth, 2018) and corporatized Black peoples' stories by packaging, branding, and conserving their stories and selling them in the marketplace (Nyaga & Torres, 2021), such an epistemological and ontological claim helps this chapter to remember ways in which Black were enslaved and sold in the market as objects/property (Pardo, 2018). Such forms of market rationalities and logics continue to operate in research; more so in quantitative studies where single truth is weighed more and remembered than Black emotions, realities, value, and histories. Black emotions are casted out, forgotten, discounted, and reduced for the purpose of truth making. Research as an industrial complex has over the years supervised and suctioned the denigration of Black peoples' ways of life, values, realities, and histories; to which this chapter argues has contributed to the social death of Black communities. This chapter calls for a return of subjugated and buried Black values and histories as a way of reimagining knowledge production differently. This chapter argues that such forms of forgetting Black values and denigration and discounting of the same in research has contributed to ever present-day forms of anti-Black racism. This is a question of value gap in knowledge production and works in complex ways to bury Black histories and ways of being at the expense of white truth. The gap in values is a space of discounting, forgetting (Pon, 2009) and burying Black truths into graveyards in ways that value more white singular truth about Black life while conforming the white researcher as the quintessential holder of knowledge. So, to speak of value gap (Glaude, 2018) is to think of material and symbolic consequences that Black peoples face in the name of truth making. It is therefore ethically imperative and responsible for research to pay attention to the issue of value gap (Glaude, 2018) when undertaking research among Black communities to start accounting the loss of Black values in knowledge production. This axiological and epistemological occasion helps to start looking at research as a process of mourning and accounting the loss of Black histories, realities, and values in knowledge production (Oviawe, 2016; Torres & Nyaga, 2021).

This chapter reads these corporate market interest and logics in research as one among the many ways through which research produces Black communities (read this as punishment, disciplining and eventual social death) through a reductive neoliberal registration and management of Black emotions, values and histories that subsequently commit Black genocide in the name of truth making. The chapter seeks to look at how such colonial thingification of Black stories is state sanctioned and driven by market and corporate rationalities, commitment, and logics of profit maximization that ignores, and discounts Black ontologies and therefore implicated Anti-Black racism. Key to this argument is that the process of reducing and simplifying people's stories forgets peoples' histories and is simultaneous the process that disappears (social death) them into neoliberal products (read this as graveyards) that can then me sold into the market. In a nutshell, the process of neoliberal production and processing of Black stories is consequently the of social genocide of Black life.

My claim is that research has been captured by markets logics and other state actors and cannot speak the language and realities of Black communities in ways that are ethical and political. The effect to such ethical corporatization is the present-day hesitation by Black communities to participate in COVID-19 vaccination, which I argue help return knowledge production to its ethical grounds of being human. This chapter argues that the current research process is meant to disappear Black life and make live a white neoliberal market through a process sustained and suctioned by profit greed. I therefore argue that there is a need to reimagine violence in research in ways that call upon non-violence (Butler, 2020) as a research method/ology of humanizing research process. Such a methodology pays attention to histories of communities, values, context, and ways of live of communities that continues to live in the shadows of the world (Smith, 2012; Torres & Nyaga, 2021). A nonviolent research process recognises the role of ethics in demystifying colonial footprints in neoliberal research; to start thinking on how to disassemble truth making and the whiteness that is present in contemporary ways of meaning making. Non-violent research praxis therefore calls for community-based research steeped in forms of allyship that are conscious of Black lateral differences and ready to transform and transverse Black psyche in ways that lays bare and displaces (read genealogy) that which we see and have been made to believe as single Black normal and reality.

1 Implicating Research and Black Loss

> The focus on personal hygiene and cleanliness at the Tuskegee Institute opened the door for alliances with public health initiatives early in the twentieth century, making the school's student population as well as residents of surrounding counties subjects of intense hygienic surveillance. In short, the residents of Macon County had been transformed into a research population well before the 1932 initiation of the syphilis experiments by the Public Health Service (PHS).
> RUSERT, 2009, p. 157

I start this section with a look at the Tuskegee experiment and the effect it had and continues to have on Black communities. Black scholars continue to implicate research in anti-Blackness, grounding their argument on Tuskegee experiment and the effect it had and continue to have on Black lives (Rusert, 2009).

According to Rusert (2009), the levels of Black objectification in Tuskegee experiment had started way before 1932. Black bodies had been registered as a disease or pathological misnomer (miasma) that required scientific control, justifying the white researcher to enter Black life to save them from self-cannibalization. That way, the white researcher was justified to commit white evil (savior syndrome and the narrative of white mans' burden) on Black bodies in the name of civilizing the broken Black other. The Black other was objectified through miasmic labels that were attached on their body to remove the human in them, mark them as a pathology, freeze their movement and simultaneously justify colonial model of surveillance on their movement. Black became a scientific object that required scientific introspection and surveillance to control its spread and therefore contain, manage, and incarcerate Blackness.

This traumatic history and the effect of Tuskegee experiment remains fresh in Black psyche. Black miasma and subsequent freezing of Black movement through everyday police surveillance helps implicates us as researcher to start interrogating how Black bodies have historically been earmarked as bio-political social excesses that can be nullified to sustain a neat and white society. Black is seen as statistical surplus and social excess that must be eliminated to make live a white and pure society. Population as a form of statistical operation work towards removing, disappearing, dispossessing, and deporting the Black miasma from infiltrating and taking hostage the White city.

This history seems to be repeated when engaging with the effects of COVID-19 on Black communities and African peoples in general. In a white dominant system, the question asked is why would Black community (notice singularization of Blackness) hesitate to be vaccinated to protect themselves from the scourge, knowing they are affected by COVID-19 disproportionately? COVID-19 has affected Black bodies in ways that are compounded and complex. As such, for such a white question to be posed about Black vaccine hesitancy, one needs to recognize violent colonial histories in research (Rusert, 2009) that have and continue to dispossess Black community of their values and ways of being while masquerading as benevolent. This is not just a simple ethical question requiring simple answers. What Black communities are calling upon is for the state and vaccine manufacturer is to engage more with histories of anti-Blackness as expressed in historical scientific experiments (Rusert, 2009). Black hesitation is a necessary ethical claim and a point of critical reflexivity in research and help guide research process to start asking questions of how we can remember and re-member our research practices. This means a change to the colonial assumptions that Black is straight and singular. Black is complex and requires researcher to engage with the miasma that is Black. This calls for researchers to imagine Black as rainbow; in that some colours are visible and have a name while others are invisible and nameless and yet they are part of the Black prism. McKittrick (2006), referencing Sylvia Wynter, says:

> Sylvia Wynter's work entails not only "deconstructing" or denaturalizing categories such as "race"; it also means envisioning what is beyond the hierarchical codes and partial human stories that have, for so long, organized our populations and the planet. This means accepting that global, human, and environmental connections—of cultural histories, exchanges, "discoveries," experiences—are evidence of a conceptual shift.
>
> p. 135

Doing research within Black communities calls for a rainbow methodology that trouble colonial assumption in research with Black communities. Remember and re-member calls for a complicated process of cognitive gathering. It means that research is not just a rational process but rather a gathering of emotions that have been subjugated over the years.

The effects of Tuskegee continue to affect Black communities and the best ethical methodology is to engage with these Black traumas in ways that account Black loss. According to Reye (2017),

In a recent economic study, researchers concluded that the "disclosure of the Tuskegee Study in 1972 is associated with increases in medical mistrust and mortality and decreases in both outpatient and inpatient physician interactions for older black men." What this means is that even older black men, particularly those with the lowest education and income levels, who did not participate in the study were also negatively impacted. The heightened mistrust of medical professionals ultimately led to worse health outcomes and a life expectancy reduced by 1.5 years which accounted for 35 percent of the 1980 life expectancy gap between black and white men.

p. 1

The effect of Tuskegee is the mistrust of Black communities on vaccine-producing companies. When Black communities sought to know how the production of vaccine was Black, the vaccine production companies justified their vaccine with claims that Black doctors were involved in the production of the vaccines and while vaccine companies provided quantitative data of how the vaccine was tested in diverse (read this as Black) communities. It is ontologically and epistemological unethical for vaccine producing companies to identify couple of Black doctors who participated in the production of the vaccines to claim being culturally competent and sensitive to Black needs. This way of accounting for leaves the vaccine Black nouns rather than verb Black and leads the preservation and freezing of Blackness (Walcott, 2003). This kind of preservation and conservation of Blackness nullifies Black histories, realities and values and seems to be grounded in whiteness and neoliberal white guilt and shame.

This by any ethical measure is a form of what (Pon, 2009) call a form of new racism (read anti-Black racism) that fail to engage with Black beyond Black (read this as Black as rainbow). Such an engagement looks at Black value, cultures, and ways of Black communities from an ethical and historical view. Subsequently, it is unethical for Black bodies employed in those vaccines to be used by vaccines companies to justify and account on how the vaccine is Black. Such form of corporate accountability reduces such Black bodies into commodities that can be sold back to Black communities for the sake of rationalizing how a vaccine is Black. Such Black bodies are reduced into advertisement board (read objectification) that need to labor to sell the vaccine to Black communities.

This corporate 'progressive' discussion, which I underwrite here as imperial, anti-Black and colonial are acts of sanitizing and whitening vaccination process and production, rendering it ahistorical and grounded on a colonial process of research that claim objectivity while simultaneously discarding and displacing Black engagement and capacity building. Such a research process is grounded on colonial believe that Black is an object of sale for profits. I understand the urgent need to vaccinate Black communities that they are affected disproportionally. While that may be the rationale for an accelerated vaccination, I would argue that an equal measure of engagement with Black communities on historical injustices meted on them is equally urgent and a fundamental ethical call for any society that claims to be just and fair. What instead we are witnessing is militarised process of vaccination that is unprepared to engage with Black traumas and grief but rather to force vaccination into the hands of Black bodies. This process of vaccination in and of itself is an expression of bio-power that enters Black bodies (read the process of inserting the needle into the body as an act of invasion) without necessarily engaging (read this as remember and re-member) with Black communities on the how and why of vaccination.

I argue that such a process devoid of Black voice and engagement is a colonial invasion and marking of Blackbodies as property that needs to be controlled and confined (Rusert, 2009). The question of Black traumas and the how of engaging with it is equally complicated and cannot be simplified through vaccinating it away or out of global psyche. The issue we as Black bodies continue agonizing with is the fact that we still see a society attempting to vaccinate itself out of its own shame and guilt of having caused pain on Black communities. We exist in a society that seeks to vaccinate itself back to a normal that never worked for Black communities in the first place. My wager in this chapter is that we cannot fail ourselves by losing this COVID-policy window of opportunity. There is an ethical necessity to allow us to engage with historical Black trauma and wounds by accelerating vaccination of research outside of institutionalized ethics in ways that are historical, psychic and political.

To understand the politics of institutionalization and corporatization of ethics, we must question the statistical composition and mechanisms of identifying population. The onus is to start engaging with the fact that Black has never been accounted as part of the population. This implicates statistics gymnastics that reduce Black as unnecessary emotion in truth making and therefore nullifying its material and symbolic existence. In short, the Tuskegee experiment opens complex discussions on the making of the state population on the backs of Black bodies. Such a process is significant in knowledge production because it inaugurates colonial art of dispossession, incarceration and simplification of Black communities while marking and producing them as disposable, dispensable and superfluous population who can be disappeared at will. Such form of disappearance is never considered a loss that counts. Black life can easily be discounted and rationalized as non-life that is ungrievable and that can easily be sold for profits.

Butler (2020), speaking about grievability, said,

> the unequal distribution of grievability might be one framework for understanding the differential production of humans and other creatures within a structure of inequality, or, indeed, within a structure of violent disavowal. To claim that equality formally extends to all humans is to sidestep the fundamental question of how the human is produced, or, rather, who is produced as a recognizable and valuable human, and who is not. For equality to make sense as a concept, it must imply such formal extension to all humans, but even then, we make an assumption about who is included within the category of the human, and who is partially included, or fully excluded; who is fully alive or partially dead; who would be grieved if they were lost, and who would not be grieved, because they are, effectively, socially dead.
>
> p. 58

To imagine these metrics of grievability and Black loss within neoliberal markets, we need to interrogate further the meaning of population and statistics metrics (read science of experimentation) that guide the process of determining who lives is protected and who life is nullified for profits. Population is a biometric measure of determining who becomes human with rights of citizenship (the populations) versus those other who are discounted or disposable superfluous immigrant populations whose life can be lost for the existence of the white nationals. Such a claim implicates science of population (statistics) in the death of Black lives.

2 Towards a Reconciling and Accounting Black Loss as a Research Methodology

> The silence, or rather the prudence, with which the unitary theories avoid the genealogy of knowledges might therefore be a good reason to continue to pursue it.
> FOUCAULT, 1980, p. 87

Research as a process of producing knowledge needs to work in ways that account and grieve Black trauma without necessary measuring such grief (read this as inconsolable mourning). The ways of accounting such Black historical traumas should intersectional and should fails colonial coding of Black life. In short, research and the ethics that guide the process of producing knowledge needs to verb Black and Blackness without necessarily commodifying and preserving the process of Black grief and loss. For a while, research has masqueraded as culturally competent or sensitive practice to Black loss (Torres & Nyaga, 2021). I call out this as another form of performance that manifest its racist practices in Black communities. These forms of research theatrics fail to engage with histories of atrocities meted on Black communities and instead collapses Black bodies into tools that are assumed as culturally important therefore reproducing Black trauma. Research that is assumes as ethical becomes the very practice of constituting and retooling black bodies for sale in the marketplace. This chapter therefore calls for a critically reflexive research exercises that looks at Black bodies as not just cultural tools and instrument of study and profits, but rather as beings that have spirits.

This chapter engages with these colonial atrocities on Black life to argue that for research to be just, humane and geared towards transformative change within Black communities, it must break from its knowledge fixation on Black as objects of introspection and embrace Black ethics as a necessary demand in knowledge production. This means that knowledge production will have to break away from institutional industrial and corporate walls and embrace Black values, histories and context as a way of decolonizing what we know and how we come to know what we know. This means that research will need to engage with it historical violence against marginalized communities in ways that are outside corporate profit maxim. To do that, research need to disappear and be buried in epistemological graveyards to come face to face with its implication in term of the continued death of participant majority of whom come from marginalized communities such as Black and Indigenous peoples. To claim that research needs to disappear is to argue for a critically reflexive research process that looks at knowledge from a place that is ethical and humane.

Such a critically reflexive research process calls for reformulation of the philosophical assumptions that guide research such that those subjugated Black truths that continue to be buried and marked as irrational acquire an ontological and epistemological muscle to speak their truths in ways that are contextual and historically oriented. Such an ethical process of knowledge insurrection is a necessary ethical demand for decolonizing research since it does not only dig deep (read archeology and truth making) but engage and displace that which has been dug in ways that are transformational and transgressive (genealogy) (Foucault, 1980). To do this, research will need to be political in ways that employs Black values, realities and ways of being Black into the production of knowledge.

The fact that we study communities comes with its own ethical dilemma, in that we can never understand communities (read reduce or quantify) but rather imagine who they are. This epistemological route pays attention to the work of Emmanuel Levina's work on the face of the other, to which this chapter argue that we are always late when we want to know the other. To place such an argument in the face of research is to argue that our knowledge of the other is premised on the fact that the other is a necessary ethical demand for our existence. To frame this ethical orientation into the research process is to demand that research cannot exist in the vacuum but rather needs to exist with the other for it to tell the truths of participant in ways that are contextual and historically placed. This chapter argues that such an ethical orientation demands that research dissolve in the face of the other to start to engage with its colonial psyche in ways that helps understand its physical world of collapsing those others it marks as irrational and savages. This ethical argument seeks to place psychic discussion as political, historical, and contextual and that their evocation will help decolonize how we come to know what we know and how we know.

A psychic analysis helps unwraps (just like a commodity) normal presentations to start asking the hidden performances that prepared what is presented in the public view. Life is a theatre (performance) and presents what is required and fails to show the hidden that prepared what is required. There is a lot that goes on in the background for such a performance to be presented to us as the reality of life. I argue that what is presented to us should be read, imagined and acted outside itself. This places the onus of misreading the performance by the audience to start asking strange question that unravel the neatness that we see with our naked eyes. This by any ethical measure means that we need to open the background of the epistemological theatre in research to start engaging with the masked realities of knowledge production.

While ethical measures are necessary safeguard of participants from unethical researchers, the process of measuring(guideline) ethics are the very process of decontaminating and concealing white and whiteness from Black death. I argue that ethical guidelines were and remains an operation that is grounded on white guilt and shame and geared towards reconciling and obscuring colonial white implication on Black death. This chapter argues that current ethical guidelines remain white and fail to safeguard Black and other marginalized groups from colonial violent research/ers. My wager is that ethical measures (guidelines) need to be made Black in ways that allow them to walk in and work in Black spaces in ways that are intersectional and complex (miasmic methodology). We need to ask how the line to guide research was drawn and the violence such lines continue to mete on Black communities and their values and realities and how such a Black epistemological sabotage may help question neoliberal logics and profit maximization present in the ethical lines. This ontological assertion opens critically reflexive conversation (read this as ethical psychic conversations) on the currency of current ethics and how it drives and incarcerated Black research within institutional policies, guideline, and law. To ground such an ethical conversation beyond ethics is to claim for a need to undertake extra-ethical mile (read this as ethical psychic miles) that breaks boundaries between knowledge and ethics in ways that deinstitutionalizes ethics from its present colonial neoliberal order and commitment to surplus value. This means that we need to defrost (read this as decolonize) the ethical guideline in ways that are Black to start asking strange questions about the logics of neoliberal commodification of Black pain and trauma mostly made real in research.

To argue that ethical guideline is incarcerated (Frozen) is to implicate white guilt and shame. The whole process of ethics was not to curtail any further Black atrocities but rather to clean and clear Black values and realities in research. It was a way of white cleaning its hand from racial atrocities and a commitment to profit as an alternative to Black ethics. Such a methodological practice deviates fundamentally from historical and ethical role that makes research accessible to communities. Instead, ethics speaks and guide research from a white privileged space away from Black miasma (experiences and values); therefore, repeating the same evil it was supposed to fix. Such an epistemological conundrum authorizes the researcher to become vile without seemingly looking evil. The epistemic distance (the line that guides) between the researcher and the participant grows and widens in ways that suspends and conceal violence inflicted and imprinted on Black skin while simultaneously committing themselves to neoliberal logics on profit maximization.

With such an ethical/epistemological reality, it seems to me that we need to open institutional flood gates to release ethics from its white and neoliberal manufactured comfort and have it engage with Black discomforts (Miasma) steeped in histories and values of Black communities. Through that, we can start to blur the ethical guidelines in ways that are Black and ethical. Research ethics need to be culturally competent and sensitive to Black lives without collaterally culturalizing them. The current ethical guides culturalize (read this as objectification/new form of anti-Black racism) Black and Blackness in ways that conserve and preserve Black into cultural items or objects that can be sold to the market. I argue that such an ontological direction of competency fails to recognize that Black is fluid, that such cultural items are in and of themselves spiritual and psychic and that they come from places that are historically Black (read this as miasma or jungle) that fails to be collapsed into a single neat Black story. In a nutshell, white ethical guides in research need to undergo Black revelation and emancipation for them to engage with Black communities in ways that are Black. Such an ontological and ethical assertion means that ethical measure needs to come to terms with the violent histories of anti-Blackness in research, in ways that fail to reconcile white guilt and shame, but rather to invite those uncomfortable conversations between research and Black communities.

Any progressive researcher needs to take COVID-19 as a teachable moment and open critical discussion on Black traumas in ways that are non-intrusive and political. That can only happen when such a society decides to dance with the Black ghost in ways that are uncomfortable, political, and non-invasive. This conversation on Black traumas calls for a different form of researching and working with Black bodies beyond the current corporate performance that seeks to name the number of black bodies that were engaged in the production of the vaccine.

This process of Black vaccination by any means is by itself an expression of research that cannot come to terms with its multiple forms of anti-Blackness. I argue that COVID-19 has opened historical windows that we cannot vaccinate ourselves through, expecting to go back to a normal society that was in the first place unequal and anti-Black. This is a great opportunity for any society that claims to be progressive to account for its Black atrocities in ways that sometimes may be uncomfortable and yet ethically essential.

3   Conclusion

To account for Black deaths, research needs to critically engages with histories of Black traumas in ways that refuse the neatness of Black stories while simultaneously accounting for the loss of Black lives. Subsequently, research needs to be a process of grieving Black loss in ways that are human and grounded in Black realities and values. This chapter therefore calls for recognition and acknowledgment of Black life as valuable and worth to be celebrated in knowledge production. To acknowledge Black life as valuable is to break away from corporate and market-based rationalities that imprisons Black values into a commodity branded for sale in the marketplace. Black values and valuation should transform research from a process of corporate value addition to activity where research disappears and embraces itself as value laden rather than an objective process. Research must engage with Black histories in ways that allow for grief with the loss of Black lives subsequently giving value to the ways that are Black and critically reflexive. This process of grief must be an act that make research to be disoriented with its past atrocities on Black lives. Through this process of ethical engagement, research comes to terms with the fact that it cannot understand Black life but rather can only imagine and acknowledge Black and Blackness as valuable and worthy of being considered as knowledge. Such a process of ethical Black action makes research face a philosophic death in ways that makes research to become the graveyard of Black lives. Such a death reframes research beyond white corporate values and that embraces Black values as necessary methodologies of producing Black knowledge and making Black meanings.

References

Butler, J. (2020). *The Force of Nonviolence: an Ethico-political Bind*. London: Verso.
Creswell, J. (2013). *Qualitative Inquiry and Research Design* (3rd ed.). Thousand Oaks, CA: Sage.
Creswell, J., & Poth, C. (2018). *Qualitative Inquiry and Research Design: Choosing among Five Approaches* (4th ed.). Thousand Oaks, CA: Sage.
Foucault, M. (1980). *Power/Knowledge: Selected Interviews and Other Writings, 1972–1977*. New York, NY: Pantheon.
Glaude. (2011). On prophecy and critical intelligence. *American Journal of Theology and Philosophy*, 32(2), 105–121.
Glaude. (2018). The whitewashing and resurrection of Dr. King's legacy. *Time* 191(13), 20–21.
McKittrick, K. (2006). *Demonic Grounds*. Minneapolis, MN: University of Minnesota Press.
Oviawe, J. O. (2016). How to rediscover the ubuntu paradigm in education. *International Review of Education*, 62(1), 1–10.
Pardo, R. I. (2018). Bankrupted slaves. *Vanderbilt Law Review*, 71(4), 1071–1166.
Pon, G. (2009). Cultural competency as new racism: an ontology of forgetting. *Journal of Progressive Human Services*, 20(1), 59–71.
Reyes (2017). *Effects of Tuskegee Study Still Felt Today*. University Wire.
Rusert, B. (2009). "A study in nature": the tuskegee experiments and the new south plantation. *The Journal of Medical Humanities*, 30(3), 155–171. https://doi.org/10.1007/s10912-009-9086-4.
Smith, L. T. (2012). Colonizing Knowledges. In *Decolonizing Methodologies: Research and Indigenous Peoples* (2nd ed., pp. 61–80). London, UK: Zed Books.

Torres, R., & Nyaga, D. (2021). Research as an Inconsolable Mourning. In *Critical Research Methodologies*. Leiden, The Netherlands: Brill. doi: https://doi-org.ezproxy.algomau.ca/10.1163/9789004445567_009.

Walcott, R. (2003). *Black Like Who? Writing Black Canada*. Toronto, ON: Insomniac Press.

CHAPTER 2

Grounded Theory: Effects of COVID-19 on Homeless Youth

Methodological Reflections

Dionisio Nyaga, Dawn Onishenko and Rose Ann Torres

> To live in the unhomely world, to find its ambivalences and ambiguities enacted in the house fiction, or its sundering and splitting performed in the work of art, is also to affirm a profound desire for social solidarity: 'I am looking for the join ... I want to join ... I want to join.'
> BHABHA, 1994, p. 26

∴

Based on a grounded theory research study looking at the experiences of 'marginalized' youth experiencing precarious housing during the COVID-19 pandemic, this chapter attempts to explores the 'how' of grounded research as a strategy to 'ground' the research in the voice of the community and considers the way in with the iterative process need be re-imagined to consider who it is that guides the research – from initiation through data collection, analysis and interpreting/reporting findings. To this end, this chapter looks at the effects of the COVID-19 pandemic among homeless Black youth living in Toronto in order to tease out grounded research approach and considerations – our reflexive musings – in undertaking this project. Thus, this research project set out to draw out the lived experiences of marginalized homeless youth in Toronto, Ontario in order to understand the differentiated challenges they face as a result of their identities and the existing policies/practices during the COVID-19 pandemic. This chapter implicates research process, since it is the quintessential definition of broken and singularized policies and practices that continue to forget and discount marginalized homeless youth.

1   Literature Review

While homelessness impacts youth in Canada, some youth with compounding identities based on race (A Way Home, 2020), Indigeneity (HomelessHub,

2020), disability (Baker Collins et al., 2018), sexual orientation (Abramovich, 2016; A Way Home, 2020), gender (Oudshorn et al., 2021) and citizenship (Ansloos & Wager, 2021), and other marginal social constructs, are disproportionately compressed by homelessness due to multifaceted factors and existing policies and practices authorized by colonial research. Racialized (Boyd, Fast & Small, 2016; Petering, 2017), LGBTQ2S (EGALE, 2020), Indigenous (Kidd & Thistle, et al., 2018) and homeless youth with disabilities (Baker Collins, et al., 2018) are more likely to experience harassment, policing, depression, and addiction on top of being homeless.

While there are many studies looking at youth homelessness in Canada (HomelessHub, 2020), there is a glaring epistemological gap left to understand and imagine the specific experiences of Black homeless youth. While some of the studies pay attention to issues facing racialized homeless youth living in Canada few attempts have been made to mark the specific experiences of Black homeless youth. In addition, there is not enough research in Canada that pays attention to the effects of COVID-19 among homeless Black youths in Canada. However, existing research on effects of COVID-19 among Black communities living in Toronto paint a grim picture on the number of Black families who have been affected by the pandemic in terms of their social, political and economic conditions (Choi, et al., 2020). The COVID-19 pandemic has had a compounded effect among Black families based on the numbers of unemployment, homelessness, and death. While this is ongoing, one can only imagine the intensified effects of COVID-19 on homeless Black youth. Thus, this chapter argues for a re-imagination of terms such as youth and homelessness through an inter-textual historical analysis to birth a new COVID-19 methodology that sits with the specific experiences of Black homeless youth.

2 Methodology

This chapter is based on a qualitative research study that used grounded theory to explore the compounded effect of COVID-19 on 'marginalized' homeless youth living in Toronto. Marginalization is a social process which is rooted in, and maintained by, inequitable power relations that produce barriers which prevent access to social protection and participation for certain populations based upon multiple, and often intersecting, axis of social differentiation (Lassiter et al., 2018; Matheson et al., 2019; Rios et al., 2021; Thumath et al., 2021). As a result of these inequalities, marginalized homeless youth populations experience a broad array of disadvantages that include lack of access to resources such as education and healthcare, as well as reduced opportunities for employment and social advancement (Lassiter et al., 2018; Rios et al., 2021; Thumath et al., 2021). Importantly, research has established marginalization as one of the key social determinants of health, demonstrating marginality's corrosive effects on physical health and wellbeing (Rios et al., 2021).

Grounded Theory was chosen as it generates theory from the 'ground up' rather than bringing pre-conceived ideas to the research – i.e., participant voice (Glaser & Strauss, 1967). Grounded theory embraces an iterative process wherein interviews inform other interviews, literature informs interviews, which in turn may lead to needing to seek more literature, different data sources inform other data sources, etc.; each one may lead us back to the other to seek deeper information. Further, this research utilized Constructivist Grounded Theory, which is an inductive approach to research, with an ongoing process of simultaneous data collection and analysis, aimed at developing a theory, or explanation, 'grounded in', and emerging from, the data, rather than "pre-existing categories and theoretical frameworks" (Charmaz, 2006).

This research employed in-depth semi-structured interviews with 18 precariously housed youth (16–24), identifying as being part of a marginalized community(ies), 11 frontline housing/homelessness workers, including shelter workers and street outreach workers, and 9 service delivery managers, including executive directors, managers and program directors. The study attempted to answer the following research questions: What challenges do marginalized homeless youth face during the pandemic in terms of accessing housing, mental health supports, substance use treatment and other services; what are the experiences of these youth in regard to bullying, social exclusion, over policing, and access to appropriate services, and; what should our responses to marginalized youth homelessness look like? Engaging with this research, and the research team, lead us to engage in reflexive discussions on such existential questions as: What is 'marginal'; What is homeless; and who is considered youth and what happens to those are discounted as lesser or non-youth?

2.1 *Existential Analysis*

Research on homelessness of youth continues to be white and hegemonically essentialist. This epistemological imperative and reality continues to disappear 'other youths' experience (read Black, Indigenous, LGBTQ +, racialized, those living with disabilities among others) by reasserting a universal experience/essence (read collapsing or social genocide) of youth. This renders others marginalized youth voice homeless (read disappear or social death), both in research and subsequent policy formulation; making research as a technology or a program of discounting and disappearing and vanishing such voice in what Foucault calls the art of biopolitical erasure and extermination of subterranean social life (Foucault, 1997). To be disappeared and rendered homeless is a social conversion and alteration of social being into unintelligible or incomprehensible matter that have no place both in research, policy, and practice; to which we argue is the new form of social death or what Gordon Pon (2009) calls ontology of forgetting. If it is not imaginable (read this as knowable, has a name and is researchable) then it is non-existent; and, therefore, nullified from social life. In a nutshell, such disappearance becomes a form of social death that cannot be grieved nor seen as a loss (Butler, 2020), because they cannot be named nor imagined as living. Since they are unintelligible social refuse/excesses, they cannot be included into the infrastructure of state care; rather they must be disposed, discounted and dispossessed of their right to life or existence while being mapped or marked as social excesses. It is this technology of dispossession or epistemological eviction of homeless marginalized youth that this chapter seeks to grapple with to reimagine research and care as a process of accounting or grieving the loss of bodies that fail to matter. It calls for us to comes to terms with the death of marginalized groups and sit comfortable with the fact that we as researcher must become the graveyards of participant, which helps us think of ways in which we can employ vulnerability (self-cannibalization) as a necessary ethical prerogative in knowledge production.

This epistemological and ontological death has differentiated material and symbolic consequences to marginalized homeless youths in terms of how they face substance use, mental health, and policing. This chapter seeks to argue that not all experiences of youth are equal and that not all youths are considered youths. From this perspective, we argue that some youths are more equal than others (borrowing from George Orwell's animal farms) and therefore to speak of youth experience is to engage with differentiated existential human development which renders Black and Africa/n youth outside this foundational western narrative of human/youth development. Such unspeakable and silenced youth experiences are marked as irrational and unintelligible and as such in need of care from the savior (the researcher). To be considered irrational in research is to argue that they cannot be scientifically constituted/ represented (read boxed as a technology of panopticon or prison complex mentality), quantified, and unified; therefore, rendering them outside what may be calculable within the metrics of scientific human development. This aspect of incalculability or lack thereof of metrics of measure help mark out this group as unable to join the human citizenhood (civilization), therefore rendering such bodies as homeless and placeless in research and policy.

We equally argue that representation of youth (as a unified quantifiable piece) in research continue to denigrate 'other youths' in ways that are materially and symbolically violent and exterminatory. When doing research among youth, there is a tendency to collapse (read social extermination/disappearance/death) youth into one universal experience, subsequently denying them social existence. This existential reality renders experiences of Black and African lives as not livable (and using Butler word ungrievable and can easily be lost (read homelessness) without being mourned) enough and subsequently erased from research, policy and practice. The art of marking such experiences as outside social life deports and nullifies these bodies as non-existent and broken and as such becomes a site of violent operation of colonial power. This chapter therefore argues that rather than boxing such lives into one universal truth, there is a need to re-engage more with their experience in ways that imagines their experience rather that methodically boxing them into one prison of existence.

Our argument therefore is for us to critically look at the psychic life of those pre-determined as socially broken or outside human life in ways that re-imagine how this groups of youth can be differentially grieved and counted as lost both in research and policy. We argue that such an imagination will have to render research and policy empathetically homeless to imagine the face of the other as grievable. To argue that research needs to be empathetic (read grievable) to the existence of such social lives outside what is considered normal homelessness is to reimagine ways of decolonizing empathy so that we are not conscripted within colonial packaging of empathy that again renders participants homeless in research and care. If we are to engage with the present corporate methodology of empathy as "being on the shoe of the other" then we can only imagine what happens to the original wearer of the shoe. Their footprints (read histories) will be lost rendering such bodies as inconsequently unimaginable. It goes without saying that such a method/ology will remove (read evict) the participant and their footprints from the shoe (read their histories), through the imprint of the researcher (read performativity) (Butler, 2004) and then invite the former wearer into a civilized shoe, bearing the saviour's footprints. Two things will have happened: first, removal of the original person/wearer of the shoe (think of Indigenous communities and colonialism) together with their footprint (read their experience) and secondly replacement of that experiences with researcher's. This by any measure is the art of colonial violence in that we can easily replace other people stories and experiences (read life) with our own and in retrospect collapse the other while masquerading as the caring saviour. It is our differentiated stories made possible by our context that marks us as human. Subsequently, any form of erasure of such stories by quantification without qualification is concurrently a process of violent death of the participant, who are deemed unrecoverable consequences. But we are also very aware that such a process of erasing other people's stories is simultaneously a process of rendering them unreadable and therefore unrepresentable. This by any term is violent and a form of social death made possible by empathy as an ethical prerogative in research.

2.2 Methodological Analysis

This chapter reflects on the research project to critically and reflexively engage with terms such as homelessness and youth and how ethics of care (Butler, 2020) in research have been rendered homeless in an environment that is COVID. We already know that research and care has always been violent (Butler, 2020; Foucault, 1979). Our wager is to disturb existing dominant colonial care technologies in research in ways that are non-violent and community based (Butler, 2020). Key to this argument is to underline the need for research and policy to become homeless (read disappear) for it to come to terms with and agonize with the desire and experience of people or communities living with homeless. This mean engaging and complicating the issue of institutionalized empathy in research as an ethical prerogative to non-violent research care. We know that empathy as a research care technology and methodology is flout with imperial industrialization and is implicated in violence (Zembylas, 2013). According to Zembylas (2013),

> Empathetic identification with the plight of others, then, is not a sentimental recognition of potential sameness—you are in pain and so am I, so we both suffer the same—but a realization of our own common humanity, while acknowledging asymmetries of suffering, inequality, and injustice. A discourse of vulnerability neither eschews questions of material suffering nor obscures issues of inequality and injustice; on the contrary, it highlights both the symmetries and the asymmetries of vulnerability. That is, although the experience of vulnerability may be more or less universal, the discourse of common vulnerability raises important critical questions such as "vulnerable to what? To whom?" to dismiss the possibility of sliding into a sentimental recognition of potential sameness—which is exactly what a politics of compassion ardently seeks to avoid. Without this double realization—that is, we are all vulnerable but not in the same manner—our actions run the danger of being a form of charity and condescension toward those who are systematically and institutionally oppressed.
> BUNCH, 2002, p. 512

This means that for research care to comes to terms with the plight of Black homeless youth, a new form of vulnerability and care informed research will have to inform the philosophical underpinning of our epistemological imagination. In a COVID-19 environment, it is easy and simple to employ empathy as a care technology. In this chapter, vulnerability informed empathy will have to grapple with the fact that we are all not in this suffering together. That will mean a differentiated epistemological assignation with the lived realities of Black homeless youth without collapsing them into quantifiable and redacted sameness. Secondly, research and care will have to move from it current expert tower and become homeless. This form of empathy informed research care should be grounded on realities and values of research participants. It comes with the loss of researcher as the expert. This form of vulnerability and loss of the expert will sanction policies and research that inform care to become pedestrian and homeless (and steeped in peoples' ways of life).

This section attempts to disappear (read homelessness) empathy in ways that employ beyond market rationalized care technologies in research that continue to bind and package emotions as a product for sale in the market. Such a form of epistemological homelessness or disappearance is a necessary ethical prerogative that throws off research from its public comfort and into places of discomfort and unknowing; such that a researcher comes to grapple with the fact that they cannot understand or collapse participant but rather imagine them as people who have rights bestowed to them as thinking beings. This imagination is an ethical necessity of allowing the self to move from academic pedestal and actively listen to the multifaceted stories of youth living with homeliness without necessarily quantifying them into metrics of care. To disappear and imagine the other must therefore be the new metrification of care that account for the loss of those we are given the opportunity and responsibility to care for. We have to look at research and care from the standpoint that is human, and be ready to be raffled by the fact that we always arrive late and that such a colonial belief that we are expert has to disappear to accommodate the other who is never grieved or whose loss is never seen as a loss. To that end, this chapter situates research as a process of inconsolable mourning and an accounting of losses of our comfort in knowledge production as a research methodology.

3 Recovering, Mourning and Critical Reflexivity as Social Justice

To that end, we must be critically reflexive of our implication in the social death of the participants even in the process of research. That being the case, this chapter proposes the need to apply a COVID-19 methodology within and without grounded research approach. This chapter argues that while COVID-19 continues to wreak havoc based on the number of countable deaths we continue to witness, there is some lessons that we need to learn from it to help bring forth relevant and critical transformative everyday research work. Our witness is a necessary place of forming a non-violent form of knowledge creation steeped in people's histories and life experiences. COVID-19 has brought forth subterranean stories to the street, while rendering the how of research homeless in ways never seen before.

Over time, transformative critical research has underlined the need for change. But all this time, such stories have been considered emotional and unspeakable. It is through COVID-19 deaths that the 'pedestrian' has spoken the need to pay attention to historical injustice meted on marginalized homeless youths. Excluded communities, such as Black communities, have suffered the social vulnerabilities of this pandemic in ways that are disproportional and compounded compared to their white counterparts. COVID-19 has therefore spotlighted these historical injustices, and as researchers, we cannot let this method/ological window close by vaccinating our way out of colonial research. This study therefore seeks to argue that such a methodology twist will help bring forth the stories of homeless youth in ways that are historical, political, ethical, and transformative. This methodological disorientation will also work closely with the uniqueness of every youth experience in ways that are not only rational but emotional and explorative.

4 Reimagining Grounded as a COVID-19-Related Approach

This chapter looks at how the COVID-19 pandemic has caused a lot of trauma among Black communities in ways that are disproportionate and compounded. A look at print and other form of electronic media paints a bleak picture of lives that continue to suffer under the current pandemic. According to recent data in Toronto, Black, Indigenous, 2SLGBTQ, racialized and differently abled groups suffer the most pain from COVID-19. The situation is even dire when you introduce issues of gender, citizenship, and postal code. It is recognized that this aspect of social life is further compounding the levels of social pain among marginalized communities.

While this is ongoing, we realize that COVID-19 has opened new conversation in terms of laying bare historical injustices that marginalized communities have and continue to suffer under current policy framework. Equally, we argue that these policies continue to breath colonial life made possible by research studies, which therefore makes it easy for the policies to speak language that is not in tune with communities. From this perspective, this chapter argues that policy and research is implicated in the social pains that marginalized communities continue to suffer then and under the current pandemic. What the COVID-19 pandemic has done is to lay bare the 'how' of policy (research) in ways that open a discussion on lived existence and context of the communities. We argue that COVID-19 has rendered policy and research epistemologically homeless in ways that will ground the how of getting to know what we know (methodology). Therefore, there is need to reinvent a new breath of life in terms of how we need to undertake grounded theory so that it is grounded in the stories of people experiencing social pain and that such lives can be grieved and counted when they are lost. We call for a grounded theory approach that is transformative and that can be vulnerable to the open historical wounds caused by colonial violence among communities. We look for a critically transformative grounded theory that is critically reflexive.

This psychic process of becoming means grounded theory will need to reimagine itself beyond its traditional assumptions. We argue that processes of saturation will need to be reimagine by asking questions like who decides when data is saturated. Bhabha (1994) speaking of back-and-forth movement may help provide some light on this process of iteration as necessary in grounded theory. He says:

> In their cultural passage, hither and thither, as migrant workers, part of the massive economic and political diaspora of the modern world, they embody the Benjaminian 'present': that moment blasted out of the continuum of history. Such conditions of cultural displacement and social discrimination – where political survivors become the best historical witness-are the grounds on which Franz Fanon, the Martinican psychoanalyst and participant in the Algerian revolution, locates an agency of empowerment.
> p. 12

The process of going back and forth will need to be reimagined psychically and ethically to begin to ask who walks through the road from analysis and back to data collection. Traditional grounded theory allows a 'male centric research' the privilege to walk that road. We call this male privilege because it seems 'he' has accessed the participant who seemingly look docile and submissive. This in and of itself is colonial violence to research participants. It is a reminder of a colonizer who enters and leaves at will and when they return to their office for analyses, they can claim they have survived barbarism of the broken other (read communities), which in itself is the gendered coloniality in research. This process reinscribes colonial violence and the role of research as a process of saving the barbarian other from self-cannibalization. The road back and forth represents colonial boundaries that are violent in ways that renders the other as fixed being living in the past and who needs to be saved by the benevolent other (read researcher). We argue that such a road needs to be psychically reconceptualized in ways that re-imagine the role of the colonized researcher in the eye of the participant and vice-versa. The boundary and the bridges between the researcher and researched need to come down and be open to the tides and waves in the river or the sea. This will mean that we will need to find different grounds and waves that connects us in ways that are political and transformative. To cross the land, we will need to engage with diversity of social waves and tides and come to the reality that even though the tides and waves may disturb our settler hood, more is to be gained if we hold our hands and build bridges that are human and fluid.

5   Conclusion

For a while, qualitative research has come out as a process that enables stories of marginalized communities to speak to the coloniality of quantification and reduction of the same. In other works (Torres & Nyaga, 2021), qualitative studies continue to maintain quantitative reductionism based on the methodologies of its different approaches. A look at qualitative approaches provided to social work research, one realizes disciplinary competition between these approaches. Each one of the approaches seeks to be scientific and equally a return to their original place of quantification. A case in point is traditional phenomenology that calls for bracketing out of the researcher so that their research can be objective. We also see divisions within this disciplinary approached each one of them trying to exist a live that can be as close to quantification of knowledge. We argue that this punitive division and subsequent boxing (read prisons) is quantitatively and colonially supervised (read surveillance) rendering these approaches (case study, grounded theory, phenomenology, ethnography) imprisoned and unable to engage deeply with the life of communities. This chapter argues that even when it seems that these approaches are grounded on the lives of marginalized communities, they have inherently re-recolonized the communities. What these approaches are doing is progressive politics of providing the communities with platforms of equity, equality and justice that is grounded in colonial epistemologies. Through that, communities are made to exist others in ways that renders then prone to everyday erasure. Our argument is that these qualitative approached are inherently colonial and need to work from a place of ethics, in ways that looks at the face of pain without necessarily understanding it but rather imagining them.

The chapter argues that these approaches need to work with communities in ways that are grounded to their context, histories, and as such ethically conscious. This will mean a change to the philosophical assumptions that undergirds these approaches so that they can start unshackling themselves in ways that are in solidarity with communities. In essence, the approaches will have to be rendered homeless for them to speak in line with the lived experiences of people. This is a psychic process of getting to know themselves through the eye of the communities. The unshackling will have to be a process of allying with communities in ways that are psychic, political and ethical.

References

Abramovich, A. (2016). Preventing, reducing and ending LGBTQ2S youth homelessness: the need for targeted strategies. *Social Inclusion*, 4(4), 86–96.

Ansloos, A., Wager, A. & Dunn, N. (2021) Preventing indigenous youth homelessness in Canada: a qualitative study on structural challenges and upstream prevention in education. *Journal of Community Phycology*, 50(4), 1918–1934.

A Way Home. (2020). Youth homelessness in Canada. https://awayhome.ca/.

Baker Collins, S., Schormans, A. F., Watt, L., Idems, B., & Wilson, T. (2018). The invisibility of disability for homeless youth. *Journal of Social Distress and the Homeless*, 27(2), 99–109.

Bhabha, H. K. (1994). *Location of Culture*. New York, NY: Routledge.

Boyd, J., Fast, D., & Small, W. (2016). Pathways to criminalization for street-involved youth who use illicit substances. *Critical Public Health*, 26(5), 530–541.

Butler, J. (2020). *The Force of Nonviolence: an Ethico-political Bind*. Verso.

Butler, J. (2004). *Undoing Gender*. Routledge.

Charmaz, K. (2006). *Constructing Grounded Theory: a Practical Guide through Qualitative Analysis*. Thousand Oaks, CA: SAGE.

Choi, K., Zajacova, A., Haan, M., & Denice, P. (2020, May 20) Data linking race and health predicts new COVID-19 hotspots. *The Conversation*. Retrieved from https://theconversation.com/data-linking-race-and-health-predicts-new-COVID-19- hotspots-138579.

EGALE. (April 16, 2020). *Newsletter: Impacts of COVID-19 on LGBTQI2S People*.

Foucault, M. (1979). *Discipline and Punish: the Birth of the Prison* (1st ed.). Vintage Books.

Foucault, M. (1997). *Society Must Be Defended*. London, UK: Penguin.

Glaser, B, & Strauss, A. (1967). *The Discovery of Grounded Theory: Strategies for Qualitative Research*. New York: Aldine de Gruyter.

HomelessHub, (2020). The use of homeless shelters by Indigenous people in Canada. https://www.homelesshub.ca/coh-awh-youth-survey-covid19-2020.

Kidd, S., Thistle, J., Beaulieu, T., O'Grady, B., Gaetz, S. (2018). A national study of indigenous youth homelessness in Canada. *Public Health*, (176),163–171.

Lassiter, C., Norasakkunkit, V., Shuman, B., & Toivonen, T. (2018). Diversity and resistance to change: Macro conditions for marginalization in post-industrial societies. *Frontiers in Psychology*, 9, 812–812. https://doi.org/10.3389/fpsyg.2018.00812.

Matheson, K., Foster, M. D., Bombay, A., McQuaid, R. J., & Anisman, H. (2019). Traumatic experiences, perceived discrimination, and psychological distress among members of various socially marginalized groups. *Frontiers in Psychology*, 10, 416–416. https://doi.org/10.3389/fpsyg.2019.00416.

Oudshorn, A., May, K., Van Berkum, A., Schwan, K., Nelson, A., Eiboff, f., Begun, S., Nichols, N. & Parsons, C. (2021). *Exploring the Approaches of Gender-Based Approaches to Women's Homelessness in Canadian Communities.* Western University: Homeless Hub. Exploring The Presence of Gender-Based Approaches to Women's Homelessness in Canadian Communities | The Homeless Hub.

Petering, R. (2017). Youth homelessness and gang involvement: Ties, trajectories, and timelines.

Pon, G. (2009). Cultural competency as new racism: an ontology of forgetting. *Journal of Progressive Human Services*, 20(1), 59–71.

Rios, S., Meyer, S. B., Hirdes, J., Elliott, S., & Perlman, C. M. (2021). The development and validation of a marginalization index for inpatient psychiatry. *International Journal of Social Psychiatry*, 67(4), 324–334. https://doi.org/10.1177/0020764020950785.

Thumath, M., Humphreys, D., Barlow, J., Duff, P., Braschel, M., Bingham, B., Pierre, S., & Shannon, K. (2021). Overdose among mothers: the association between child removal and unintentional drug overdose in a longitudinal cohort of marginalised women in Canada. *The International Journal of Drug Policy*, 91, https://doi.org/10.1016/j.drugpo.2020.102977.

Torres, R. A., & Nyaga, D. (2021). *Critical Research Methodologies: Ethics and Responsibilities.* Leiden: Brill.

Zembylas, M. (2013). The "crisis of pity" and the radicalization of solidarity: Toward critical pedagogies of compassion. *Educational Studies*, 49(6), 504–521.

CHAPTER 3

Reflexivity, Recursion and Re-evaluation
Some Reflections On 'Institutional Ethnography'

Nob Doran

1 Adding Recursion to Reflexivity[1]

I grew up on 'reflexivity'.[2] My very first published article was entitled "Jumping Frames: Reflexivity and Recursion in the Sociology of Science" (Doran 1989). And it was my earliest (peer-reviewed) attempt at going beyond my unconventional undergraduate fascination with ethnomethodologically-inspired writers (Drew 1978; Wootton 1975; Blum and McHugh 1971; Turner, 1974b; Filmer et al., 1972; Sandywell et al., 1975). In that early paper, when I was still using my birth name (Chris Doran), and had not yet worked out my textual identity,[3] I showed the 'tangled loop' (Hofstadter 1979) that even reflexively-aware sociologists got into, when debating each other. In other words, I documented how these scholars went around 'in circles' while arguing the merits of their respective positions about 'constructionist' sociology. More interestingly perhaps, I foregrounded the problem of 'recursion' in these nascent sociological debates about this notion of 'reflexivity' introduced by the ethnomethodologists Wieder (1974), and Mehan and Wood (1975). And my suggestion was that, once scholars (even reflexive scholars) discover that they may be going around in circles in such debates, they might consider 'jumping frames' and cease living[4] and writing, within an epistemic field pre-occupied with the will to truth

---

1 A version of this chapter was presented at the 2022 Canadian Sociology Association's annual meetings, held virtually, on May 19th 2022. The session was entitled 'Feminist sociology: Theorising past, present and future' (12noon to 1.30pm Atlantic time).
2 At least, the ethnomethological version of it, as displayed in the writings of authors like Garfinkel (1967) and Wieder (1974). For a recent overview of how the meaning of this term has changed considerably, see Lumsden, Bradford and Goode (2019).
3 Unlike Gloria Jean Watkins, whose 'textual identity' seems to have been in place from a relatively early age. See hooks, b. (1981) for an example.
4 The importance of this notion of 'living' within paradigms will become clearer, once we have discussed Foucault's final writings on 'parrhesia' (Foucault, 2010, 2011), and the assembling of what I call a 'parrhesian' self. That is, someone who engages in a form of truth-telling associated with 'fearless speech' (Foucault 2001) and an entire 'way of life'.

(Foucault, 1980, pp. 92–3), and perhaps move to a different one; such as the Foucauldian paradigm of power/knowledge.[5]

And this suggestion, that we move to this meta-level 'frame' of power/knowledge, was informed by my early realization that ethnomethodologically-informed scholars not only insisted that one always begins sociological analysis from one's own, shared 'common sense reasoning' (Turner, 1974a; Smith, 1974b), but that it also opened up a route for mounting a powerful critique of sociology's privileged status, as a social science (Douglas, 1970; Cicourel, 1964; Cicourel, 1968). And in this respect, I was closer to Smith's ethnomethodologically-aligned[6] critique of sociology's methods (Smith, 1974a), but I felt unable, at that time, to use her 'standpoint' in women's experience (Smith, 1974b) on which to base my emerging critique. So, instead, I tried starting from the standpoint of these (Social Studies of Science) scholars who also wanted to keep the critique of science a central component of their research.[7]

Of course, having been weaned on ethomethodological insights, there was never a time when I wasn't aware of issues of 'frame' and 'content' (or, as it is sometimes called, 'topic and resource', see Dennis, 2019). And that was because my first ever sociological seminars introduced me to the ethnomethodological revelation regarding the gap between what traditional sociology said at the level of content (based on its asserted social scientific 'expertise'), and what it actually did, at the level of frame (based, instead, on its tacit reliance on mundane 'common sense reasoning') (Zimmerman and Pollner, 1970; Douglas, 1970; Cicourel, 1968). And as it wasn't long before some ethnomethodologically-influenced scholars turned their attention to the 'natural sciences', and not just the 'social sciences', I was intrigued by this work, as well (Woolgar, 1976; Garfinkel, Lynch and Livingstone, 1981). And my ongoing sensitivity to, and awareness of, contradictions (between theory and method, content and frame) was then incorporated into that early critique of mine regarding reflexivity in the 'sociology of science'.

---

5 The term 'power/knowledge' is utilized here so as to situate this Foucauldian thinking in its appropriate socio-historical context. Obviously, Foucault went on to develop this concept in a number of different directions (Foucault 1979, 1980, 2007, 2008).

6 Her pioneering article "The Ideological Practice of Sociology" (1974a) was also published, in abridged form, in the 1974 edited collection, entitled "Ethnomethodology" (Turner, 1974b). And, thus, my introduction to her work was to see her as some type of (innovative) ethnomethodologist.

7 By this time, much ethnomethodology was devoting itself to the study of work (Garfinkel (Ed.), 1986), or of conversation (Atkinson and Drew, 1978). The early challenge to traditional social scientific ways of knowing (e.g., Cicourel, 1968; Cicourel and Kitsuse, 1963) was no longer as prominent.

Basically, the early research in the 'social studies of science' field had been inspired by the critique of the 'social sciences' put forward by the early ethnomethodologists. (e.g., Cicourel, 1964). For example, scholars like Latour and Woolgar documented the 'social construction of science' in their groundbreaking book "Laboratory Life" (1979). And because Woolgar, at least, had a strong concern with 'reflexivity', the book was very aware of the position in which it found itself. As I said, in my 1989 paper,

> A wary reader might have noticed already an obvious problem with this radical critique of science. If the thrust of the new 'constructionist' scholarship is to claim that 'all science is constructed' through the social actions of scientists, surely the same criticism can be applied to their own sociological reports. Thus appears the problem of reflexivity.
> DORAN, 1989, p. 516

And to counter this possible critique, "Laboratory life" had gone out of its way to demonstrate, in its textual methods, that it too was a 'constructed account'. Moreover, it sought to draw attention to its ironic stance and reflexive standpoint. As Woolgar commented on the reception, from traditional researchers, that the book received:

> [T]he first photograph in the photograph file is labelled 'view from the laboratory roof. Now, presumably, a determined instrumentally-minded reader will take this at face value, and go away happy that he is better informed about the character of laboratory roofs (and views therefrom). For such readers we are naturally pleased to increase their sum of knowledge about the world. But unfortunately, the main point of the exercise would then have been lost. Our wish was that the inclusion of such a photograph might at least make such readers stop and think about what is involved in the juxtaposition of textual imagery, and how this affects the reader's relationship with the facts as represented by the text. An instrumental reading of the ethnography will miss the irony intended to alert the reader to issues in reflexivity.
> quoted in DORAN, 1989, p. 518

Thus, Woolgar shows that he is self-reflective about the status of his own 'constructionist account', via both his content and his (textual) methods. However, the intent of my paper was to push this understanding of 'reflexivity' and 'self-reflection' even further. And in this respect, I adopted the textual method that Mulkay (1984) proposed. For him, the issue of 'reflexivity' had become central to scholarly analysis; and he wanted to explicitly foreground the 'constructed' nature of his own analysis. And that meant him abandoning traditional research formats. Instead, he used the format of a 'play'.[8] And in this play, he showed how social scientists (sociologists in the 'social studies of science' field), *and* natural scientists went around in circles, when they did not pay enough attention to the issue of reflexivity.[9] And I built on Mulkay's method to push this argument even further. That is, I went on to show that a reflexive scholar, like Woolgar, also fails to be sufficiently self-reflective in his own writings, when he engages in debate with another 'reflexively-aware sociologist'.

Not surprisingly then, this constant examination of 'frame' versus 'content' has remained with me ever since. And, thus, the interrogative stance, adapted from Mulkay's 1984 work, that I had first used in that 1989 paper, was subsequently modified and deployed on several other writers. Interestingly, these examinations were aimed at my early teachers.[10] That is, although the ethnomethodologically-inspired writers had often critiqued traditional sociology, I wanted to interrogate my 'teachers' to see if they displayed similar paradoxical, contradictory stances in their analyses; or whether they were able to demonstrate a harmony between what they said, and what they did.[11] And Dorothy Smith was next on this list; as she not only critiqued traditional sociology but she insisted that any 'alternative sociology must be reflexive (Gouldner, 1970), i.e., one that preserves in it the presence, concerns and experience of the sociologist as knower and discoverer' (Smith, 1974b: 11). In other words, a version of reflexivity was at the heart of Smith's enterprize, as well.[12]

Thus, my next interrogation of these 'teachers' led me to revealing the (first half of the) 'recursive loop' that Dorothy Smith (Doran, 1993) got caught in,

---

8 For other examples of 'new literary forms' which draw attention to their 'constructed nature', see the papers collected together in Woolgar (1988).
9 Mulkay is heavily dependent on Hofstadter's (1979) work here, which thoroughly displays these problems of 'recursion', 'tangled loops' etc.
10 To be clear, these scholars were not actually teachers in the literal sense of the word. I never took classes from any of them or studied with them. I simply immersed myself in their works. Thus, it constituted a form of self-education, as much of it was carried out on the margins of my 'formal education'. And some of these teachers inspired me (the ethnomethodologists, Smith etc) while others annoyed and frustrated me (Hall et al., 1978).
11 It was the Analysis school which, most fervently pursued this goal of seeking a harmonious relationship between the content of one's scholarly writings, and its 'form'. See Blum and McHugh (1984) and McHugh et al. (1975) for examples.
12 And Smith's 'reflexive' alternative continues to be widely embraced today. And although Smith originally intended 'institutional ethnography' to be a theory/method, it has become frequently re-interpreted as an 'alternative methodology'. See Rankin (2017), for an example.

when she failed to self-reflect enough, on her own practices. I then followed that with similarly-informed analyses of scholars in the fields of 'ethnomethodology' (Doran, 1996) and then 'cultural studies' (Doran, 2008). Most recently, however, my interrogation of Foucault (Doran, 2015) has demonstrated the opposite, with regard to frame versus content. Whereas the scholars I had interrogated up until then, had all been found wanting because of the contradiction between what they said, and what they did, in their textual practices; I now discovered that Foucault had actually done the opposite. His embodied methods (of assembling a 'self') actually constructed a harmonious fit between what he said, and what he had done over the course of his career. That is, he had become a truth-telling 'parrhesian' in his embodied methods of 'caring for himself' (Doran, 2015, p. 149–55).

And this realization has made me think that I perhaps need to re-evaluate my earlier interrogations. That is to say, I could return to one of these teachers at least, Dorothy Smith, and re-examine her from this meta-level; this Foucauldian perspective of the parrhesian. And this may constitute itself as a radical turning point for any contemporary understanding of Smith's work. This is because if we *jump frames* (again) to this Foucauldian perspective, of embodied life-long activity (albeit always situated within 'agonistic' fields), we might see that Smith, although she may go around in circles in her textual work, might actually have assembled herself as a 'parrhesian intellectual' over a long period of arduous educational struggle, of trans-forming her embodied 'self' into a feminist self.[13]

Of course, asking readers to make this leap with me, is perhaps a little premature, as there is one crucial step in this journey which remains somewhat hidden right now. As suggested earlier, after showing the recursive loop in which several sociologists of science got themselves entangled, I then went on to examine Dorothy Smith's work for similar paradoxes and contradictions. And although my 1993 paper displayed the first half of that loop, the second half (although written at the same time) never did get published.[14] And as that unpublished paper not only completed the full display of this recursive loop, but also showed a crucial problem with Smith's macro-sociological theorizing, it is an important missing step. And that is because it not only displays Smith's

---

13   Of course, this would involve the examination of the conversion process (Foucault, 2005) that Smith may have worked on, in transforming herself from the Dorothy Place of Northallerton, England to the Dorothy E. Smith of international recognition.
14   Interestingly, while the paper containing the first half of this loop was accepted for publication immediately, without any revisions, the paper containing the second half of the loop was rejected at almost the same speed (albeit by a different journal).

'ideological practices' with regard to historical materials, but it paves the way for the replacement of Smith's Marxist frame, with Foucault's 'power/knowledge' frame.

2   Completing Smith's Recursive Loop: the 'Paper' within a Paper

In 1993 I had published the first half (Doran, 1993) of my interrogation of Smith, into the harmony, or lack thereof, between the content of what she said, theoretically, and her textual practices. In that paper, I demonstrated that even though she began her feminist career critiquing traditional sociology for converting everyday experience (the 'actualities' of social life)[15] into the official discourse (typically 'statistical' and 'conceptual') of sociology(Smith, 1974a), when she went on to formulate her own version of (a feminist) sociology (Smith, 1987), she repeated those practices (albeit at a higher logical level), by converting historical experience into the official discourse of "Marxism". Moreover, I drew attention to the constructed nature of my own account, by adopting the textual format of an 'autobiographical discovery';[16] that of demonstrating what I had learnt, and also what I had had to 'unlearn',[17] in my academic self-formation.

However, at that time, I also completed my demonstration of the second half of the 'recursive loop' that Smith, herself, was caught up in. That is, I showed that she then went on to develop a more historically informed analysis, but once again tacitly converted the everyday experiences of late 19th century women into the theoretical discourse of the (Marxist-inspired) 'ruling relations'.[18] And so, what I would now like to do is actually display the completion of this loop.

---

15 For a specific discussion of some of the issues involved in the use of this term see Hart and McKinnon (2010).

16 The initial aim was to attempt a 'form' of presentation which eschewed 'traditional forms' of research writing, while, at the same time, not writing in a format which would be widely understand as 'completely fictional'. In this regard, 'autobiographical writing' appeared attractive; as it not only sits between the two formats just mentioned, but it sheds light on one great mystery of academia; how do academics assemble the sociological 'selves' that they become. This paper tries to shed a little more light on this typically backgrounded process.

17 As Foucault suggests about the process of 'conversion of the self' involved in becoming parrhesian, it involves a considerable amount of unlearning (Foucault, 2005), as will become clearer later on.

18 Smith's usage of this concept went on to become quite central in the institutional ethnographic studies informed by Smith. For an early example, see Campbell and Manicom (1995).

So let us return to the specifics of this chapter. And in a similar fashion to how playwrights sometimes insert a play within a play, or how novelists may insert a story within a story, this chapter will insert a paper within a paper, in order to draw attention to the recursive and nested nature of this analysis; that is to say, one must always be aware of the level at which one is operating. In other words, my early paper is now being 'nested' within this paper.[19] And for ease of exposition, and to help clarify these different levels, this old paper[20] will be reproduced with its original footnotes, as can be seen below.

INSTITUTIONAL ETHNOGRAPHY AS PROBLEMATIC: IDEOLOGICAL PRACTICES IN DOROTHY SMITH'S MACRO-SOCIOLOGY

Chris Doran

The latter half of Dorothy Smith's career has been systematically concerned with linking lived experience to institutional structures, and has resulted in the formulation of 'institutional ethnography' as a means of both uncovering contemporary ideological practices and of formulating a specifically feminist sociology. Unfortunately, despite Smith's groundbreaking work in linking micro with macro, this paper argues that her own work is also ideological (in her own sense of that term). Through a textual analysis of Smith's research, I demonstrate her tacit ideological practices (operating at the level of frame rather than content) in her treatment of working class mothers in nineteenth century England. As a consequence, she ends up adopting an 'ideological' position similar to the one she began her career criticising with regard to conventional social science. That is, she completes a strange recursive loop in which she curiously reverses her theoretical positions regarding both ideology and embodied experience.

Vocalising an Ambivalence

Dorothy Smith's work is often taken as a prime example of the standpoint perspective in contemporary feminism (Harding, 1986a, 1986b, 1990;

---

19 Of course, for readers today, familiar with reading texts online, the idea of stories, report etc., being 'nested' within other stories, reports, etc., is routinely taken for granted.
20 According to my records, this paper was sent off to "Women's Studies International Forum" on 09/12/94.

Hawkesworth, 1989) and has been frequently cited in recent discussions comparing the merits of standpoint feminism (Hartsock, 1983; Smith, 1987) and postmodern feminism (Fraser & Nicholson, 1990; Haraway, 1988, 1990; Nicholson 1990). However, as much of this debate has taken place within philosophical circles, this has resulted in a rather narrow understanding of Smith's work; usually only focussing on her early critique of sociology as ideological or her subsequent call for a sociology starting from women's experience. And although there have recently emerged several critiques of Smith's experientially based micro-sociology (Clough, 1993; Doran, 1993), so far little attention has been paid to her later development of a feminist macro-sociology.

In contrast, I grew up on Smith's work as sociology. Thus I was able to better appreciate both the particulars of the disciplinary context out of which her work emerged and the subsequent development of her early critique into an alternative feminist sociology. Nevertheless, that appreciation has not been without reservations. For some time now, I have been ambivalent about Smith's sociological amalgamation of a 'realist' version of Marx with the 'relativism' of the phenomenologically inspired ethnomethodology so as to create the macro-sociology she calls 'Institutional Ethnography'. However, with Smith's publication of three book length pieces in recent years, it has now become clear to me that this ambivalence is because her Institutional Ethnography, like the conventional sociology she originally critiqued, is ideological. Moreover, it is ideological in Smith's own specific sense of that term (Smith, 1974a, 1990a, 1990b; cf Abercrombie, Hill & Turner, 1980; Larrain, 1979, 1983). That is, it is ideological in its methods rather than its content.

To present this belated realization, I will proceed as follows. Beginning at that critical point in her career when she called for a sociology beginning from experience, I then examine the temporal development of her feminist macro-sociology. First, I contextualize Smith's work by showing how she tried to develop her early insights into a 'critical' ethnomethodology, despite the fact that ethnomethodology usually shows 'relativistic indifference' (Atkinson, 1988, p. 459) to questions of power. Second, I show how Smith later attempted to move beyond these ethnomethodological limitations, by arguing that ethnomethodology itself was also ideological. That is, it was unable to move beyond mere surface description. She then proceeded to develop a research strategy (Institutional Ethnography) for moving beyond this surface towards the underlying social organization which the ethnomethodologists ignored. Third, I argue that when Smith actually conducts her institutional ethnographic analysis, it too is ideological in its practices. In fact, it uses methods parallel to the ones she identified as ideological in her early critiques of conventional sociology and ideological theorizing more generally.

Initial Explorations: Pursuing a 'Critical' Ethnomethodology

In order to fully understand Smith's later work, it is first necessary to resituate Smith's project within the specifically sociological, rather than feminist, context from which it emerged. That is, in her formative years Smith had few feminist contemporaries within sociology upon whose work she could draw. Thus, it is perhaps not surprising that her work is heavily dependent upon existing sociological perspectives; but which she bends and reshapes in a peculiarly feminist fashion. In this case, that early context was marked by the rather caustic emergence of ethnomethodology into a sociological canon dominated by the conservative tendencies of American structural functionalism (Garfinkel, 1967). Inspired by the phenomenological insights of Alfred Schutz, the early ethnomethodology not only introduced a concern for the mundane activities of everyday life and the inter-subjective basis of social order (Douglas, 1970; Turner 1974b), it also mounted a critique of existing sociological research for being tacitly dependent upon common sense methods of data collection (Cicourel, 1964). As a consequence, ethnomethodology insisted that the cultural competence of the analyst had to become an explicitly acknowledged feature of the research endeavour and that any future analysis had to begin from embodied experience (Filmer, Phillipson, Silverman & Walsh, 1972; Turner, 1974a).

Not surprizingly, Smith adroitly used such insights to mount her own critique of conventional sociology as being both ideological and as having silenced women's voices through its research methods. Yet ethnomethodology was less helpful in other regards. Despite its early empirical forays into the realms of law, delinquency and deviance (Cicourel, 1968; Douglas, 1967; Sudnow, 1965), much of this ethnomethodology, and the conversation analysis which grew out of it (Sacks 1963, 1972; Sacks, Schegloff & Jefferson, 1974; Psathas, 1990), still preserved an overwhelming pre-occupation with merely describing the 'social grammar' of mundane interaction, rather than challenging these tacit rules of everyday life in any critical fashion (Atkinson, 1988; Benson & Hughes, 1983; Heritage, 1984; Garfinkel, 1987; Maynard and Wilson, 1980; cf Murray, 1987; Zimmerman and West, 1975). In fact, it took quite some time before a 'critical' stance (Baker, 1989; Emmison, 1989; Fairclough,

1985, 1992; Grahame, 1985; McHoul & Luke, 1989; Silverman and Torode, 1980; Torode, 1989; Van Dijk, 1993) emerged out of this linguistic turn in sociological analysis.

The beauty of Smith's work, however, is that twenty years ago, she had started to go beyond Garfinkelian ethnomethodology (Garfinkel, 1967) and give her own work both a critical direction and a macro-sociological linkage (cf Alexander, Giesen, Munch & Smelser, 1987; Collins, 1981). For example, Smith's work on the formulation of K's mental illness (1978, reprinted in 1990b) used insights from conversation analysis to document the common sense "facticity" of mental illness. But she then went beyond conversation analysis to discuss the issue of whose voice was rendered silent in the construction of that text. Starting from the typical conversation analytic injunction to present all of the data (See Atkinson & Drew 1979, ch. 1 for a discussion), Smith explicated the members' resources used to stigmatize a prior friend as mentally ill. But she then went on to contrast this version with another possible interpretation, of K having been frozen out of the previous relationship. Smith did this by showing the 'contrast structures' and the 'instructions for reading' which were utilized by K's 'friends' so as to silence and discount K's voice.

Smith's 1974 work, 'The social construction of documentary reality' is also significant because it instituted her research agenda of linking the micro and the macro. This was to be accomplished, in part, via analyses of the textualization of everyday experience and the simultaneous construction of a documentary reality. As nowadays, "a documentary reality is fundamental to the practices of governing, managing and administration of this form of society" (Smith, 1974b, p. 257).

Although businesses, governments, the professions (including the social sciences) etc., all use such documentation as their primary mode of action, the social construction of such documents had rarely been analysed. Using the work of ethnomethodologists like Zimmerman (1969), and Zimmerman and Pollner (1970), she not only investigated the social construction of facticity, but she showed that 'documentary facts' constitute a knowledge which is,

> ideological in the sense that this social organization preserves conceptions and means of description which represent the world as it is for those who rule it, rather than as it is for those who are ruled. (1974b, p. 267)

Hitherto, Marxism and ethnomethodology had had little to say to each other (Bandyopadhyay, 1971; Chua, 1977; Mehan and Wood, 1975). Yet from these early insights, Smith began to develop this concern with ideology at the level of the everyday (Eichler, 1985). Ethnomethodology by itself, was inadequate, as it made no connections to institutional structures. But it took some time before Smith was able to develop a detailed critique of ethnomethodology to show exactly why it was inadequate. As might be expected, Smith discovered that ethnomethodology was ideological.

Researching the Macro through the Micro: Going beyond Ethnomethodology

According to Smith, ethnomethodology is ideological because it fails to move beyond the surface descriptive level to reach the primary level underneath, and she uses Tuchman's (1973) work on newsrooms to display this problem. Although Tuchman had improved upon conventional sociological accounts by using phenomenological insights, she, nevertheless, failed to get beyond these members' descriptive accounts.

Smith's alternative is to attempt to reach the primary level[1] where we would find a different structure operating. In order to get there, one has to move from the level of describing a social context to the level of using and being competent in that social context. It is a question of learning how to 'mean'.

> It is a familiar experience - the sense of not knowing quite how to speak, quite how to use terms correctly, at the stage when we are only beginners in a setting ... Thus, learning how to 'mean' with words correctly in that setting is learning how it is socially organized. (1990b, p. 166)

Thus although Tuchman used members' typifications, she was unable to get to the primary level, where competent newspeople (who have learnt this social organization and now take it for granted) operate in their daily lives. Smith finishes by briefly suggesting the primary level which

---

1 Although it is not easy as Smith herself admits "the proposal for an alternative is simple to state, and difficult to do. It is to proceed by explicating the implicit social organization" (1990b, p. 109).

Tuchman's analysis misses. In talking about 'spot news', Smith claims that it is probably not used frequently to 'describe', but rather to communicate between people who share a common background,

> it is a term which is not likely to be used to identify a class of events; it will be used rather in talking to the next shift about what happened, when the city editor reports to the managing editor, or the like. (1990b, p. 113)

But it is not just a product of local circumstances. It gets its comprehensibility from the wider social relations in which the newspaper is embedded. It is not just that type of news which requires a reporter to be 'on the spot' (1990b, p. 113), but rather it has to be understood within the wider context of the newspaper industry.[2]

> It arises in social relations among newspapers and other news sources. These are competitive. Newspapers and other news sources compete with one another directly when they publish on the same time band. (1990b, p. 113)

In other words, the competitive context in which newspaper organizations exist today is indispensable for understanding newsrooms' behaviour (1990b, p. 113).

Although Smith's critique of Tuchman introduces this concern with the primary level and the problem of learning how to 'mean', she develops it more systematically when she examines the discourse of 'femininity' (Smith 1990b). Today, of course, 'femininity' is

> a textual discourse vested in women's magazines and television advertisements, the appearance of cosmetics counters, fashion displays and to a lesser extent books ... Such discourse is clearly articulated to a commercial process. (1990b, p. 163)

Women learn the discourse of femininity, its social organization, through the mutual elaboration of appearances and their underlying pattern. This

---

2 Other types of news are governed by other constraints. Developing news "is that information which is sufficient to make a news story but is incomplete, arrives just in time to be covered in a preliminary way, and gets into the paper that day" (1990b, p. 112).

is accomplished in a manner similar to Garfinkel's 'documentary method of interpretation'. In Smith's adaptation of Garfinkel's process, Smith emphasizes the temporal nature of this method, its open-endedness, and its more general use in giving us our sense of underlying reality.

> This interpretive practice is essential to the way in which we organize the speakable and reportable 'reality' of our world. What is there for us arises as accountably what it is in an active process of finding in what we see, hear, or otherwise sense, the evidences of an underlying pattern. Doors, windows, walls, and roof evidence the rest of a whole house lying in back of them. (1990b, p. 178)

In other words, we don't hesitate over outward appearances wondering whether there is, in fact, an underlying pattern lying behind, "we open the door of the house and walk in without stopping to determine whether there is anything else behind it" (1990b, p. 178).

According to the normal workings of the documentary method of interpretation, the locking together of the document and the underlying pattern is instantaneous, or should be. But the discourse of femininity, because it is textual, works more often via an ideological circle rather than an interpretive one. The difference between the two circles is crucial.

> There is a documentary method of interpretation organized within textual discourse. It differs from the 'experiential' in one important way. The underlying pattern is not open-ended, shifting as local historical processes add new constituents in the ongoing play between document and pattern. Rather, instead of a shifting pattern, the documents are provided with fixed forms determined by discursive texts. (1990b, p. 178)

And a girl-growing-into-woman is often oppressed by the fixity of the latter's terms, because she doesn't fit the rigid terms of the category of 'feminine'. "My 16-17-year-old body was an abberation, a freak of nature. Femininity eluded me and without its confirmation I was vexed with questions about who or what I was" (quoted in Smith 1990b, p. 179). Thus the ideological circle 'locks in a fixed relation between the textually given images and interpretive schemata'(1990b, p. 179). It insists on a fixed relation between the textual discourse of femininity and the actual physical body, with the body being given little voice in this discourse.[3] Consequently, the body is invited to rectify its own deficiencies (1990b, p. 187). In other words, 'learning how to mean' within the contemporary textual discourse of 'femininity' is a profoundly alienating socialization.

Nevertheless, in the second half of the 'Everyday World as Problematic' (Smith, 1987) Smith explicitly specifies a research strategy to enable researchers to get to this primary level of social organization, which Tuchman had missed. In the first half, Smith had shown why a feminist sociology must start from women's experience. But she then emphasizes the necessity to move beyond the everyday.

Institutional Ethnography is the name Smith gives to this research strategy. It is quite different from traditional sociology.

> It means finding a method that does not begin with the categories of the discourse, approaching the actualities of the social world with a view to discovering in it the lineaments of the theoretical object. Rather it proposes an inquiry intended to disclose how activities are organized and how they are articulated to the social relations of the larger social and economic process. (1987, pp. 151–2)

She even shows how this larger social structure impinges constantly upon the otherwise mundane occurrence of taking a dog for a walk. More seriously, she notes how the usage of the term 'single parent' works to fit families into certain areas of the 'ruling apparatus': to locate my experience as that of a single parent, enters it into the generalized and generalizing relations of an institutional process (1987, p. 159). And it is the exploration of the 'extralocal determinations' (1987, p. 161) of this experience which is the task of an Institutional Ethnography.

Ethnomethodology's concern with accountability (1987, pp. 161–2) is helpful in this regard. Smith contrasts this notion of members' accountability with the accountability procedures of institutions which render only some things visible. Thus social workers have traditionally rendered invisible, and thus not accountable, the work that gets done in families. Instead focus is concentrated on the family 'in terms of interpersonal relations and roles'. For Smith, what is and what is not made accountable

---

3 Smith speculates that without this ideological circle of femininity, there would be the open-ended evolution and joint articulation of the body and its underlying pattern. "In the absence of such an ideological circle, growth and aging would gradually modify how someone's presence would be seen and interpreted" (1990b, p. 179).

is of essential importance to her research; "we are specially conscious of work essential to the accomplishment of accountable order, that is not itself made observable-reportable as work" (1987, p. 165). And Smith can now set up a method by which these hitherto invisible practices can be revealed.

The work of mothering done on behalf of the school system, is a good example of work which has typically been ignored.

> The Ontario Ministry of Education publishes for parents a little pamphlet containing suggestions about how parents (but in fact mothers) can improve their/her child's reading and writing. The specific exclusion of the suggested practices from the category of work is marked in recommendations for what mothers can do to promote reading skills that can be done "as you go about your daily work." Work and encouraging reading skills are mutually exclusive. (1987, p. 168)

But Smith also wants to work outwards towards those social relations only implicit in the world of mothering.

By 'making a design', Smith aims to provide a rough map of the larger terrain which needs to be filled in. It is deliberately open-ended so that, like the making of a quilt, it can be finished at a later time (1987, p. 177). It tries to map the interpenetrations of the different levels of these extra-local relations, such as class, the state, professional discourse, etc.[4] A first move out of the everyday world of mothers entailed entering the complementary organization of the school. Here, as Smith shows, the school's ability to document the child's performance as an individual within the larger context of certain generalized standards, gives it significant power over families (1987, p. 200).

The third stage of this process would then be to work out once again to the 'overall ecology of education'(1987, p. 201). Smith's research does not go this far. But she speculates that such work might be very revealing.

> I could be talking about, in a sense I am talking about, the way in which a traditional division of labour between women and men in the home has been foundational to the development of the North

---

4 See her diagram (1987, p. 171) for a rough sketch of the types of interpenetrations which she has in mind under this rubric of 'making a design'.

American educational system, the way in which the division has been built into the system as its working "assumption". (1987, p. 203)

Smith's work thus stands as a powerful and compelling version of a feminist sociology. It builds slowly yet progressively from a critique of conventional sociology to suggest a promising alternative for both empirically and theoretically inclined sociologists. Nevertheless, I still was unclear as to how well it resolved the nagging problems which I had had with Smith's curious mixture of Marxism and ethnomethodology.

Unanticipated Consequences

Unfortunately, despite Smith's sophisticated understanding of the ideological practices implicit in the methods employed by the ethnomethodologists, she herself is also ideological when she tries to move beyond embodied experience. However, she is ideological in her frame not her content. That is, she tacitly parallels the ideological methods which she herself had identified in the practices of conventional social science. Beginning from everyday embodied experience, Smith wants to move beyond the ideology of ethnomethodology so as to reach the primary level of social organization. But in this process, she too acts ideologically. Specifically, she constructs ideological narratives out of primary narratives. Not only that, but her procedure is an almost exact parallel to an ideological one she had identified in her 1983 (reprinted in 1990a) work "No one commits suicide".

In the first part of that paper, Smith identified the workings of a simple ideological circle concerning depression.

> When we return to the primary narrative with the assembly instructions derived from the clinical description, we can then find "depression" in the primary narrative account. We set up this relation using the procedures of an ideological circle. We discard those aspects of the primary narrative that do not "belong" and retain only those that do. We then have locked the two together, schema and particulars, so that the latter can "find" the former and the former will interpret and describe the latter. (1990a, p. 165)

But in its second half, she spends time analysing a more subtle form of the ideological procedure. This is concerned not just with the discarding of particulars, but with their "selection, assembly and ordering" (1990a,

p. 165). And this analysis of how a woman, Harriet, had her own experience transformed by a medical resident into an ideological narrative of psychiatric illness, is later paralleled in how a woman, Mrs T, also has her own experience transformed by Smith, herself, into an ideological narrative. But before getting to Smith, let us first examine the details of Harriet's transformation. It works as follows.

For both Smith and the resident, the case record was their prime source of information,[5] but they put it to very different purposes. The resident worked up this information into a set of particulars[6] which became Harriet's 'case history'.[7] "The sequence we are looking at begins this time with the particulars in the form of an extract from a case history prepared by a psychiatric resident for formal clinical presentation" (1990a, p. 165). But interestingly, the details of the case history intend a certain interpretive framework, which although being named in the case history's title, is not explicitly found in the narrative itself. In other words, the connecting links between the particulars and the ideological schema are not made explicit. And although Smith appears to make this point in passing, she returns to it at the end of her paper. Here its importance is made clear, as we shall also see later.

Next, this case history is then compared with the reconstructed 'pseudo' primary narrative. The latter was created by Smith from the original case record[8] so as to show the ideological procedure at work. Crucially, the case history had a different order and different selection of narrative clauses than the primary narrative. As a consequence, it operated to tell the reader to read Harriet's story in only one way. It "opens with general instructions for reading what follows: it is to be read as a narrative of an illness" (1990a, p. 167). In the slot immediately after these 'instructions' came the required symptom of psychiatric illness. That symptom was identified by the resident as Harriet's worry "that God was

---

5   According to Smith, the case record consists of "a loose assemblage of records from admission interviews, diagnostic interviews, ward notes, interviews with relatives and treatment prescribed and given" (1990a, p. 165). It also consists of such things as "nurses' observations, perhaps an interview by the social worker with the family, possibly an interview by the psychiatrist himself with the husband" (1990a, p. 166).
6   Smith's use of this term 'particular' comes from police practices. They are "the description of what happened as prepared by the police on the basis of which specific charges are brought. They are not a neutral description" (1990a, p. 160).
7   which was "prepared by a psychiatric resident for formal clinical presentation" (1990a, p. 165).
8   As Smith says, "it is based on notes made by the psychiatric resident from the case record in the course of preparing the case history" (1990a, p. 165).

going to punish me for this unnatural insemination with the birth of a deformed child" (1990a, p. 166).[9] The resident then acknowledged that Harriet had, in fact, undergone artificial insemination some time previously. But Smith countered this acknowledgment by arguing, taken out of context like this, "the worry that God would punish her for the unnatural insemination with the birth of a deformed child appears to come from nowhere, to have no ground" (1990a, p. 168), and thus allowed these worries to be seen as symptoms of an underlying mental illness.

In contrast, Smith who had constructed Harriet's 'pseudo' primary narrative from materials available to the resident but overlooked in the preparation of his case history, presented an interpretation in line with the experiential unfolding of Harriet's story. This account led to a quite different conclusion. "I could find material to make up clauses that can be read to occasion Harriet's behaviour, that is, to provide for it out of the context of illness as a frame" (1990a, p. 168). By including information about Harriet's sickness during pregnancy, medication taken, the baby's small size at birth etc., Smith's 'pseudo' primary narrative allowed Harriet's worries to take on quite a different meaning. That is, her problems arose out of her 'lived situation' rather than from a mental illness.[10]

Finally, Smith returned to her earlier discussion and showed how the case history's construction had been assembled so as to display little of the larger theoretical and interpretive schema which guided it, yet it was readily comprehended by other professionals. The case history's only explicit suggestion of this interpretive schema was in its title; 'A case of recurrent psychiatric disturbance involving Para-natal factors'. But Smith showed that this narrative was guided in its construction by the larger interpretive schema of "affective disorder associated with pregnancy and childbirth"(1990a, p. 169). Thus professionals skilled in this language could easily see this minimally theoretical narrative exemplifying this underlying reality. In effect, the larger interpretive schema "instructs the assembly and ordering of particulars"(1990a, p. 170) as well as suggesting which information needs to be omitted. Consequently, as Smith concluded,

---

9   In the case history, the resident cites it as "she began lying awake at night worrying that 'God was going to punish me for this unnatural insemination with the birth of a deformed child'" (quoted in Smith, 1990a, p. 167).

10 Yet when these additional features are not included, Harriet's worries lack context. "They don't make sense. They are thus available as symptoms to be interpreted in terms of the underlying psychiatric schema" (1990a, p. 168).

At the point of reading (or hearing) the case history, those who know the psychiatric schema and how to apply it can read the connections into the particulars ... [and] a fully "psychiatrized" story can be told that unites particulars and schema. (1990a, p. 170)

Unfortunately, Smith's exemplification of her 'institutional ethnography' research strategy in the second half of the "Everyday World as Problematic" displays strong parallels to the work of the resident in the case above. In both cases, ideological rather than primary narratives are produced,[11] and the procedures used for producing them are amazingly similar. In Smith's case it works as follows.

Unlike the resident, Smith enacts her transformation not on a case record but on a British research monograph; "Round about a Pound a Week" (Pember Reeves, 1913 - reprinted 1979). From this, Smith assembles certain particulars to produce her own authoritative analysis. But interestingly, the details of Smith's analysis intend a certain interpretive framework. Furthermore, although this framework is hinted at in the section's title (namely 'Exploring the Social Relations Determining the Everyday'), it is not explicitly found in the analysis itself. In other words, the connecting links between the particulars and the ideological schema are not made explicit. I too will return to this point near the end of this section.

Next, this analysis can also be contrasted with a reconstructed primary narrative created from the original text of Mrs Pember Reeves, so as to show the ideological procedure at work in Smith's analysis. In other words, Pember Reeves's original text includes aspects of typical primary narratives of these working class women. For example, one anonymous woman begins a narrative of her day's work, as follows,

> Me young man 'as ter be up abart five. E's a fair whale at sleep. If I didn't wake 'im 'e'd be late all the days in the year: I tell yer. E' come 'ome abart six, 'n soon's 'e's 'ad 'is tea 'e's that sleepy agen you'd 'ardly get a word off 'im. (1979, pp. 159–60)

Crucially, Smith's analysis has a different order and different selection of narrative elements than the primary narrative. As a consequence, it tells

---

11 Where the resident constructed a case history from a case record which concealed a pseudo-primary narrative, Smith constructs an analysis from an original text which also conceals pseudo-primary narratives.

the reader to read these working class mothers' stories in one particular fashion only.

Smith's analysis also gives 'general instructions for reading'. She begins the section in which these women's lives are discussed, by reminding the reader of the importance of Marx's analysis of commodity fetishism. Moreover, by imitating such an analysis this will lead to an understanding of "the social relations in back of the everyday worlds ... of exploring these relations as they really are" (1987, p. 134). These instructions act like the resident's. They tell the reader how to read the upcoming analysis; to read it as a narrative of these 'real', underlying social relations. In the slot immediately after these instructions comes the required indicator of these underlying relations. That indicator is identified by Smith as 'an account of Mrs T's working day' (1987, p. 136). She then proceeds to display Mrs Pember Reeves's original account of Mrs T's sixteen and a half hour workday, looking after her husband and six children. Although Smith then acknowledges that this study of Mrs T and other working class women in Lambeth had been originally undertaken to ascertain the overall health of these women and their babies, that point is curiously minimized. As Smith insists about this study of nutrition, "its very existence is grounded in class relations, and class relations are at work in how the text is constructed as an account of the lives of working class women for an 'educated' middle class" (1987, p. 137). Through this type of textual work, the study of nutrition seems to come from nowhere, to have no ground, and thus allows it to be also seen as an indicator of these underlying social relations.

In contrast, it is possible to construct the outline of a 'pseudo' primary narrative of these mothers' lives, from materials in Pember Reeves' text and available to Smith, which leads to rather different conclusions. To paraphrase Smith, one can even find material to make up clauses that can be read to occasion Mrs T's behaviour (and others) which provide for it outside of the context of class relations as a frame.[12] If we include information which seeks to context Mrs T's life in the local and historical situation of early twentieth century Britain, then a different interpretation is possible. Firstly, the focus on Mrs T and others came about from an initial concern not with economic or capitalist relations, but with the state's concern for children. Pember Reeves' research started from questions concerning the health of children. "Had they been well housed, well

---

12 Compare with Smith's discussion of the resident (1990a, p. 168).

fed, well clothed, and well tended from birth, what kind of raw material would they have shown themselves to be" (1979, p. 7)? As a result, research was begun to examine the effects of sufficient or insufficient nourishment on mothers and children of the poor. And this necessitated weekly visits to working class homes to ascertain the specifics of their daily lives. Contacts were originally made through a local lying in hospital of expectant mothers, and visitors were then to visit the homes. These visits were frequently seen as intrusions.

> A sympathetic stranger walking through the length of one of these thoroughfares feels the atmosphere of criticism. The rent collector, the insurance agent, the coal-man, may pass the time of day with worn women in the doorways, but a friendly smile from the stranger receives no response. (1979, p. 4)

And the mothers reacted with hostility to the visitors' imposition on them of having to keep accounts.

> The women were with one consent appalled at the idea of keeping accounts. Not that they did not "know it in their heads", but the clumsy writing and the difficult spelling, and the huge figures which refused to keep within any appointed bounds, and wandered at will about the page, thoroughly daunted them. (1979, p. 12)

Furthermore the visitors humiliated some of these mothers, when it was discovered that they could not read or write (1979, p. 12). They routinely hurt the women's feelings by being unable to understand the local dialect (1979, p. 14) and as a consequence the women "were suspicious and reserved" (1979, p. 15), steeling themselves "to sit patiently and bear it while the expected questions or teaching of something should follow" (1979, p. 16).

> Sometimes, the visitors would be humoured by being invited to sit in a draught. If the mother was subsequently congratulated on her knowledge of the value of fresh air, "she might repeat in a weary manner commonplaces on the subject which had obviously been picked up from nurse, doctor, or sanitary inspector" (1979, p. 16). Othertimes, 'teachings' would be less politely handled. One mother reacted to the 'gospel of porridge' (1979, p. 57) being taught to her, by replying quite simply that her family, "they 'eaved at it". (1979, p. 58).

Mrs Pember Reeves' research finishes by devoting a chapter of her research to the 'State as Guardian'. Here she explicitly details the growing influence of the state vis-a-vis simple economic relations.

> During the last century the State prohibited the employment of children under a certain age--an age which, as wisdom grows, tends to become higher and higher. By this necessary action the State formally invested itself with the ultimate responsibility for the lives and welfare of its children, and the guardianship thus exercized has continually been enlarged in scope until it has assumed supreme control of the nurture and training of the youth of the nation. (1979, p. 214)

When these considerations are included, Mrs T's life can be understood quite differently. These working class mothers' lives, at this historical juncture, make sense in the wider context of increased state intervention into their everyday lives. It is not just a simple reduction of those lives to the playing out of class relations.[13] Yet when these additional features are not included, as with the resident's narrative, it is all too easy to accept the authoritative version produced by Smith.

Finally, let me return to our earlier discussion and show how Smith like the resident, has assembled her narrative of these mothers, without giving the full interpretive schema which guides it. Yet it is readily comprehended by other professionals. The section of her book, like the Resident's case history, hints at the interpretive schema, but doesn't spell it out. Yet any competent professional trained in that discourse can make the connections like readers of the resident's account did. In effect, the larger interpretive schema "instructs the assembly and ordering of particulars" (1990a, p. 170) as well as suggesting which information needs to be omitted. Professionals familiar with Marxist political economy, (like those doctors familiar with 'affective disorder associated with pregnancy

---

13 For example, Davin's (1978) work (which Smith herself cites) emphasizes the importance of 'imperialism' for understanding the state's concern with motherhood and health in this historical period. In fact, it is almost a common sense observation that the power of the state increased in this period (Bruce, 1966; Donzelot 1980, 1988). Yet many Marxist-inspired analyses (Poulantzas 1973, 1978) then want to reduce this increase in power to the workings of a specifically capitalist state (albeit a relatively autonomous one). The other trap, which Foucault (1977, 1979) falls into, is that of seeing power everywhere. In both cases, a theoretical reduction is involved, which downplays primary narrative.

and childbirth') will not only be competent at reading Smith's account to discover an underlying cause in terms of capitalist social relations, but they will be equally competent at reading the connections into the particulars. They will know instinctively how to assemble and order the particulars and which information to omit. To paraphrase Smith,

> At the point of reading (or hearing) Smith's analysis, those who know the Political Economy schema and how to apply it can read the connections into the particulars ... [and] a fully "Marxized" story can be told that unites particulars and schema. (1990a, p. 170)

Thus Smith's analysis of the social relations lying behind these mothers' primary narrative has been found to be ideological.[14] Just as Harriet's voice was subdued when the resident imposed an authoritative psychiatric account, Mrs T's voice was subdued when Smith imposed her authoritative Marxist account. As Smith rightly concludes, although not about herself,

> this is the ideological procedure ... [it] works a transformation on narratives speaking from people's actual experience so that the active presence of subjects is discarded and the objectified version entered into the relations of ruling is installed as the authoritative account. (1990a, p. 171)

Summary: Going beyond Ideological Analysis

It has now been shown that Smith's position is ideological, albeit ideological in terms of its methods rather than its content. Furthermore, it has been shown to be ideological in a sense close to the one she herself had identified in the traditional human sciences at the beginning of her career. But perhaps a more general point to be concluded from this analysis is not just that Smith's work is ideological but that it is also recursive. That is, her textual formulation of 'institutional ethnography' brings to a close the recursive 'strange loop' which her career has followed. As Mulkay explains, strange loops are "potentially endless sequences of

---

14   Her critique (1990b, chapter 4) of Tuchman's analysis also contains a similar 'ideological' account. Although the 'primary level' which Smith wants to reach is not explicitly described as capitalist, Smith's description implicitly assembles those particulars which will suggest that as an adequate description.

discourse which constantly invert and undermine initial assumptions, yet which return us unexpectedly to the original point of departure" (1984, p. 267). Although this paper only documented the second half of the loop, its complete structure is something like the following.

At the beginning of her career, Smith criticised conventional sociology for its ideological transformation of everyday experience and called for a sociology which prioritized such experience. But, by the time she completes the formulation of her Institutional Ethnography (in the second half of the 'The Everyday World as Problematic'), she has almost totally reversed this original position. Here she criticizes ethnomethodology (that form of sociology which prioritizes everyday experience) as ideological and calls for a sociology which goes beyond everyday experience to an underlying reality. But when she actually performs such an analysis, she too is guilty, (like the early conventional sociologists she herself criticized) of ideologically transforming everyday experience.[15]

Nevertheless, despite these problems, Smith's work is still extremely useful in suggesting future directions for empirical and theoretical analysis. The beauty of Smith's work has always been its portrayal of the transformation of embodied experiences into the official world of textual relations. Her major mistake, as we have seen, was to suggest, in her 'institutional ethnography', that one could only reach this primary narrative through the prism of Marxist theorising. As a result, even in her own analysis, she missed the crucial importance of the state in these nineteenth century women's lives. This is even more ironic when one considers that in other areas of her work, most notably in her textual analyses, Smith, herself, is very much concerned with everyday state practices. Nevertheless, it is becoming increasingly clear from other empirical research influenced by Smith that a prioritization of the economic is not an essential feature of this type of research. Rather, the unity around which this empirical work seems to be organizing itself is the more general sense of domination by, or exclusion from, existing official discourses, which women (and others) have experienced, or are presently experiencing. For example, Walker's (1990) work stresses the experiential and textual primacy of violence, Smart (1989) accents the need to incorporate both the diversity of women's experiences and of

---

15   For initial explorations into this property of recursion see Hofstadter (1979), Keeney (1983) Poundstone (1985). For specifically sociological examples of recursion see Doran (1989), Mulkay (1984), Platt (1989). For an example of Smith's recursive tendencies in her micro-sociology, see Doran (1993).

theoretical approaches into any feminist analysis of law, while G. Smith (1988) has displayed the applicability of Smith's method to experiences other than women's.

Finally, because of Smith's early start in this field, her work may also serve the very useful function of highlighting some of the difficulties encountered when one starts to challenge these dominant discourses. Thus, I want to finish by briefly identifying two general areas of concern which have arisen out of Smith's pioneering work. The first concern is with the problem of 'frame and content' in Smith's own research. Although Smith has always been explicitly aware of the problems generated by traditional sociology's framing of women's experiences so as to silence them, she has also demonstrated an implicit awareness of the problem of 'framing' her own work. Not only did she intuitively realize that embodied writing (Haraway, 1990) was a first step towards empowerment against dominant discourses, but she realized that the articulation of these experiences had to be framed in quite specific ways. In other words, Smith understood that one can't simply write about one's experiences, as this is likely to be appropriated or ignored by dominant discourses. Instead, one must write using the frame of the dominant discourse, but simultaneously resisting any appropriation, as Smith herself did. That is, her work framed itself as sociological, she was a sociologist writing in sociological journals. But in her content, she talked about the disqualification of women's voices by sociology itself. In this sense, Smith challenged the prior official expertize of traditional sociology. Perhaps more importantly, through this process, Smith seriously challenged prior understandings of the relationship between expert and lay person. Rather than silencing lay voices as previous sociology had done, she insisted on prioritizing them. And in this sense, she helped re-define the scholar-lay person relationship. The problem which arises from this, however, is the temporal one of the success of Smith's endeavour. Because Smith has been successful in getting that voice heard, there is now the danger that it too will be seen, by those still excluded, as merely part of the dominant discourse rather than as a challenge to it.[16] That is, Smith may now become the authoritative voice which excludes other voices. And that problem does not come from the content of Smith's work but rather from

---

16 Thus, it is perhaps not surprising that women of colour have recently begun to object to the rather monolithic viewpoint which previous feminism had imposed on their experiences. See Hurtado (1989), Collins (1989).

its success at getting itself heard; a process which only emerged during the course of Smith's career (Smith, 1992).

The second concern which Smith's work raises is with regard to the relationship between personal experience and structural explanation. More specifically, it raises the question of the 'subject' in an interesting fashion. That is, Smith's work may be understood as the creation of a speaking 'subject' at the level of textual discourse; namely Smith herself. But it is a subject who learned to speak rather differently than expected. In fact, Smith created herself as a subject with attitude (Probyn, 1993). She 'learned to mean' within the discourse of sociology, but she learned it differently than her sociological teachers expected. More importantly, Smith's creation of herself as a feminist rather than the conventional sociologist which would otherwise have been her lot, gave her not just an understanding of herself but also of how the world 'really' worked. And Smith's demonstration of this process, this locking in together of self and world view, via something like an academic equivalent of the 'documentary method of interpretation' has been enormously instructive for subsequent readers. The problem which arises from this, however, is that this approach results in something like a 'situated knowledge' (Haraway, 1988). As Smith's body was produced locally, in a specific gendered, classed, ethnic, spatial, temporal, etc, location it spoke primarily to those who shared similar circumstances. And as its animating impetus was to get this hitherto ignored voice heard, it spoke against the dominant discourse which excluded it rather than to other voices, albeit dissimilar ones, which have also been excluded. And although Smith is now reaching out to other women whose experiences are quite dissimilar to her own, it is unclear how her own research agenda may change as a result, because it has been so dependent in the past on the authority of its own experiential voice.

References

Abercrombie, Nicholas, Hill, Stephen, & Turner, Brian S. (1980). *The Dominant Ideology Thesis*. London: George Allen and Unwin.

Alexander, Jeffrey, Giesen, Bernhard, Munch, Richard, & Smelser, Neil (Eds.). (1987). *The Macro-Micro Link*. Berkeley: University of California Press.

Atkinson, J. Maxwell, & Drew, Paul. (1979). *Order in Court*. London: Macmillan.

Atkinson, Paul. (1988). Ethnomethodology: A critical review. *Annual Review of Sociology*, 14, 441–65.

Baker, Carolyn. (1989). Knowing things and saying things: How a natural world is discursively fabricated on a documentary film set. *Journal of Pragmatics,* 13, 381–393.

Bandyopadhay, Pradeep. (1971). One sociology or many. *Sociological Review,* 19, 5–29.

Benson, Douglas & Hughes, John, A. (1983). *The Perspective of Ethnomethodology.* London: Longman.

Bruce, Maurice. (1966). *The Coming of the Welfare State.* New York: Schocken Books.

Chua, Beng-Huat. (1977). On the commitments of ethnomethodology. *Sociological Inquiry,* 44, 241–55.

Cicourel, Aaron. (1964). *Method and Measurement in Sociology.* New York: The Free Press.

Cicourel, Aaron. (1968). *The Social Organization of Juvenile Justice.* New York: John Wiley and Sons.

Clough, Patricia T. (1993). On the brink of deconstructing sociology: critical reading of Dorothy Smith's standpoint epistemology. *The Sociological Quarterly,* 34.1, 169–182.

Collins, Patricia Hill. (1989). The social construction of black feminist thought. *Signs: Journal of Women in Culture and Society,* 14.4, 745–773.

Collins, Randall. (1981). On the microfoundations of macrosociology. *American Journal of Sociology,* 86, 984–1014.

Davin, Anna. (1978). Imperialism and motherhood. *History Workshop: A Journal of Socialist Historians,* 5, 9–65.

Doran, Chris. (1989). Jumping frames: reflexivity and recursion in the sociology of science. *Social Studies of Science,* 19, 515–31.

Doran, Chris. (1993). The everyday world is problematic: Ideology and recursion in Dorothy Smith's micro-sociology. *Canadian Journal of Sociology,* 18.1, 43–63.

Donzelot, Jacques. (1980) *The Policing of Families.* London: Hutchinson.

Donzelot, Jacques. (1988). The promotion of the social. *Economy and Society,* 17.3, 395–427

Douglas, Jack, D. (1967). *The Social Meanings of Suicide.* Princeton: Princeton University Press.

Douglas, Jack, D. (Ed.) (1970). *Understanding Everyday Life.* Chicago: Aldine.

Eichler, Margrit. (1985). And the work never ends: feminist contributions. *Canadian Review of Sociology and Anthropology,* 22.5, 619–644.

Emmison, Mike. (1989). A conversation on trial? The case of the Ananda Marga conspiracy tapes. *Journal of Pragmatics,* 13, 363–80.

Fairclough, Norman. (1985). Critical and descriptive goals in discourse analysis. *Journal of Pragmatics,* 9, 739–763.

Fairclough, Norman. (1992). *Discourse and Social Change*. Cambridge, MA: Blackwell.

Filmer, Paul, Philipson, Michael, Silverman, David & Walsh, David. (1972) *New Directions in Sociological Theory*. Cambridge, MA: The MIT Press.

Foucault, Michel. (1977). *Discipline and Punish*. London: Vintage.

Foucault, Michel. (1979). *The History of Sexuality, Volume 1: An Introduction*. London; Allen Lane.

Fraser, Nancy, & Nicholson, Linda. (1990). Social criticism without philosophy: An encounter between feminism and postmodernism. In Linda Nicholson (Ed.), *Feminism/Postmodernism* (pp.19–38). London: Routledge.

Garfinkel, Harold. (1967). *Studies in Ethnomethodology*. Englewood Cliffs, NJ: Prentice-Hall.

Garfinkel, Harold. (1987). A reflection. *The Discourse Analysis Research Group Newsletter*, 3, 5–9.

Grahame, Peter. (1985). Criticalness, pragmatics, and everyday life: Consumer literacy as critical practice. In John Forester (Ed.), *Critical Theory and Public Life* (pp. 147–174). Cambridge, MA: MIT Press.

Haraway, Donna. (1988). Situated knowledges: The science question in feminism and the privilege of partial perspective. *Feminist Studes*, 14.3, 575–599.

Haraway, Donna. (1990). A manifesto for cyborgs: Science, technology and socialist feminism in the 1980's. In Linda Nicholson (Ed.), *Feminism/Postmodernism* (Pp. 190–233). London: Routledge.

Harding, Sandra. (1986a). The instability of the analytical categories of feminist theory. *Signs: Journal of Women in Culture and Society*, 11.4, 645–665.

Harding, Sandra. (1986b). *The Science Question in Feminism*. Ithaca: Cornell University Press.

Harding, Sandra. (1990). Feminism, science, and the anti-enlightenment critiques. In Linda Nicholson (Ed.), *Feminism/Postmodernism* (pp.83–106). London: Routledge.

Hartsock, Nancy. (1983). The feminist standpoint: Developing the ground for a specifically feminist historical materialism. In Sandra Harding & Merril Hintikka (Eds.), *Discovering Reality* (pp.283–310). Dordrecht: D. Reidel.

Hawkesworth, Mary. (1989). Knowers, knowing, known: feminist theory and claims of truth. *Signs: Journal of Women in Culture and Society*, 14.3, 533–557.

Heritage, John. (1984). *Garfinkel and Ethnomethodology*. Oxford: Polity Press.

Hofstadter, Douglas. (1979). *Godel, Escher, Bach: An Eternal Golden Braid*. New York: Vintage.

Hurtado, Aida. (1989). Relating to privilege: Seduction and rejection in the subordination of white women and women of color. *Signs: Journal of Women in Culture and Society*, 14.4, 833–855.

Keeney, Bradford P.(1983). *Aesthetics of Change*. New York: The Guildford Press.
Larrain, Jorge. (1979). *The Concept of Ideology*. Athens: University of Georgia Press.
Larrain, Jorge. (1983). *Marxism and Ideology*. London: Macmillan.
Maynard, Douglas W. & Wilson, Thomas, P. (1980). On the reification of social structure. *Current Perspectives in Social Theory*, 1, 287–322.
McHoul, Alec & Luke, Allan. (1989). Discourse as language and politics: An introduction to the philology of political culture in Australia. *Journal of Pragmatics*, 13, 323–332.
Mehan, Hugh & Wood, Houston. (1975). *The Reality of Ethnomethodology*. New York: John Wiley & Sons.
Miller, Leslie. (1990). Violent families and the rhetoric of harmony. *British Journal of Sociology*, 41.2, 263–288.
Mulkay, Michael. (1984). The scientist talks back: A one-act play with a moral about replication in science and reflexivity in sociology. *Social Studies of Science*, 14, 265–82.
Murray, Stephen O. (1987). Power and solidarity in 'interruption': A critique of the Santa Barbara school conception and its application by Orcutt and Harvey (1985). *Symbolic Interaction*, 10.1, 101–110.
Nicholson Linda (Ed.). (1990). *Feminism/Postmodernism*. London: Routledge.
Platt, Robert. (1989). Reflexivity, recursion and social life: elements for a postmodern sociology. *Sociological Review*, 37.4, 636–667.
Poulantzas, Nicos. (1973). *Political Power and Social Classes* (Timothy O'Hagan, Trans). London: NLB and Sheed and Ward
Poulantzas, Nicos. (1978). *State, Power, Socialism* (Patrick Collier, Trans). London: NLB.
Poundstone, William. (1985). *The Recursive Universe: Cosmic Complexity and the Limits of Scientific Knowledge*. New York: Morrow.
Probyn, Elspeth. (1993). *Sexing the Self*. London: Routledge.
Psathas, George. (1990). *Interaction Competence*. Lanham, MD: University Press of America.
Reeves, Mrs. Pember. (1979). *Round about a Pound a Week*. London: Virago (originally published 1913).
Sacks, Harvey. (1963). Sociological description. *Berkeley Journal of Sociology*, 8, 1–16.
Sacks, Harvey. (1972). On the analyzability of stories by children. In John Gumperz & Dell Hymes (Eds.), *Directions in Sociolinguistics* (pp. 325–45). New York: Holt, Rinehart and Winston.
Sacks, Harvey, Schegloff, Emmannuell, & Jefferson, Gail. (1974). A simplest systematics for the organization of turn taking for conversation. *Language*, 50, 696–735.

Silverman, David & Torode, Brian. (1980). *The Material Word: Some Theories of Language and its Limits*. London: Routledge.
Smart, Carol. (1989). *Feminism and the Power of Law*. London: Routledge.
Smith, Dorothy E. (1974a). The ideological practices of sociology. *Catalyst*, 8 (Winter), 39–54.
Smith, Dorothy E. (1974b). The social construction of documentary reality. *Sociological Inquiry*, 44.4, 257–268.
Smith, Dorothy E. (1977). *Feminism and Marxism - A Place to Begin, A Way to Go*. Vancouver: New Star Books.
Smith, Dorothy E. (1978). K is mentally ill. *Sociology*, 12.1, 25–53.
Smith, Dorothy E. (1983). No one commits suicide: Textual analyses of ideological practices. *Human Studies*, 6, 309–59.
Smith, Dorothy E. (1987).*The Everyday World as Problematic*. Toronto: University of Toronto Press.
Smith, Dorothy E. (1990a). *The Conceptual Practices of Power*. Toronto: University of Toronto Press.
Smith, Dorothy E. (1990b) *Texts, Facts and Femininity*. London: Routledge.
Smith, Dorothy E. (1992) Sociology from women's experience: A reaffirmation. *Sociological Theory*, 10.1, 88–98.
Smith, George. (1988). Policing the gay community: An inquiry into textually-mediated social relations. *International Journal of the Sociology of Law*, 16, 163–183.
Sudnow, David. (1965). Normal Crimes. *Social Problems*, 12, 255–76.
Torode, Brian. (1989). *Text and Talk as Social Practice*. Dordrecht: Foris.
Tuchman, Gaye. (1973). Making news by doing work: Routinizing the unexpected. *American Journal of Sociology*, 79.1, 110–131.
Turner, Roy. (1974a) Words, utterances and activities. In Roy Turner, (Ed.), *Ethnomethodology* (pp 197–215). Harmondsworth, Middlesex: Penguin.
Turner, Roy. (1974b). *Ethnomethodology*. Harmondsworth, Middlesex: Penguin.
Van Dijk, Teun A. (1993) *Elite Discourse and Racism*. Thousand Oaks, CA: Sage.
Walker, Gillian (1990). *Family Violence and the Women's Movement: The Conceptual Politics of Struggle*. Toronto: University of Toronto Press.
Zimmerman, Don. (1969). Record-keeping and the intake process in a public welfare agency. In S. Wheeler, (Ed). *On Record: Files and Dossiers in American Life*. (pp. 319–54). New York: Russell Sage.
Zimmerman, Don & Pollner, Melvin. (1970). The everyday world as a phenomenon. In Jack D. Douglas (Ed.), *Understanding Everyday Life* (pp. 80–103). Chicago: Aldine.

Zimmerman, Don & West, Candace. (1975). Sex role, interruptions, and silence in conversation. In Barrie Thorne and Nancy Henley (Eds.), *Language and Sex* (pp. 105–29). Rowley, MA: Newbury House.

3   Concluding Remarks: Reflecting on Smith; Re-evaluating Smith

Now that we have seen the major accomplishment of that paper; – showing the completion of the 'recursive loop' in which Smith got entangled, because of her reliance on Marxist theorizing, it should not be a surprize that this self-clarification of mine re-assured me that the Foucauldian paradigm that I had already been utilizing, empirically (Doran, 1986, 1994a, 1994b) could provide me with a much more useful macro-structure, for the issues that pre-occupied me then, and still pre-occupy me today. That is to say, my animating impulse to become a scholar was bound up with the totally inadequate representations of people like me that I discovered in my sociological education.

Thus, supposedly 'working class (youths and their) families' like mine, were typically represented in ways, by sociologists, both traditional and Marxist, which appeared to not only mis-represent us (Goldthorpe, et al., 1968a, 1968b, 1969; Hall and Jefferson, 1975; Hebdige, 1979), but which also tended to limit our potential for 'agentive action'. And this was especially problematic for people like myself: the first generation of supposedly working class children to benefit from a university education, as we were either being 'taught' these findings or being exposed to them, in university collections. Thus, it is not surprizing that the early ethnomethodologically-inspired writers attracted me immediately, because they suggested the possibility of 'talking back' (Jeffrey and MacDonald, 2006) to these problematic 'academic knowledges'. And this 'talking back' was to be done from the standpoint of one's own culturally shared, embodied experience.

But even though Smith's standpoint feminism did allow her to 'talk back' to traditional (positivist and functionalist) sociology, her use of Marxism, as I have just shown, was similarly problematic. And it was Foucault's macro-theorizing which enabled me to go beyond Smith in those early days. But now, some decades later, I have not only continued to follow Foucault's intellectual journey (Foucault, 1985, 1986, 2001, 2005, 2007, 2008, 2010, 2011) but I have discovered his final excavations regarding the individual *at the micro-level*, as well. And it was my 2015 paper that first put forward the notion of the 'parrhesian standpoint', something which Foucault hinted at in his writings, but exemplified in his embodied practices, his way of life (Foucault, 2011, pp. 141–74).

And this parrhesian is someone who has struggled to convert her/himself (Foucault, 2005) over many decades, so as to know her/his place in the world, and to know the nature of that world as well. (Foucault, 2005, pp. 276–85) Moreover, this process also involves unlearning as much as one learns (Foucault, 2005, pp. 95–6). And thus now, when I look back on Smith's life, not just Foucault's, I see her, in a potentially new light. That is to say, I think it would repay analysis to discover in what ways, Smith, in her embodied practices, assembled herself, (after a long conversion process entailing much agonism, struggle and 'unlearning') as a parrhesian intellectual; one who courageously spoke her truth (Foucault, 2001, 2011), as she knew it, from her position as an underdog (Smith, 1994), while also striving to explain the world which she inhabits, and equally importantly, her own position within that (her feminist standpoint).

References

Atkinson, J. M. & Drew, P. (1978). *Order in Court*. Atlantic Highlands, N.J.: Humanities Press.

Blum, A. & Mchugh, P. (1971). The social ascription of motives. *American Sociological Review*, 36, 98–109.

Blum, A. & McHugh, P (1984). *Self-Reflection in the Arts and Sciences*. Atlantic Highlands, N.J.: Humanities Press.

Campbell, M. & Manicom, A. (Eds.) (1995). *Knowledge, Experience and Ruling Relations*. Toronto: University of Toronto Press.

Cicourel, A.V. (1964). *Method and Measurement in Sociology*: New York: The Free Press of Glencoe.

Cicourel, A. V. (1968). *The Social Organization of Juvenile Justice*. New York: Wiley.

Cicourel, A. V & Kitsuse, J (1963). A note on the use of official statistics. *Social Problems*, 11, 131–39.

Dennis, A. (2019). The influence of topic and resource. *Journal for the Theory of Social Behavior*, 49(3) 263–400.

Doran, C. (1986). *Calculated Risks: an Alternative History of Workers' Compensation*. (Unpublished doctoral dissertation). University of Calgary, Calgary.

Doran, C. (1989). Jumping frames: Reflexivity and recursion in the sociology of science, *Social Studies of Science*, 19(3): 515–531.

Doran, C. (1993). The everyday world is problematic: Ideology and recursion in Dorothy Smith's micro-sociology. *Canadian Journal of Sociology*, 18(1), 43–63.

Doran, C. (1996). Ethnomethodology's recursive dilemma: Some problems for a contemporary anti-science. *The D.A.R.G. Newsletter*, 12(1).4–15.

Doran, N. (1994a) Maintaining the simulation model, in the era of the 'social': the 'inquiry' system of Canadian workers' compensation, 1914–1984. *Canadian Review of Sociology* 31: 446–469. doi: 10.1111/j.1755-618X.1994.tb00830.x.

Doran, N. (1994b) Risky business: Codifying embodied experience in the Manchester Unity of Oddfellows, *Journal of Historical Sociology*, 7 (2), 131–154.

Doran, N. (2008). Decoding 'encoding'. moral panics, media practices and marxist presuppositions. *Theoretical Criminology*, 12(2), 191–221.

Doran, N. (2015). Beyond phenomenological anti-sociologies: Foucault's "care of his self" as Standpoint Sociology: *Canadian Journal of Sociology*, 40(2), 131–162. https://doi.org/10.29173/cjs21786.

Douglas, J. D. (1970) Understanding Everyday Life. In Douglas, J. D. (Ed.) *Understanding Everyday Life: Toward the Reconstruction of Sociological Knowledge* (pp. 3–44) Chicago: Aldine Publishing Co.

Drew, P. (1978). Accusations: the occasioned use of members' knowledge of 'religious geography 'in describing events. *Sociology*, 12, 1–22.

Filmer, P., Philipson, M., Silverman, D. & Walsh, D. (1972) *New Directions in Sociological Theory.* London: Collier-Macmillan.

Foucault, M. (1979). *The History of Sexuality*, London: Allen Lane.

Foucault, M. (1979). *The History of Sexuality, Volume 1: an Introduction.* London: Allen Lane.

Foucault, M. (1980) Two Lectures. In C. Gordon (Ed.) *Power/Knowledge, Selected Interviews and Other Writings, 1972–1977* (pp. 78–108). New York: Pantheon.

Foucault, M. (1985) *The Use of Pleasure. Volume 2 of the History of Sexuality.* New York: Pantheon.

Foucault, M. (1986) *The Care of the Self. Volume 3 of the History of Sexuality.* New York: Random House.

Foucault, M. (2001), *Fearless Speech.* Cambridge, MA: Semiotext(e).

Foucault, M. (2005). *The Hermeneutics of the Subject.* New York: Palgrave Macmillan.

Foucault, M. (2007). *Security, Territory, Population.* New York: Palgrave Macmillan.

Foucault, M. (2008). *The Birth of Biopolitics.* New York: Palgrave Macmillan.

Foucault, M. (2010) *The Government of Self and Others*, New York: Palgrave Macmillan.

Foucault, M. (2011) *The Courage of Truth.* New York: Palgrave Macmillan.

Garfinkel, H. (1967). *Studies in Ethnomethodology.* Englewood Cliffs, NJ: Prentice-Hall.

Garfinkel, H (Ed.) (1986). *Ethnomethodological Studies of Work.* London: Routledge.

Garfinkel, H., Lynch, M., Livingstone, E., (1981) The work of a discovering science construed with materials from the optically discovered pulsar. *Philosophy of the Social Sciences*, 11(2), 131–158.

Goldthorpe, J., Lockward, D., Bechhofer, F., Platt, J., (1968a), *The Affluent Worker, Industrial Attitudes and Behaviour.* Cambridge: Cambridge University Press.

Goldthorpe, J., Lockward, D., Bechhofer, F., Platt, J., (1968b), *The Affluent Worker, Political Attitudes and Behaviour*. Cambridge: Cambridge University Press.

Goldthorpe, J., Lockward, D., Bechhofer, F., Platt, J., (1969), *The Affluent Worker in the Class Structure*. Cambridge: Cambridge University Press.

Gouldner, A. (1970). *The Coming Crisis of Western Sociology*. New York: Basic Books.

Hall, S., & Jefferson, P., (1975). *Resistance through Rituals: Youth Subcultures in Post-war Britain*. London: Hutchinson.

Hall, S., Critcher, C., Jefferson, T., Clarke, J, Roberts, B. (1978). *Policing the Crisis: Mugging, the State and Law and Order*. London: Macmillan.

Hart, R., & McKinnon, A., (2010). Sociological epistemology: Durkheim's paradox and Dorothy E. Smith's actuality. *Sociology*, 44(6), 1038–1054.

Hebdige, D., (1979), *Subculture: the Meaning of Style*. London: Methuen.

Hofstadter, D.R., (1979), *Gödel, Escher, Bach: an Eternal Golden Braid*, Basic Books,.

hooks, b., (1981), *Ain't I a woman?*. Boston: South End Press.

Jeffrey, L., & MacDonald, G., (2006), *Sex Workers in the Maritimes Talk Back*, Vancouver: UBC Press.

Latour, B., & Woolgar, S., (1979) *Laboratory Life: the Social Construction of Scientific Facts*. Beverley Hills: Sage.

Lumsden, K., Bradford, J., Goode, J., (2019), *Reflexivity: Theory, Method, and Practice*, London: Routledge, DOI https://doi.org/10.4324/9781315692319.

McHugh, P., Rafel, S., Foss, D., Blum, A., (1975). *On the Beginning of Social Inquiry*. London: Routledge and Kegan Paul.

Mehan, H., Wood, H., (1975) *The Reality of Ethnomethodology*, New York: John Wiley and Sons.

MulKay, M., (1984), The scientist talks back: a one-act play, with a moral, about replication in science and reflexivity in sociology, *Social Studies of Science* 14, 265–282.

Rankin J., (2017), Conducting analysis in institutional ethnography: Analytical work prior to commencing data collection. *International Journal of Qualitative Methods* https://doi.org/10.1177/1609406917734484.

Sandywell, B., Silverman, D., Roche, M., Filmer, P., Phillipson, M., (1975), *Problems of Reflexivity and Dialectics in Sociological Inquiry*, London: Routledge and Kegan Paul.

Smith, D. E. (1974a). The ideological practice of sociology. *Catalyst, 5,* 39–54.

Smith, D. E. (1974b) Women's perspective as a radical critique of sociology. *Sociological Inquiry.* 44(1): 7–13.

Smith, D. E. (1987) *The Everyday World as Problematic.* Toronto: University of Toronto Press.

Smith, D. E. (1994) A Berkeley Education. In K. P. Meadow Orlans, & R. Wallace. (Eds.) *Gender and the Academic Experience: Berkeley Women Sociologists* (pp. 45–56) Lincoln: University of Nebraska Press.

Turner, R. (1974a) Words, Utterances and Activities. In R. Turner (Ed.), *Ethnomethodology* (pp 197–215). Harmondsworth: Penguin.

Turner, R. (Ed.). (1974b) *Ethnomethodology*. Harmondsworth: Penguin.

Wieder, D.L., (1974) *Language and Social Reality: the Case of Telling the Convict Code*. The Hague: Mouton.

Woolgar, S. (1976) Writing an intellectual history of scientific development: the use of discovery accounts. *Social Studies of Science*, 6, 395–422.

Woolgar, S. (Ed.). (1988). *Knowledge and Reflexivity: New Frontiers in the Sociology of Knowledge,* London: Sage.

Wootton, A., (1975) *Dilemmas of Discourse: Controversies about the Sociological Interpretation of Language*. London: Allen & Unwin.

Zimmerman, H., Pollner, M., (1970) The Everyday World as a Phenomenon. In J. D. Douglas, (Ed.) *Understanding Everyday Life: toward the Reconstruction of Sociological Knowledge* (pp. 80–103) Chicago: Aldine.

PART 2

Overview of Critical Reflexive Research Methodologies

CHAPTER 4

Resisting through Research

Developing a Qualitative "Mixed Methods" Approach in Research with Sex Workers

Laura Winters

> One of the biggest challenges to building bridges between sex workers and researchers is the large ideological disjuncture in conceptualizations of prostitution. This divide, in turn, informs methodological practice
>
> VAN DER MEULEN, 2011, p. 379

∴

1   Introduction

Although the sociological study of stigma has typically been researched using conventional qualitative methods (Link and Phelan, 2001), my own research on sex worker resistance to stigma has required more unconventional approaches. While mixed methods are common in the social sciences (Luker, 2008), the version utilized here is rather unique. In part, that is because it is not a combination of quantitative and qualitative methods, but rather a combination of different qualitative methods. Perhaps its most important contribution is that it deals very concretely with certain of the specific issues one faces in the field, and especially in research with marginalized communities (from an initial concern with sampling, to the more complex issues of power, trust and exploitation, to the routinely ignored issue of the researcher as insider or outsider). In the process of confronting these issues, one sees that the issue of the 'standpoint' of the researcher becomes of central importance.

Initially, the project in question (Winters, 2020) began from a traditional qualitative approach, by carrying out qualitative interviews with sex workers in St. John's, Newfoundland (NL) and Labrador. In the course of my research, however, other more specifically appropriate methodologies were subsequently explored. Community Action Research (CAR) (van der Meulen, 2011) most directly addressed the specific methodological issues (regarding trust and power differentials when working with marginalized groups) that

I was encountering in my own research. Yet, despite CAR's potential utility for my research, the actual practical difficulties involved in carrying out research in St. John's meant that such a strategy could not be easily employed. Fortunately, Miller's (2000) theoretical/methodological form of discourse analysis allowed me, as a researcher, to satisfactorily resolve these issues. Collectively, my use of qualitative 'mixed methods' produced some very insightful results; this chapter follows the development of this methodological approach which encourages the researcher to examine both what words 'say' and what words 'do'.

2 Conventional Methodological Considerations

Because my project began as an extension of Jeffrey and MacDonald's (2006b) research (to St. John's), it initially sought to simply reproduce their methods. Moreover, it followed a tried and trusted formula, as similar methods have informed much of the Canadian research on sex work. In fact, many scholars have become trailblazers in prioritizing the voices of sex workers by using such methods.

This particular methodology is informed, primarily, by the symbolic interactionist tradition frequently associated with the study of stigma pioneered by Goffman (1963). And because this perspective is concerned with how human beings "construct, share, resist, modify or reject various aspects of the social world" (Given, 2008: 849), it has great potential for showing the nuances and details of everyday interaction. Moreover, its primary aim is to collect and analyze data from people's experiences; sometimes via ethnographic research in naturalistic settings, at other times via focus groups, informal interviews etc. So, my research project began by adhering to its standard interviewing practices and protocols, as the following discussion shows. However, it also had to first take into account one or two exceptional circumstances.

2.1 Location

Whereas Jeffrey and MacDonald (2006a) had studied the Maritime provinces, this research was (and still is) exceptional in that it takes place in the small city (Anderson and Papageorgiou, 1992; Bourne, 1989) of St. John's, NL, rather than in the large urban areas where the majority of sex work research has previously occurred (a notable exception in Canada includes Hannem's (2018) research in rural southern Ontario). Moreover, before my project, there had been no locally conducted studies of the sex industry in Newfoundland; an island which at the time of research had no sex work-specific services and a culture unique to the rest of Canada (Chafe, 2003). Nevertheless, my aim was to interview sex workers in St. John's to discover more about the relationship between sex work and stigma in this urban area. Perhaps not surprisingly, one issue that was immediately confronted was that of carrying out research on the typically hard-to-reach population of sex workers.

2.2   Sampling and Access

There are numerous challenges inherent in research involving hard-to-reach populations (Benoit, et al., 2005; Shaver, 2005) and as no sampling frame existed for sex work research specifically (Bungay et al., 2016), conventional random sampling methods were practically impossible. Nevertheless, this challenge was addressed through the use of diverse sampling methods.

That is to say, participants were contacted through advertisements placed on the online sites where sex workers advertise their services, as well as through various work locations such as escort agencies and massage parlours, through advertisement at local universities and colleges, posters hung at local bars, coffee shops, grocery stores, etc. The variety of advertisement locations acknowledges the fact that sex workers have lives outside of sex work. Snowball, or word-of-mouth sampling (Emmel, et al., 2007; Atkinson & Flint, 2001) was also used, as well as referrals by community agencies.

In addition, I already had relationships of trust with community partners that far pre-existed the research, and this proved extremely helpful in gaining support for the research project. These organizations both helped to advertise the research and provided interview space. Furthermore, prior to conducting the interviews, I had many years' experiences volunteering with a street outreach organization in St. John's.

Also related to relationship building, my cultural knowledge (Smith, 1987) as a resident of St. John's was important. In a city with a unique dialect (Kirwin et al., 1990) and culture; being "of this place" was key for establishing rapport with interviewees. Also, the fact that I lived in the area where the majority of street work occurs was helpful for the interviews with people doing street work, as researcher presence in the area, through both volunteer work as well as mundane activities such as dog walking, meant visibility to, and contact with, some of the participants.

In terms of the way that the research was presented in advertisements, the posters mentioned stigma and conveyed participation in interviews as an opportunity for sex workers to "talk back" and "have their voice heard" – in other words, there was an inherent politicality in the project. Thus, I was aware that this type of methodological framing of the research could affect "sampling", with regard to who participated in the study and, in turn, the results. Initially, that was a question that worried me. Fortunately, as will be shown, I was eventually able to resolve this uneasiness, but in the meantime, I was still concerned with following standard practices regarding qualitative research.

2.3 Interview Process

The interviews took the form of approximating as close to informal conversations (Silverman, 1998) as possible. Many participants just dove in and were very forthcoming with their information and opinions. Initially, I did develop an interview guide, but quickly abandoned it; it was not necessary because participants had much to say, and the interviews were able to very quickly approximate natural conversation. Participants very much directed the conversation within the confines of the research themes, which were made explicit in the advertising, posters, and initial recruitment phone call. These conversations revolved around stigma and "talking back"; that is to say, each participant discussed what they would say to those who hold stigmatizing views of sex workers, if given the chance.

Colloquially, Newfoundlanders are known to have the "gift of the gab" and indeed, conversations did flow naturally. This was a good learning experience for me as a researcher in that my expectation around the need for a set of questions was incorrect, and I was able to gain much richer data by "going with the flow" and allowing for the expertise of lived experience to be the driver of the discussions. In that sense, these interviews resembled 'naturally occurring conversation', a point that will become more important later on. Clarification questions were asked throughout, and in the few instances where questions or probes were needed in a more formal way, people were asked to talk about themselves, their work, its place in their lives, how they felt others in St. John's saw their work, and most importantly what they would say to those people. In the end, open-ended interviews (Carlin, 2009; Fontana and Frey, 1994; Lichtman, 2010; Luker, 2008) were conducted with thirty-two individuals who do sex work.

In many ways, the fact that the interviews quickly approximated friendly conversation spoke to the advantage of being "of this place", as being local helped with the trust-building necessary to have people open up in that way. In terms of trust, the small nature and inter-connectedness of St. John's helped as well, as people quickly spread the word and I became known as a safe person to talk to.

3 Going beyond Traditional Qualitative Methods

3.1 Feminist Qualitative Methods for Researching Sex Work

Although the methodological guidelines described, in detail, above are conventional ones (especially for scholarly research emanating from the symbolic interactionist tradition), as this research was also informed by feminist theorizing, I found myself exploring other methodologies more attuned to the theoretical and methodological issues that feminist theory has raised for traditional social scientific research (as well as for some of the practical issues I was facing in my own research project). Moreover, when I turned my attention to these feminist-inspired methodologies, I found that they sought to address a number of the blind spots associated with conventional methods; blind spots that I was already experiencing in my own research project and that were already causing me to be uneasy about my project.

The issues I had to grapple with can be summarized as follows. First, although intending to be guided by feminist theorizing, I was already well aware that certain forms of feminist research (Barry, 1995; Dworkin, 1981, 1993, 1997; Jeffreys, 1997, 2004; MacKinnon, 1983, 1985, 2005; Millet, 1990; Raymond, 1998) seemed to be denying the agency to sex workers that early feminism had demanded for women, when challenging traditional "malestream" (Smith, 1974) sociology.

Fortunately for me, van der Meulen (2011) has drawn attention to this problem, as it affects sex work research. For her,

> One of the biggest challenges to building bridges between sex workers and researchers is the large ideological disjuncture in conceptualizations of prostitution. This divide, in turn, informs methodological practice.
> p. 379

More concretely, those research projects that are grounded in the understanding of sex workers as victims "have helped to facilitate a relationship of distrust between sex working communities and feminist researchers" (van der Meulen, 2011, p. 371). My first concern was that such research may, in turn, be contributing (albeit unwittingly) to sex work stigma.

Second, early on in my project, I quickly became aware of the tacit power relationship which is conventionally assumed when one is seen as a professional expert on the issue of sex work. Specifically, I was asked to display my supposed professional expertise and give a media interview on sex work, even though, at that time, I had done almost no research on the topic. Before considering representing local sex workers publicly, I needed to understand what messaging people wanted about their work, and also to explore whether there was anyone with current or former experience doing sex work who was open to speaking.

Third, I was also aware that issues of sex worker – researcher trust were often of paramount concern for many sex workers, and I was determined to do as much as possible to ensure that any trust relationship I formed, would be a strong and lasting one. This was especially important seeing as many sex workers feel that previous scholars have done them a disservice in the portrayal of them as victims.

Fortunately, van der Meulen's work tackles both of these problems directly, when she discusses how it is possible to carry out action research with sex workers. Moreover, she not only addresses the specific worries that I had, but she suggests other methodological guidelines aimed at reducing the effects of misplaced agency, tacit power assumptions and participants' distrust of researchers.

3.2 *Community Action Research*

Community Action Research is founded on many of the same principles as Participatory Action Research (Whyte, 1991) but distinguishes itself by paying attention to issues oftentimes associated with marginalized communities being researched. Perhaps most crucially, issues of exploitation and trust that may exist between researchers and communities are addressed directly. With regard to the latter, van der Meulen argues that "conventional social science research projects and processes have helped to facilitate a relationship of distrust between sex working communities and feminist researchers" (2011, p. 371). She notes that many sex working communities are weary of researchers who come, take these communities' knowledge and time, and then leave and build research careers, while the sex work communities themselves receive nothing of real value to them, in return. Similarly, she cites Dudash's (1997) interviews with strip-club dancers who "felt that sex workers are constantly misrepresented by academics and journalists from outside the industry" (van der Meulen, 2011, p. 373). To counter such trust issues, CAR encourages a breaking down of the problematic academic researcher/community member relationship. Hitherto, the academic researcher was the "outsider" coming into the community, carrying out their research (perhaps in collaboration with community members) and then leaving.

In contrast, CAR envisages a completely different role for the researcher. As Brydon-Miller et al. (2003) suggest; the researcher becomes a

> hybrid of scholar/activist in which neither role takes precedence. Our academic work takes place within and is made possible by our political commitments and we draw on our experiences as community activists and organizers to inform our scholarship.
>
> cited in VAN DER MEULEN, 2011, p. 375

As van der Meulen (2011) continues; "those who engage in action research are often already engaged with the local stakeholders as organizers and activists"

(p. 375). Such a strategy, she believes, goes a long way to help mediate the issue of trust that has dogged sex work research in recent years. The intended end result is that researchers within the CAR tradition not only become hybrids of activists/researchers, concerned with social justice for the communities they research with, but they also work hard to ensure that issues of trust do not emerge.

The other related issue that CAR directly confronts is that of "the exploitative nature of social science research" (van der Meulen, 2011, p. 374). With regard to sex work specifically, "the absence of praxis in most studies ... has, among other things, contributed to a production of knowledge that many sex workers claim does not reflect realities" (Wahab, cited in van der Meulen, 2011, p. 371). Not only that, but "radical feminist writing has argued that sex workers are only ever the victims of male violence and sexual exploitation" (van der Meulen, 2011, p. 372). This conclusion has been reached by researchers "glossing over complexity and diversity in order to present homogenous images of the sex industry" (van der Meulen, 2011, pp. 371–2). That glossing over is coupled with "a research framework that positions sex workers as unable to participate in research about their lived realities" (van der Meulen, 2011, p. 372).

Thus, in order to counteract these concerns about exploitation, and to hopefully bring egalitarian and democratic principles to the research process, CAR promotes the active involvement of sex workers in research design, process, dissemination and implementation of solutions. In addition, it necessitates that researchers "prioritize their political convictions" (p. 375) in their work, drawing on their experiences as community activists and organizers to inform their scholarship. The hope is that the problematic power dynamic of the researcher/researched relationship can be challenged. This approach actually informed van der Meulen's own research. That is, she utilized action research methodology and community involvement in research alongside her activism and involvement in the sex workers' rights movement. Moreover, she noted that her "strong sex workers' rights perspective was central to building the trust and solidarity needed for successful research" (p. 379).

When carrying out research with marginalized groups such as sex workers, issues that may have been backgrounded in more traditional research designs, not only foreground themselves, but insist on being confronted. In this regard, van der Meulen's approach shows significant promise; as it tackles thorny, but usually backgrounded issues. As we have seen, CAR promotes a very novel understanding of the researcher. That is, s/he is no longer an objective outsider to the research process. CAR also promotes a very different understanding of the trust relationship between researcher and researched. Whereas traditional methodologies spend little time on this topic, assuming for the most part, that this is not a significant problem, van der Meulen highlights the necessity of paying explicit and close attention to this issue, because sex workers have become wary of research that misrepresents them. Thus, the researcher must constantly attend to this concern.

Finally, and relatedly, van der Meulen links this issue of "exploitative research methods" (2011, p. 372), to the theoretical considerations which inform those methods. For example, when "radical feminist researchers ... conceptualize sex workers as victims in need of protection, unable to make decisions about their lives and work" (2011, p. 379), their choice of research methodology will reflect the theoretical conceptualization that they bring to bear on the people they are going to study.

In order to challenge such an inadequate conceptualization, van der Meulen suggests that an action research framework, where sex workers are actively involved in the research design, implementation, analysis and dissemination, can be a highly effective way to challenge problematic conceptualizations and to ensure the voices of the community are not overshadowed by ideology (2011, p. 379). In other words, questions about transparency and the politicality of sex work research are now being given serious consideration.

Van der Meulen's promotion of CAR methodology certainly does address many of the issues found in sex work research, and also addresses some of the issues I found in the early days of my own research. Nevertheless, her approach assumes a number of features of sex work research that may not always be present in any actual research endeavour. For me, the major issue with adopting this method in St. John's was that there was no cohesive community of sex workers at the time, no outreach or advocacy program for sex workers, and as such, no space where sex workers were coming together in any way that would facilitate this type of research.

While informing the development of a front-line advocacy and outreach program was not an original goal of my research project, that is the work that I began to carry out, work that then went on to inform and support the development of services for people doing sex work in the province. In many ways, this involvement not only took the suggestions of Community Action Research seriously, but in some respects went beyond it. That is, by staying in the community and devoting time and effort to community development work and advocacy, the issue of exploitation and trust between myself as a researcher and the community of people engaged in sex work in St. John's was minimized. By staying present and engaged well beyond the life of carrying out the interviews, I avoided the problem of simply taking people's stories for my own academic work, and not giving something back, in return, to those individuals I had researched with. In addition, my active involvement, in collaboration with several sex workers, in the design, process and implementation of SHOP as a solution to the lack of services and advocacy in St. John's also deepened trust to a level that is typically unknown in conventional (and CAR-inspired) research methodologies.

However, that work occurred after the completion of interviews; thus, CAR did not so much inform my initial research method as it re-assured me of the ethical need to take extreme care about issues of "trust" and "exploitation". Fortunately, Miller's (2000, 2003) work suggested a theoretical/methodological solution that attends to several of the concerns that van der Meulen identified (the need to amplify the embodied voices of the marginalized, the need to consider methodological and theoretical concerns as informing each other, the standpoint of the researcher), but it does that without recourse to the necessity of already having an organized community of the marginalized accessible.

4   Beyond Community Action Research

4.1   *Qualitative Methods from the Theoretical and Methodological Margins*

The lack of sex worker advocacy or organizing in the province was uniquely relevant for this research, as the majority of work on stigma resistance examines organized activism (Benoit et. al, 2018; Bruckert and Hannem, 2013; Hannem and Bruckert, 2012). Nevertheless, Miller (2003) suggests a powerful way of demonstrating how the marginalized, those on the underside, find ways of talking back to relations of power, even as single individuals. Her preference is for a form of discourse analysis; but it is not a simple utilization of the insights of conventional conversation analysis to study the naturally occurring conversation of the marginalized. Instead, Miller's mature work (2000, 2003) deals with the issues that marginalized groups face when trying to get their voices heard. Although she does not deal with sex work specifically, in many ways she suggests a theory/method which addresses the issues left unanswered in van der Meulen's work. So, let us deal with each in turn.

4.2   *Amplifying the Embodied Voice of the Marginalized*

The fundamental premise of Miller's discourse analysis is "that language constitutes rather than reflects reality, and that speakers use talk strategically to accomplish their purposes in particular settings" (2000, p. 317). In their talk, all people promote one version of the world and disqualify another; thus, in this methodology, all language is analyzed as a "claims-making" enterprise, and these claims are stories or accounts designed to further some practical goal. Yet, for practical methodological purposes, Miller is instructing us to pay extremely close attention to the naturally occurring talk of the marginalized, at the level of the individual her/himself. By paying attention to the strategic use of language; wherein language is analyzed as a "claims-making" enterprise (Miller, 2000), one can identify the subtle strategies individuals use to get their voices heard. But this can only be done by analyzing language inside, rather than outside of, its context of use. It is by paying such close attention to how individuals do things with words, that one can also identify the politicality that is inherent in the everyday talk of the "subaltern". Not surprisingly perhaps, a methodology like this, certainly held promise for someone like myself, wanting to amplify the voice of the marginalized, especially when this could be done in situations when the marginalized did not have anything remotely like a collective voice. Yet Miller's writings were also useful in addressing another issue raised by van der Meulen.

4.3 Considering Theoretical and Methodological Concerns Informing Each Other

Van der Meulen (2011) makes a strong case that methodological concerns are often informed by theoretical stances, and that in order to carry out CAR, one needs to problematize both theoretical and methodological concerns. Specifically, she critiques radical feminism for using its conceptualization of sex workers as victims to inform its methodologies and thus to foreground and highlight only certain features of sex workers' lives. Not surprisingly, many sex workers ended up very distrustful of research like this, which turns them into "victims". Thus, the trust issue is a very serious one.

To counter this, van der Meulen argues that Community Action Research starts from the community and includes community members' views in the entire methodological process. She exemplifies this with her own research project in which she, a confessed "Marxist-feminist" (2011, p. 376) scholar with a "strong sex workers' rights perspective" (2011, p. 379) worked with Toronto sex workers' organizations to collectively design a research project. Perhaps not surprisingly, elements of that theoretical stance infuse the project, as it becomes a project on "the ways in which workplace improvements can be achieved through policy change and labor organizing" (2011, p. 379). In other words, van der Meulen's own theoretical stance (Marxist-feminism) tacitly shape the project into being one about labour practices, and about improving the workplace for its workers; all concerns that follow naturally from Marx's theoretical understanding of the central importance of 'labour'.

In certain ways, Miller's approach goes even further than van der Meulen's. Because Miller's theoretical point is to prioritize everyday language at the level of theory, as well as at the level of method. She follows the 'conversation analytic' injunction to study how members themselves construct their sense of 'shared reality' through their interaction, (through their mundane sense-making practices, one might say) rather than imposing upon that interaction, an 'analytic interpretation' informed by the researcher's prior theorizing on the topic. Thus, Miller is advocating that we listen to how individuals themselves, through their talk, 'make sense' of power relations, rather than imposing (previously formulated) 'theoretical' interpretations of power relationships (e.g., victim status) upon them.

4.4 The Standpoint of the Researcher

The third, and related, issue that van der Meulen addresses in her promotion of Community Action Research is the "exploitation problem" that surrounds certain forms of sex work research. Oftentimes, this is linked with the "insider/outsider" dichotomy, where "insider research is understood to be research that is conducted by a member of the community in question, whereas outsider research is when a non-group member designs and conducts the project" (van der Meulen 2011, p. 375). More importantly for van der Meulen, outsider research has not only resulted in distrust, but it has also resulted in a form of exploitation where researchers complete their research and then return "to the campus, institution or suburb where they write up their data, publish and build careers – on the backs of those they took data from" (O'Neil, cited in van der Meulen, 2011, p. 373). In order to challenge this type of exploitation, van der Meulen's suggestion is to blur the insider/outsider dichotomy. By involving herself in the sex work community and engaging in research design with them, she temporarily blurs that distinction. Her standpoint, at least for the duration of the research is both outsider and insider. That is, CAR researchers "prioritise their political convictions and their academic work" (van der Meulen, 2011, p. 375)

In contrast, Miller's work puts forward a potentially more radical standpoint. Whereas van der Meulen conjoins political conviction and academic work, while at the same time understanding them as different activities, Miller brings politicality into academic work itself. She construes them as inseparable, because, for her, much academic work entails forms of 'claims-making', and thus displays its own tacit politicality. Thus, academia mirrors, in certain ways, the claims-making that occurs outside the academy. In other words, Miller is pointing out talk's routine politicality wherever it occurs. The theorist's account is an enactment of power and a moral claim in much the same way as that of the participant's. By returning us to that politicality wherever we find it (i.e., in the theorist's "talk" as well as in the participant's), this discursive approach "persistently reminds us of our ongoing complicity in the constitution of reality" (Miller, 2000, p. 331). As a result, the researcher/researched dichotomy is rethought in a different way than van der Meulen's. For Miller, her scholarly stance of prioritizing lay talk over theoretical talk and invoking the politicality of both lay and theoretical talk, results in a standpoint which sees research itself as inherently political, not just community activism being political. Whereas van der Meulen sees a distinction between the researcher as 'scholar' and the researcher as 'activist', and mainly wants to bring them closer together (the insider and outsider working together), Miller suggests the potential formation of the hybrid scholar/activist. The scholar/activist may inhabit the same corporeal body, and the theoretical stance of the scholar is to acknowledge the politicality of 'theorising' as well as that of 'activism'.

5   Conclusion

Traditional qualitative methods assume a researcher whose scholarly standpoint is outside the community s/he is studying. This methodological standpoint was undertaken, in a somewhat taken for granted fashion, at the outset of this research, in line with much of the research on stigma. And it certainly proved useful in this project, to the extent that it was able to provide us with a wealth of interview and demographic information about sex workers in St. John's. In contrast, CAR builds on its feminist origins and assumes a researcher whose standpoint is (at least, temporarily) inside the community s/he is studying, by virtue of her/his social position as a community activist. Its strengths are that it deals with issues of trust, exploitation and activism, typically downplayed in more traditional qualitative methods. This methodology has also proved useful to me, as it reminded me to the real necessity of paying serious attention to issues of 'trust' and 'exploitation' in the carrying out of research in sensitive areas such as 'sex work'. Furthermore, it has justified my work in building relationships of 'trust', which at the time, I thought were ancillary to the research process, but which I now consider to be an essential part of the research.

Lastly, and perhaps most importantly, Miller's methodological perspective does not simply assume a researcher who is both an academic on the one hand, and an activist on the other, but rather assumes that the researcher's embodied standpoint is one of becoming a scholar/activist, both methodologically and theoretically. For her, activists are obviously engaged in claims-making activities, but Miller, in her mature work concludes that scholars, themselves, are tacitly engaging in similar activities. In other words, we all are constructing our world and ourselves through agentive talk, but Miller is perhaps the first scholar to explicitly articulate this theoretical/methodological standpoint.

Her methodological suggestions also seemed to offer me a way of going beyond certain of the limitations I encountered with CAR. Thus, whereas CAR's approach necessitated working closely with already existing community groups, Miller's approach allowed me to conduct my analysis in the absence of such groups. Also, whereas CAR's approach premises itself on the distinction between the outsider (the scholarly researcher) and the insider (the community group member), Miller's approach seeks to dissolve that distinction, via her theorizing of the researcher as a 'claims-making activist', engaged in similar activities to activist members of marginalised groups. As a result, this methodology allowed me to document the mundane 'politicality' of the agentive talk of sex workers in St. John's, Newfoundland.

My long-term immersion in sex-workers' lives occasioned by my position establishing SHOP, meant that I had become passionate about sex worker rights, and that I had also helped construct a community agency similar to the ones preferred by CAR. However, a crucial difference still separated my situation from typical CAR research. I was not an established scholar coming to a community group to collaborate on a research project together, while at the same time, paying attention to issues of trust and exploitation. Instead, I was a graduate student who had started doctoral research, and then temporarily left that project, to engage more concretely in 'activist' work, because my original methodological perspective had not equipped me to deal with certain issues I found in the field. One possible route forward would have been to abandon my earlier interviews and start again from a CAR perspective. But that would also have been difficult, as my embodied position was closer to being that of a community activist who was also a (fledgling) scholar, rather than that of an activist scholar coming to collaborate with community activists. Fortunately, as suggested earlier, it was Miller's activist/scholar's approach that allowed me to resolve this dilemma, as it allowed me to use the information from my original interviews to demonstrate the politicality of individual sex workers, through the analysis of their resistance to stigma in their everyday talk.

Because my research and my scholarship in general have been deeply informed by my initial activism, as well as my subsequent academic education and then my work with SHOP, I was no longer the traditional researcher content to follow standard methodological guidelines. On the other hand, I was not simply a 'community activist' hoping to engage with CAR researchers in future research projects. Instead, I was closer to the hybrid scholar/activist that Miller articulates. To be sure, CAR went beyond traditional methods by its attention to the issues of trust and power that had made me so uneasy, but it was Miller's work that showed me how to address these issues in a way that reflected the standpoint I now occupy; that of an activist and a researcher, someone who understands the politicality of both endeavors.

References

Anderson, W., & Papageorgiou, Y. (1992). Metropolitan and non-metropolitan population trends in Canada, 1966–1982. *The Canadian Geographer,* 36(2), 124–144.

Atkinson, R., & Flint, J. (2001). Accessing hidden and hard-to-reach populations: Snowball research strategies. *Social Research Update,* 33, 1–4.

Barry, K. (1995). *The Prostitution of Sexuality: the Global Exploitation of Sexuality.* New York: New York University Press.

Benoit, C., Jansson, M., Millar, A., & Phillips, R. (2005). Community-academic research on hard-to-reach populations: Benefits and challenges. *Qualitative Health Research.* 15 (2), 263–282.

Benoit, C., Jansson, M., Smith, M., & Flagg, F. (2018). Prostitution, stigma and its effect on the working conditions, personal lives, and health of sex workers. *The Journal of Sex Research,* 55(4–5), 457–471.

Bourne, L. (1989). Are new urban forms emerging? Empirical tests for Canadian urban areas. *The Canadian Geographer,* 33(4), 312–328.

Bruckert, C., & Hannem, S. (2013). Rethinking the prostitution debates: Transcending structural stigma in systemic responses to sex work. *Canadian Journal of Law and Society,* 28(1), 43–63.

Brydon-Miller, M., Greenwood, D., & Maguire, P. (2003). Why action research? *Action Research,* 1(1), 9–28.

Bungay, V., Oliffe, J., & Atchison, C., (2016). Addressing underrepresentation in sex work research: Reflections on designing a purposeful sampling strategy. *Qualitative Health Research,* 26(7): 966–978.

Carlin, A. (2009). Edward Rose and linguistic ethnography: an ethno-inquiries approach to interviewing. *Qualitative Research,* 9(3), 331.

Chafe, P. (2003). Hey Buddy, Wanna buy a Culture. In J. Gifford & G. Zezulka-Mailloux, (Eds), *Culture and the State: 3* (pp. 68–76). Edmonton: CRC Humanities Studio.

Dudash, T. (1997). Peepshow Feminism. In J. Nagle (Ed.), *Whores and Other Feminists* (pp. 98–118). New York: Routledge.

Dworkin, A. (1981). *Pornography: Men Possessing Women.* London: The Women's Press.

Dworkin, A. (1993). Prostitution and male supremacy. *Michigan Journal of Gender and Law,* 1, 1–12.

Dworkin, A. (1997). *Intercourse*. Chicago: Free Press.
Emmel, N., Hughes, K., Greenhalgh, J., & Sales, A. (2007). Accessing socially excluded people – trust and the gatekeeper in the researcher-participant relationship. *Sociological Research Online*, 12(2), 43–55.
Fontana, A. & Frey, J. (1994). Interviewing: the art of Science. In *Handbook of Qualitative Research*, N. Denzin and Y. Lincoln, (eds.). Los Angeles: Sage Publications.
Given, L. M. (2008). *The Sage Encyclopedia of Qualitative Research Methods*. Los Angeles: Sage Publications.
Goffman, E. (1963). *Stigma: Notes on the Management of Spoiled Identity*. Englewood Cliffs: Prentice-Hall.
Hannem, S., & Bruckert, C. (2012). *Stigma Revisited*. Ottawa: University of Ottawa Press.
Jeffrey, L. A., & MacDonald, G. (2006a). "It's the money, honey": the economy of sex work in the maritimes. *The Canadian Review of Sociology and Anthropology*, 43(3), 313–327.
Jeffrey, L.A., & MacDonald, G. (2006b). *Sex Workers in the Maritimes Talk Back*. Vancouver: UBC Press.
Jeffreys, S. (1997). *The Idea of Prostitution*. North Melbourne: Spinifex Press.
Jeffreys, S. (2004). Prostitution as Harmful Cultural Practice. In C. Stark & R. Whisnant (Eds.), *Not for Sale: Feminists Resisting Prostitution and Pornography* (pp. 386–300). North Melbourne: Spinifex Press.
Kirwin, W. J, Story, G. M, & Widdowson, J.D.A. (1990). *Dictionary of Newfoundland English: Second Edition*, Toronto: University of Toronto Press.
Link, B., & Phelan, J. (2001). Conceptualizing stigma. *Annual Review of Sociology*, 27(1), 363–385.
Litchman, M. (2010). *Qualitative Research in Education: a User's Guide* (2nd ed). Los Angeles: Sage Publications.
Luker, K. (2008). *Salsa Dancing into the Social Sciences*. Cambridge: Harvard University Press.
MacKinnon, C. (1983). Feminism, Marxism, Method, and the State: an Agenda for theory. In E. Abel & E. K. Abel (Eds.), *The Signs Reader: Women, Gender and Scholarship* (pp. 277–356). Chicago: University of Chicago Press.
MacKinnon, C. (1985). Pornography, civil rights, and speech. Harvard Civil Rights-Civil Liberties. *Law Review*, 20, 1–70.
MacKinnon, C. (2005). Pornography as trafficking. *Michigan Journal of International Law*, 26(4), 993–1012.
Miller, L. (2000). The poverty of truth-seeking: Postmodernism, discourse analysis and critical feminism. *Theory and Psychology*, 10(3), 313–352.
Miller, L. (2003). Claims-making from the Underside: Marginalization and Social Problems Analysis. In J. A. Holstein & G. Miller (Eds.), *Challenges and*

Choices: Constructionist Perspectives on Social Problems (pp. 92–119). New York: Aldine de Gruyter.

Millet, K. (1990). *Sexual Politics*. New York: Simon & Schuster.

Raymond, J. (1998). Prostitution as violence against women: NGO stonewalling in Beijing and elsewhere. *Women's Studies International Forum,* 21(1), 1–9.

Shaver, F. (2005). Sex work research: methodological and ethical challenges. *Journal of Interpersonal Violence.* 20(3), 296–319.

Silverman, D. (1998). *Harvey Sacks: Social Science and Conversation Analysis*. New York: Oxford University Press.

Smith, D. (1974). Women's perspective as a radical critique of sociology. *Sociological Inquiry,* 44, 7–13.

Smith, D. (1987). *The Everyday World as Problematic: a Feminist Sociology*. Toronto: University of Toronto Press.

van der Meulen, E. (2011). Action research with sex workers: Dismantling barriers and building bridges. *Action Research.* 9(4), 370–384.

Whyte, W. F. (1991). *Participatory Action Research*. Newbury Park: SAGE.

Winters, L. (2020). *Resistance on the Rock: Sex Workers in NL "Talk Back"*. [Unpublished doctoral dissertation]. University of New Brunswick.

CHAPTER 5

Beyond Codified Logics of Ethics
Jungle and the Ethics of Non-violence

Dionisio Nyaga

> And finally, if philosophical discourse is not just a moral discourse, it is because it does not confine itself to wanting to form an ethos, to being the pedagogy of a morality, the vehicle of a code. It never poses the question of ethos without at the same time inquiring about the truth and the form of access to the truth which will be able to form this ethos, and (about) the political structures within which this ethos will be able to assert its singularity and difference.
>
> FOUCAULT, 2008, p. 67, on the courage of truth

∴

1   Introduction

We live in a microwave society where knowledge production is fast paced, and ethical values are nullified. Such a society pays more attention to the quantity of knowledge produced (Creswell, 2013; Faulkner & Faulkner, 2014) and fails to hesitate and qualify such knowledge production (Deliovsky, 2017). Time as a resource is compressed to allow mass production of knowledge that is reduced and simplified in ways that objectify the human in them. The process of objectification takes out emotions from stories told by the participant (Elliot, 2005); which I argue in this book is a form of epistemological genocide. We live in a consumerist society where machines and robots have taken over knowledge production, while the role of the human is to only received and consume rather than to produce and imagine. Such loss of imagination is in essence the fall of the human in what I call epistemological death.

This chapter therefore argues for ethical qualification of knowledge to allow a return of imagination, emotion, values and realities as an ethical requirement in knowledge production. It is a call for the return subjugated philosophical assumption in knowledge production as a necessary ethical demand that can also help us reimagine the human as a reflexive being. Maybe it is time to rethink the being in the human so that the violence that continue to guide knowledge production can be rethought in ways that are non-violent (Butler, 2020). This chapter calls for non-violence research process as a necessary ethical requirement to start thinking how knowledge can be produced without necessarily eliminating emotion but rather celebrating difference, histories, values and realities in knowledge production.

Research as a process of knowledge production is rife with colonial civilizational narrative meant to kill the instincts and emotions in participants' stories (Elliot, 2005; Torres & Nyaga, 2021). These genocidal practices in research are concealed and rationalized as necessary evil in knowledge production. Such a necessity, they argue, will help develop and civilize society. But such forms of civilizational narratives are the same ones that have been implicated in the violent elimination of Black and other marginalized communities (Dei, 2011; Foucault, 1980; Fraser, 2004; Torres & Nyaga, 2021, Smith, 2012) I argue that failure to recognize such hidden eviction of emotions in ethical guidelines is epistemologically unethical and irresponsible. To argue for ethics beyond ethical is to call for a re-imagination of institutional ethics in ways that bring to life these hidden, nullified, discounted and subjugated practices and knowledges in ways that account and grief the loss of live and ways of being in knowledge production.

2   Critical Ethics

My wager in this chapter is to acknowledge the need for ethics beyond ethics (para-ethics) as the necessary requirement in research process and that knowledge production should be grounded on ethics of care and the philosophy of non-violence. We are aware that care is violent (Butler, 2020; 2004) and that current models of institutional ethics affirm, conceal, and authorize such care. While research is meant to develop (read this as care or save) society, it simultaneously violently denigrates, nullifies, and eliminates marginalized communities. Research is a process is a bio political process meant to account some life through discounting others in terms of race, gender, sexual orientation and other marginalizing social markers (Foucault, 1997; Butler, 2020). If such is the truth about research, it fundamentally important to start rethinking institutional ethics beyond ethics in ways that are philosophically responsible of the historical violence that research process continue to mete on Indigenous and Black communities (Dei, 2011; Smith, 2012). Such a philosophical declaration means that researchers need to break the duality of mind and body split that is the ground of codes of ethics and recognizing the fact that the in between and beyond of the codes (gaps between and beyond the mind and body) could provide us with histories, values and realities that Black and Indigenous people exist and that are fundamentally necessary in research process.

While such gaps have been spaces of epistemic violence and disappearance of marginalized communities, it is ethical for any researcher to start reimagining such spaces as infused in communal solidarities, values and emotions that provide a requisite space for non-violence. A non-violent form of research is grounded on community, their histories, values and realities as necessary ethical requirement in knowledge production. Non-violent research practice calls for reimagining emotions as capable of imagination. Non-violent care calls for a new form of resistance that is not grounded on colonial gendered violence where physical might is the definition of strength. Vulnerability and humility are necessary and responsible methodologies of resistance in non-violent research. Non-violent research processes are transformative rather than performative and calls for substantive change in people's lives. In a nutshell, emotions are a necessary ethical requirement in the research process.

The claim is that ethics are emotional relationship we have with research participants; and that helps check and transform the how of knowledge production. As such, I argue that research needs to be comfortable in discomfort presented by duality of emotions and rationality. Sitting in such discomfort helps recognize histories, value, and realities of participants as fundamental ethical necessity in research process. Such an ethical argument contests the politics of rationality and objectivity and looks at fundamental critical inclusivity of emotions and instincts in knowledge production. With the current ethical framework where emotions are contained, detained, and deported from knowledge production. Such containment and deportation of Black and Indigenous emotions and instincts are in and of themselves a form of current colonial institutional ethical framework, which I argue herein as unethical and against community empowerment and non-violence.

As an ethical researcher, one should not pay attention to knowledge as an end, but rather start asking how they can produce knowledge with communities in ways that are non-violent and human. The claim I make in this chapter is to imagine research as an ethical human praxis. I therefore call for ethics of critical care as necessary in research praxis.

3 Theoretical and Philosophical Analysis

3.1 *Foucault and Care of the Self*

Ethics of critical care is not a new praxis in research practice. Foucault et al. (2005) demonstrates ethics of critical care by looking at Greek and Roman communities and how they conceptualized and utilized the care for the self. There are multiple inflections of care of the self-meant to prepare one to lead others. The act of caring for the self helps one to imagine the other and act in ways that disappear the self in the eyes of the other. This kind of care of the self is a fundamental spiritual and psychic praxis where one requires the other for them to know themselves (Foucault, et al., 2005). The eye or the face of the other is an ethical requirement to knowing the self. We require the pupil of the other who may not know to start knowing ourselves and subsequently for them to know themselves through our pupil. To see the self in the eye of the other is a psychic process that allows us to engage with ourselves with the help of the other who mirrors us back and fails us to understand or even know them. This means that such a form of care helps create a form of solidarity between us and the other who prepares us to focus on our repressed self in ways that make them public. To make the repressed self-public is a process of critical care of the self-grounded on transformative critical reflexivity (flexing out). In this sense, the other is an ethical requirement for transformative care of the self and getting to know the self.

In a sense, one needs to disappear in the eye of the other for them to get to know themselves. This act of self-disappearance is a form of vulnerability and loss that cross-stitches one when they see the face of the other. Emanuel Levinas (Saldukaitytė, 2021) says that by looking in the eyes of the other, we have already been contracted by the other even before they commit themselves. The other fails us to understand them and that our knowing the other is always late. He says that we always arrive late when we attempt to know the other. The failure to understand or collapse the other reminds us that we are ethically tied to each other and that any effort to distinguish ourselves as expert researchers is failed by the other who drifts away from our grip. This form of failure to know the other calls for self-reflexive exercises to acknowledge the presence of the other as an ethical requirement in knowledge production. If I see the self in the eye of the other, I am broken, lost and vulnerable and therefore in need of the other for me to know the self. Brokenness and vulnerability remain critical in knowledge production and returns us to our human ethical self as critical care providers in knowledge production. This Lacanian mirroring is a necessary ethical response in the production of knowledge and helps recognize our limitations as human. My will to know fails without the other. These human limitations help underline why researchers need to be vulnerable, transformative change makers, critically reflexive, collaborative, and aware that knowledge cannot be without ethics. Foucault calls for infusing spirituality and psychic engagement with knowledge production as a necessary ethical requirement.

This chapter pays attention to the act of knowing the self through others as an ethical demand of researching Black communities. To know the self through the other employs an ethical methodology of being disappeared (losing the familiar) by others in ways that allow vulnerability and loss to define the how of knowing. Such an epistemological methodology helps us understand that we can only imagine (ethics of care and the role of psyche) the other without necessarily understanding (read reductionism, simplification, and objectification) them. Understanding (knowledge) becomes a secondary necessity since our role in research is not to quantify and reduce the others but rather to displace ourselves as researchers in the face or the eyes of the other. The other's eyes become a place of displacing our place as expert and knower, in modalities that make us more visible and public. The eye of the other acts as a reflective and reflexive space of our becoming as ethical researchers. The other becomes an ethical reminder of our humanity.

4   Critical Ethical Care and Research Process

The art of transposition of self becomes a necessary part of knowing and caring for the other since it connects researchers to communities that we research with (read also as participants). To be displaced is an act of being vulnerable. This aspect of vulnerability prepares any researcher to give up their privilege of being an expert and disappear into the miasmas of communities' face. From this place of being and miasmatic displacement, researcher becomes a learner rather than a knower. This means that the researcher disappears in the eyes of the other and can see their reflection of themselves in the miasmatic pupil of the other. In this sense, the other must be present for the researcher to be vulnerable and critically ethical enough to know the self and as such be able to care for the self. The other opens an ethical psychic space through which the researcher comes to understand themselves while imagining the desires and pain of the other. The act of seeing the self in the eye of the other is an act of being exposed and susceptible (read this as Levinas' hostage) to philosophical death under the direction of the other.

But while we are held hostage by the other, it is equally important to recognize the role of the other in the dislocation of the self. The other acts as the graveyard through which we disappear and appear to recognize and acknowledge their desire. This may sound like a process of empathy as an ethical process of knowing the self. The other must be present as an ethical responsibility and necessity of getting to know and care for the self for us to be a researcher. While participants' presence is a necessary ethical demand for our disappearance, we are also required to provide ourselves as graveyard for them to reflect on us and be able to psychically come to know their place in knowledge production. This act of getting to know the self in the face of the other (both the researcher and participant) orients us to the act of research as a non-violent act of disappearing the other to care and know the self. It is a nonviolent act of knowledge production because it brings communities together (Butler, 2020) in ways that produce knowledge for communities by the communities (George, 2017).

5 Critical Ethical Principles

The ethics of displacement and disappearance is grounded on several philosophical and critical principles of ethical methodologies. This chapter pays more attention to the role of human rights and values as an ethical requirement in the research process. According to Foucault (1997):

> The system of right and the judiciary field are permanent vehicles for relations of domination, and for polymorphous technique of subjugation. Right must, I think, be viewed not in terms of a legitimacy that has to be established, but in terms of the procedures of subjugation it implements. As I see it, we have to bypass or get around the problem of sovereignty- which is central to the theory of rights and the obedience of individuals who submit to it, and to reveal the problem of domination and subjugation instead of sovereignty and obedience.
>   p. 27

When we speak of right giving and coronation of the human to a speaking subject, we seek to engage more with who gives that right that inaugurate the other (read subhuman or non-being) as intelligible human; as well as the how/ methodology of right giving that gives right to that which is never considered life or speaking subject. Such a philosophical conception asks what happens to the inaugurated other when they start speaking the language of right from which they become. Who do they become and what does that do to their former self? Who speaks when the other so considered non-being is made to speak in the language of the right giver? The process of right giving becomes the same process that destroys bare lives. Those given rights simultaneously disappeared from themselves in ways that multiplies (read this as the art of corporation/profits and multiplication) they who gives rights. That said, right giving is a form of self-repetition on the bodies of others in ways that makes live the giver of rights while letting die the receiver of the rights.

Research is a colonial inauguration and coronation of the speaking subject 'I' which simultaneously disappears the researcher. While researchers are expected to be right giving subject, who produce the other through analyzing and sanitizing their stories, they simultaneously disappear into the epistemological abyss. A double form of violence against the participant and the researcher is committed in colonial research process. The process used to produce the other (read participants) simultaneously works to expunge the other (researcher) from the process of research. This is because the very process of production of the other speaks colonialism and as such when we fail to ask questions of who speaks when we speak, we continually render ourselves irrelevant in the process of speaking and producing others. So, the process of righting one as speaking subject and as such a citizen (intelligible other) becomes the very process through which we are disappeared psychically. Key to this process of elimination is psychic violence that keeps us comfortable with what we can see and are familiar with and fails us to engage with psychic discomfort. For us to engage critically and reflexively with participatory research, then it is important to reimagine the process of inaugurating the speaking subject as those who deserve (read value and valuation) to have rights to be human. To speak of human rights as a fundamental ethical principle in knowledge production should be guided by questions such as who is human, and which methodology of rights giving is followed when one is becoming human.

To make sense of human rights and right giving in knowledge production, I argue along an Aristotelian conception that those who produce knowledge are considered human and they who consume knowledge are seen as subhuman or lesser being whose fate can be sacrificed for safety of producer. This bio-political conception places the researcher as human and having rights to determine who ascend or is exulted as human with rights. In this sense, research, sense making, and production of knowledge is in and of itself the very process of right giving and determination of those who are human and citizen. Those others who are not producers of knowledge must be rendered as aliens, placeless, violent and in need of salvation from their emotions, which helps justify the need for colonial researcher as the savior of the other who is buried in their emotions. In this perspective, emotions become an economy through which the human must be produced and saved from in order for them to attain full rights to be human. This in essence means denigration of emotion (read social death) as a process of civilizing the other.

While we may utilize the works of Aristotle to argue for rights giving, we recognize how such a process was gendered, raced and classed and a space to white heterosexual man to epitomize humanity and become the standard of measure for human rights and right giving. Whiteness became the currency of determining those who would be considered human while discarding those others who fell outside this social determination of humans and the rights thereof. This argument helps to argue that research process is white and casts out anything that is otherwise from the process of knowledge production. In a nutshell, whiteness sees others as beings without a face. Such a conception argues that the others need white savor to have a face. The white other is seen and imagined as rational and objective being that does not require the other since they have been able to settle their emotional issue. This form of perspective defined research ethics in ways that give credence to knowledge while subsuming ethics. This kind of whiteness in research has decanted spirituality and psychic aspect in knowledge production and instead belief that physical aspects of life are more believable. This chapter argue that the psyche is a necessary ethical requirement of understanding the physical.

The process and method/methodologies of right giving, which herein I refer as white savior ship is also an important aspect of engagement that helps us unravel research process as reductionist, simplistic and engaged in capital and colonial violence of those pre-determined as emotionally broken. This means that the process of knowledge making is the very process through which emotions are discarded, casted out and deported from knowledge production and the other is coronated by being offered rights to be human which simultaneously kills their bare life. In other works (Torres & Nyaga, 2021) I used the metaphor of mincemeat machine to argue that when one is producing knowledge (read data collection and analysis), it is like bringing down a cow, cutting a slice of meat from dead cow and putting it into the mince meat processor, which then squeezes the meat into minute pieces of meat called mincemeat which is then sold in the market place. Such a processing of meat into mincemeat becomes the very process of redacting emotion in the form of the blood and water that comes from the meat. Such forms of simplification have material and symbolic consequences. The loss of relationship (Blood) and life (water) is one among the many consequences of current research ethics that continue to support profits and market logics at the behest of communities.

6   Values (Axiology)

> Reality, for once, requires a total understanding. On the objective level as on the subjective level, a solution has to be supplied.
> FANON, 1967, p.11

Axiology and ethics of care looks at the place of values in knowledge production. The current research process white and corporate and expunges Black life. It is important to engage with the value gap in research to claim that research needs to be ground in Black values as an ethical prerogative. Black values continue to disappear in the research process. To speak of research as ethical value addition is to claim that ways of life of a people must be considered as central to any research process. Such an argument puts research as a process through which some values (whiteness) are celebrated while others are nullified (Blackness). Such a disappearance renders Black values emotional, and unnecessary in determination of what can be termed as rational knowledge. Cahn (1977), quoting Plato on a conversation about virtue and knowledge, says:

> For true beliefs, as long as they remain, are a fine thing and all they do is good, but they are not willing to remain long, and they escape from man's mind, so that they are not worth much until one ties them down by (giving) an account of the reason why. And that Meno my friend, is recollection, as we previously agreed. After they are tied down, in the first place they become knowledge, and they they remain in place. That is why knowledge is prized higher than correct opinion, and knowledge differs from correct opinion in being tied down.
> p. 25

In a society that is market and corporate oriented, Black values must be disappeared for them to appear as rational. This disappearance of Black values in knowledge production and meaning making has material, symbolic and historical consequence in terms of shaping Black life. Among those consequences is the material Black losses in terms housing, and other basic Black needs. Any research that devalues Blackness (Black emotions, values, and realities) is anti-Black. This value gap has a place in Black histories where Black voices and ways of life's are disappeared by researchers in physical and psychic ways. This form of Black racial disappearance is the testament to the ways in which Black life is never considered a life but rather one that needs white savior (read researcher) to be considered valuable. Such savior mentality in research redacts and simplifies Black ontologies and values and therefore the need to callout current research practices as anti-Black. It is therefore necessary to reimagine research ethics in ways that celebrate realities, values and ways of being of Black peoples.

7   Concluding Words

As a caveat, I would like to point out that this chapter looks at ethics beyond the ethical guidelines and breaks institutional ordering of ethics. This helps make ethics homeless and pedestrian so that it speaks in accents that are grounded in peoples' experiences. Subsequently, this chapter looks at ethics from a perspective that is de-institutionalized and fluid; allowing ethics to be freed from institutional and corporate shackles.

As discussed in other works on how we exist stories (Torres & Nyaga, 2021), I argue that when researcher collect data in the form of stories and collapse them using quantitative analytical tools, they commit a form of social genocide on the participants. Of grave reference is the simultaneous death of the researcher who works hard to become an expert through the death of the participant. It is important to reimagine current institutionalized ethics to start speaking the language of marginalized communities in ways that are decolonial and grounded in peoples' realities, values and ways of being.

References

Butler, J. (2004). *Undoing Gender*. Routledge.
Butler, J. (2020). *The Force of Nonviolence : an Ethico-political Bind*. Verso.
Cahn, S. M. (1977). *Classics of Western Philosophy* (4th ed). Indianapolis/Cambridge: Hackett Publishing Co., Inc.
Creswell, J. (2013). *Qualitative Inquiry and Research Design* (3rd ed.). Thousand Oaks, CA: Sage.
Dei, G. J. S. (2011). *Studying, Researching and Teaching African Indigenous Knowledge: Challenges, Possibilities and Methodological Cautions*. Pretoria, South Africa: University of South Africa.
Deliovsky, K. (2017). Whiteness in the qualitative research setting: Critical skepticism, radical reflexivity and anti-racist feminism. *Journal of Critical Race Inquiry*, 4(1), 1–24.
Elliott, J. (2005). *Using Narrative in Social Research: Qualitative and Quantitative Approaches*. London, UK: Sage.
Fanon, F. (1967). *Black Skin, White Masks*. New York, NY: Grove Press.
Faulkner, S., & Faulkner, C. (2014). *Research Methods for Social Workers: a Practice-based Approach* (2nd ed.). Chicago, IL: Lyceum Books.
Foucault, M. (1997). *Society must be Defended*. London, UK: Penguin.
Foucault, M. (1980). *Power/Knowledge: Selected Interviews and Other Writings, 1972–1977*. New York, NY: Pantheon.

Foucault, M., Gros, F., Ewald, F., & Fontana, A. (2005). *The Hermeneutics of the Subject: Lectures at the Collège de France, 1981–1982* (iii). London: Picador.

Fraser, H. (2004). Doing narrative research: Analysing personal stories line by line. *Qualitative Social Work*, 3(2), 179–201.

George, P. (2017). Critical Arts-based Research: an Effective Strategy for Knowledge Mobilization and Community Activism. In H. Parada & S. Wehbi (Eds.), *Reimagining Anti-oppression Social Work Research* (pp. 29–38). Toronto, ON: Canadian Scholars' Press.

Saldukaitytė, J. (2021). Emmanuel Levinas and ethical materialism. *Religions* 12(10), 870. https://doi.org/10.3390/rel12100870.

Smith, L. T. (2012). Colonizing Knowledges. In *Decolonizing Methodologies: Research and Indigenous Peoples* (2nd ed., pp. 61–80). London, UK: Zed Books.

Torres, R. A., & Nyaga, D. (Eds.). (2021). *Critical Research Methodologies: Ethics and Responsibilities*. Leiden: Brill.

CHAPTER 6

Africa beyond Africa
Afro-pessimism as an Ethical Demand

Waywaya Nyaga and Dionisio Nyaga

> The basic argument of this article is that, in order to account for both the mind-set and the effectiveness of postcolonial relations of power, we need to go beyond the binary categories used in standard interpretations of domination, such as resistance v. passivity, autonomy v. subjection, state v. civil society, hegemony v. counter-hegemony, totalisation v. detotalisation.
> MBEMBE, 1992, p. 3

∴

> No matter how far they travel, mi grants maintain tight links with their places of departure. Something of the nature of an image attaches them to their places of origin and compels them to return. Identity, then, is created at the interface between the ritual of rootedness and the rhythm of distancing, in a constant passage from the spatial to the temporal, from the imaginary to the orphic.
> MBEMBE, 2017, p. 99

∴

> Black is a Black man; that is, as the result of a series of aberration of affect, he is rooted at the core of a universe from which he must be extricated.
> FANON, 1967, p. 8

∴

In the mindset of a White corporate world, Africa is imagined and understood as tabula rasa—a childlike place, mired in emotional and instinctual turmoil (Mbembe, 2001) that needs the West to save it from its miserable state of nature and war. Through Western modern research, African is painted as a space of degeneracy and violence, desperately in need of Western salvation to stave off self-cannibalization (Webhi, 2017). Western media has played a pivotal role in the dissemination of this false narrative in the world. When I speak of media, I want to reflect beyond the dominant media and start looking at other forms of representation that are not physical (what you see and know) but rather psychic (what you cannot see or feel, and thus has no obvious meaning). It is my contention that for us to understand the how (read mapping or representation) of physical Africa (that which we can see), we first need to get lost in the jungle of the African psyche. As such, Afro pessimism as a research methodology should be grounded in the African psyche as a point of decolonizing the Western view of Africa as a broken, child-like, and garbage place (a veritable shithole).

Over time, the African continent has been produced and consumed through research and in the Western mind, respectively, as a dark space in need of White rational illumination for it to be considered as a community of the world. In the process of such representation of Africa, research becomes the only tool that brings life to the lifeless African body. With such White dominant narration and representation of Africa, major technologies of research and media control and manipulation work together in complex ways to inter and intern the continent into a child-like, out-of-space place, thereby concocting the rationale for the West to enter Africa and develop it into adulthood that is the world. The art of developing and saving the child from its deplorable state becomes the very process of shaming and punishing Africa for its backwardness. The issue in such form of African salvation assumes that Africa and Africans have not fully undergone child development (which is a privilege) and as such the world presence in and on Africa (read figuratively) will emancipate them/it from its state of war and nature. In as much as Africa and Africans remains marked as and with nature, the White savior must appear to protect it (a thing) from self-cannibalizing instincts.

The vision of Africa as a thing that is grounded in nature (immobile and stuck in the past) continues to affect Africans both on the continent and in the diaspora, in that they are never expected to move socially and economically, neither physically nor psychically. Based on such a natured and naturalized conception of Africa, African diasporas are never seen beyond their skin color. Afro-pessimism therefore becomes a methodology of imagining Africa beyond the color-coated Western mindset. Afro-pessimism is therefore a methodology of verbing rather than nouning Africa and Africanness, of breaking colonial boundaries (continental social prisons) to come to imagine Africa beyond Africa. Africa must be seen beyond the physical map and that will mean (re)imagining the psychic nature of Africa. Such a methodological conception cannot understand Africa but rather imagine the jungle that is Africa—and that cannot be collapsed into a consumable and corporate Africa map. Rather than simplifying Africa into an object (read map) and in the process kill its emotions, an afro-pessimist methodology works with Africa in ways that are African centered.

Africa is expected to remain (read this as state of deportability) Africa (read child and immobile) waiting to be saved from nature (itself). The research-based Western colonial representation of Africa as social remains or human receptacle earmarks Africans as deportable and conceives of them as sub-human in the Western mind. Such a Western belief about Africa and African diaspora collapses (read this as social death through internment and interring) Africa into a geographical colonial grid (social prisons) while simultaneously pronouncing the West as benevolent savior of the broken other. Fanon (1967) says that the White man looks at the Black as a point of reminder of their childlike experience. In the same breath, my wager is that in Western minds, Africa has become a place where the West can visit and be reminded of their past childlike life. Africa must be constructed as a place where the West can pass time (read White tourism as overcoming itself through the death of the other) while confirming itself as human with rights. An afro-pessimist methodology breaks this colonial perspective and starts imagining Africa as fluid and beyond these colonial markers. This methodology argues that child development is a privileged process infused with power to determine which child dies and, in the process, allows the other to live. The very process of saving the Africa/n child must be open to the complex interlocking biopolitical viewpoints that seemingly present the West as the benevolent other while simultaneously committing cultural and social deaths on the other. The process of adulting Africa (read as saving Africa) is in and of itself meant to kill the child in Africa while enabling the West to imagine itself as a right-holding subject.

It is in Africa that the White/West confirms its whiteness while marking Africa a cauldron of evil desires and cultures that needs to be tamed. The violent geopolitical mapping of Africa as an evil space in need of control and salvation is replicated in the ways in which African immigrants are mistreated when in the West. As Wilderson (2017) puts it,

> In other words, there is a global consensus that Africa is the location of sentient beings who are outside of global community, who are socially dead. That global consensus begins with the Arabs in 625 and it's passed on to the Europeans in 1452. Prior to that global consensus you can't think Black. You can think Uganda, Ashanti, Ndebele, you can think many different cultural identities, but Blackness cannot be dis-imbricated from the global consensus that decides here is the place which is emblematic of that moment the Choctaw person is spun out from social life to social death. That's part of the foundation.
>
> pp. 20–21

To imagine the mistreatment of Africa in diaspora, my doctoral study investigated the living experiences of Kenyan men living and working in Toronto, Canada—specifically the role of accent in determining how labor, education, and immigration policies earmarked Kenyans as deportable aliens whose presence was a threat to the existence of White Canada. Deportability in this sense must be considered beyond the usual semantics and incorporate the different interlocking biopolitical modalities that mark out Kenyan men from participating in economic practices that sustain life.

This chapter, therefore, engages with the physical markings of African borders through research as a psychic production and internment of Africa and Africans in ways that render it/them as social remains that are deportable. This way of looking at Africa and Africans helps identify a new decolonial praxis that may provide substantive means of breaking African boundaries beyond their physical colonial mapping. It is this process of African production in the Western mind that this chapter seeks to disentangle to bring forth African-centered research that is critically reflexive about the plights of Africans both in the continent and beyond.

1   Literature Review

African was colonized by Britain, Italy, France, Belgium, Portugal, and other colonial powers through colonial methods such as direct and indirect rule (Cappelen & Sorens, 2018; McNamee, 2019). Direct rule entails the colonizer being omnipresent in Indigenous lands; indirect rule means the colonizer applied Indigenous power structures to control and manipulate communities (McNamee, 2019). Indirect rule allowed some Indigenous autonomy in terms of internal administration. This form of colonization was mostly applied by French and British colonizers (Müller-Crepon, 2020).

British colonization in Kenya exploited Indigenous chiefs to monitor and administer the African Indigenous communities on their behalf (Bolt & Gardner, 2020). According to Bolt and Gardner (2020),

> Kenya's 1902 Village Headmen Ordinance, which made village headmen responsible for law and order in their villages, called for the appointment of said headmen by European officials and gave them little power (Hailey 1951, p. 92). Similarly, in Nyasaland, the 1912 District Administration (Native) Ordinance mandated the appointment of village headmen and principal headmen. It did not exclude "the use of traditional Native

> Authorities as agencies of local rule" but intended the headmen to act "mainly as executive agents of the Administration."
>
> p. 1195

Indirect rule was only applicable in places where Indigenous communities were not a major threat to British rule. This kind of rulership and colonial administration would not be neat and without contradiction, both in Africa and in Kenya (Bolt & Gardner, 2020; McNamee, 2019). There are some scenarios where some Indigenous communities in Kenya would fight back colonial rule, thus necessitating direct rule. The practice of direct colonial rule was driven by the levels of resistance from African Indigenous communities, whereby they would be controlled and ruled by heavy presence of the White colonizer in Indigenous spaces. Direct rule was mainstream control over Indigenous communities. Indirect and direct colonial practice was applied to divide and rule the community, which in essence made it economical in terms of colonial administration (McNamee, 2019).

In Kenya, the British colonizer took over the most fertile land for agricultural purposes and left dry lowlands to Indigenous Africans, giving birth to colonial spaces such as the White Highlands and the African schemes or reserves (Parsons, 2011). This process of mapping interned, administered, and controlled Kenyan Indigenous peoples in their geographical spaces by ethnically prescribing and mapping social spaces (Parson, 2011). Such colonial spatial prescription helped separate and control tribal movements from one tribal reserve to another, making it an economical administrative venture while simultaneously producing African carceral spaces and systems that were disciplinary, penal, and punitive in/on nature. The colonial government monitored the movement and settlement of the Indigenous peoples of Kenya through technologies that interned and contained social movement, therefore minimizing social uprisings. This kind of rule was without challenges, more so when some reserves faced overcrowding and Indigenous communities crossed colonial reserve boundaries, thereby challenging, and resisting colonial carceral grids. Such anti-establishment circumstances where a boundary was re-marked and resisted elevated direct rule over the communities.

The need for labor in the White Highlands also provided the re-marking of the colonial boundary in ways that were colonial in nature. The colonial government introduced the *kipande*—a small tag that the African man had to hang in his neck for the sake of identification—that allowed African men (not women) to cross over into White Highlands. This crossing was gendered, and it controlled who entered White space to work in the White Highlands. I will look at the kipande system as another technology of social incarceration of the

African body for the purpose of labor exploitation. I argue that the kipande system as a colonial technology was a policy bred, raised, authorized, and sanctioned by Western research to distill and simplify the collective African other of their emotions and humanness, consequently earmarking them as tools and objects of exploitation and violence. What is considered work in this chapter was a form of slave labor wherein the colonizer introduced a hut tax and forced Africans to work for them to pay the tax; failure to do so would result in punishment. While the kipande system acted as a passport to the White Highlands, it simultaneously produced gendered social life in the African schemes/reserve where African women were produced as children-rearing subjects while simultaneously marking them as emotional beings. This gendered construction helped sustain the commandment (Mbembe, 1992) through the colonial method/ology of divide and rule. The system authorized who was to be considered the citizen and the immigrant deportable other, respectively. To be a "citizen" meant to disappear into the tag. The kipande tag, I argue, provided the roadmap for citizenship in the Kenyan colonial narrative. This process of citizenship became the very process through which social disappearance of the other was a necessary evil to attain citizenship.

In the words of Mbembe (2001), we

> need to examine the way the world of meanings thus produced is ordered, the types of institutions, the knowledges, norms and practices that structure this new "common sense" as well as the light that the use of visual imagery and discourse throws on the nature of domination and subordination.
>
> p. 4

The White man examined the African body through the kipande tag to determine their worth to citizenship as an "economic man" (read a slave laborer). The body of the African other became a template of study earmarked for reductionism, simplification, and collapsing (read this as social death) into a kipande metal plate. This research model of simplification helped determine citizenship through social punishment, disciplining, and social death. Kipande tags employed a panoptic technology of internment of the lowland African species in ways that simultaneously concealed and wrapped (imagine this as corporatization of the body through packaging) the body while making it readable as human worth of joining the community of men and human. This technology was supposed to fade away and disappear the African into the tag for them to be considered for slave labor in the White Highlands. This technology meant to disappear the African played multiple roles of reducing and simplifying the colonized other into an object that could be transacted upon. This form of objectification was a form of surveying, inspecting, and collapsing the Africa body into a colonial data system that is manageable, controllable, and convenient while in the White Highlands. Through this form of bodily operation, African emotions were rationalized and simplified in ways that removed and discarded Africa (darkness and childlike) in the African man. I argue that this form of surveying of the African body interned them into racial boundaries/categories that were readable in the mind of the colonizer. The tag helped keep and sustain racial returns of African body (deport) while instantaneously consuming their labor.

This chapter argues that the kipande system as a racial panoptic system incarcerated the African other into an object that in turn could manipulate their racial identity in ways that were economical and unverifiable, while simultaneously exploiting their labor. The kipande system and policy was a technology of racial internment meant to control the African bodies and spaces while making colonial governance a reality. According to Mbembe (1992),

> Colonialism was to a large extent a way of disciplining bodies with the aim of making better use of them: docility and productivity go hand in hand. But how brilliant power could become, how magnificent its display, depended on that increase in productivity. So, if as on several occasions atrocities against Africans were found to be excessive, the right to punish in this way was nonetheless generally justified in terms of an overriding concern for profits and productivity (Coquery-Vidrovitch, 1972). Yet it would be wrong to reduce the meaning of colonial violence to mere economics. The whip and the cane also served to force upon the African an identity concocted for him, an identity that allowed him to move in the kind of spaces where he was always being ordered around, and where he had unconditionally to put on show his submissiveness-in forced labour, public works, local corvee labour, military conscription.
>
> p. 12

The tag as a colonial administrative tool swallowed (read this as the power of the leviathan to consume other sea animals) the Kenyan men the moment they crossed over to the White Highlands. The tag represented the power of the sovereign to decide who lives and who dies. Speaking of the role of commandment in postcolonial Africa, Mbembe (2001) says,

> The actions that signal sovereignty have to be carried through both with style and with an adequately harsh firmness, otherwise the splendour

of those exercising the trappings of authority is dimmed. To exercise authority is above all to tire out the bodies of those under it, to disempower them not so much with a view to increasing their productivity as to ensure the maximum docility.

p. 9

This form of regulation consigned Kenyan men as "worthy subjects" for entering the White Highlands through a practice of loss and disappearance. The African man remained lowland while the White Highlands (internment) constituted a form of continuous, unverifiable, and consistent deportation based on skin color. The tag interned them in ways that were deportable, displaceable, and easily expendable, while making them visible and accessible to the colonizer.

The tag system collapsed the African man (read social death) into an object (tag), reducing him into a means of production (an economic implement). This technology monitored and regulated the African in the highlands through a process of documentation and recording of their movement and their eventual deportation, making the African body a superfluous and expendable object. Kenyan men had to be disappeared (read as social death) into an object/tag for them to be considered human and worthy of citizenship. For the Kenyan men to be considered as intelligible and deemed worthy of citizenship, they had to be objectified quantitatively in ways that interned and interred them. The tag became a colonial graveyard through which Africa was laid to rest. Researchers must come to terms with these graveyards and their attendant ghosts. An afro-pessimist research methodology must implicate itself with the role of research and researchers in the social death of Africa and African bodies.

This technology of concealment of the African sociality into the kipande system incarcerated the Kenyan man while making him labor the incarceration, which in effect reduced him into moving to a prison within the White Highlands. This social technology of control reduced and simplified the Kenyan man into a comprehensible object that could be economically managed and controlled. This quantitative operation and industrialization of the Kenyan body into a simplified rational implement is in and of itself a form of colonial social violence meant to design the architecture of the African body as emotional and in need of being saved from its cannibal instinct while instantaneously presenting and confirming the White subject as the benevolent and rational being. The tag was therefore presented as a necessary tool of saving the broken Kenyan man from his heathen self. It is through such salvation of the other that they were conscripted and interned and made to carry the cost of internment.

According to Foucault (1980), the panoptic system works in ways that economize the operational cost of the prison complex by transferring it to the prisoners who must watch over themselves and others while making the whole system self-sufficient. Through the kipande tag system, Kenyan men were made to feel self-conscious of themselves and in the process watch over themselves while in the White Highlands. Their intelligibility as human and speaking beings was through the tag. The tag refined them (because they are considered crude) into beings who had rights and were worthy of joining the human community. The tag was a violent launching space of the African other into a human world space of commodification meant for the White farmlands. Such launching of the African other was a quantitative necessity meant to denigrate and vilify their emotional instincts into numbers that could be reduced into the tag. It is through this form of production of the other that a particular form of colonial market violence was meted on the African other in ways that interned them into a product that could be sold into the marketplace for the purpose of profiting the White settlers in Kenya.

This aspect of tagging was replicated by colonial administrators during the scramble for Africa, albeit in ways that were writ large. Africa collapsed into smaller silos (consider them as countries) which could them be used to provide raw materials for the colonial masters. Among the raw materials was the African man's free labor to the White man. There was a need to demarcate and partition Africa into countries that could be economical in terms of administration of resources. Such forms of partitions supposedly meant the dispersal of African communities into reserves/schemes to allow greater control and manipulation. Such African dispersal fostered the disintegration and mitosis of African ways of life, therefore rendering them easily manipulatable. Through these social displacements and dispersal, the African other was tagged and produced into a human that could be controlled, manipulated, and ultimately dispensed with.

This form of African dispersal has taken on a global dimension. Following the introduction of Structural Adjustment Programs (SAPs) in Kenya and other African countries in the 1990s, there has been a consistent movement of Africans from Kenya and other African countries to the West in search of greener pastures. We now have international passport (read this as *kipande*) systems that provide information for African immigrants to cross over to the West (read this as White Highlands). This helps us understand and imagine how a kipande colonial system is writ large and global to work together in complex and interlocking ways to mark African bodies in postcolonial transnational environments as broken and expendable. It becomes necessary therefore to open new racial and colonial operations in a global context to understand the role of the passport system in determining the lived experiences of African bodies in diaspora. This chapter, therefore, looks at the effect of accent in terms of marking Kenyan men as expendable and deportable bodies in the global politics of education, immigration, and labor. The chapter seeks to identify how local carceral technologies local employ a global perspective and their effect on African bodies. The chapter looks at how the passport system employs this carceral technologies to earmark Kenyan men as expandable and deportable bodies. I use accent as one among many racial markers that work together with passport systems to denigrate Africans in diaspora.

2   Findings

In my doctoral dissertation on the effects of accent on the employability, immigration, and schooling of Kenyan men in Toronto, it was very clear that they will face unemployment or be underemployed because of their accents. This would be compounded by the ways in which immigration, education, and labor policies worked together in complex and interlocking ways to deny them a chance of ever becoming substantive world citizens. For instance, education is a key element of immigration for one to be employable in Canada. Immigration policies expect immigrants to have a certain amount of experience to access job placements in Canada. While expressing the need for experience and linguistic ability as a prerequisite for employable immigrants, Canadian immigration policies implicitly conceal accent as an important element for one to access employment. Those without Canadian accent disguised as Canadian experience are rendered unemployable. This accenting of Kenyan men marks such immigrants as social excesses or deplorables, easily deportable and expendable. Accenting the body of the African immigrant is a technology that marks out the immigrant even in their absence. In this chapter, accent is beyond language and occupies the ways in which spaces are painted and highlighted for racial elimination.

Most participants in my doctoral study said that the process of immigration from Kenya was supposedly a difficult one. Participant 1 noted that

> Coming to Canada as an immigrant took so long. The immigration process is too long. I have to pay and again something is forgotten and I have to pay again for the Visa. I almost told my spouse to go because it is eating my pocket and is wasting my time.

The process of Canadian immigration in Kenya is tailored in ways that keep the violent Kenyan (read Africa) in its place. The process rationalizes the Kenyan immigrant (read this as an industrialization or processing of the Africa/n body) to a bare minimum to be accepted in Canada. It seems to be that the immigration is more like unveiling the other, which I argue makes the immigrant public while simultaneously impressing that Westerners are self-sufficient and rational beings. This violent processing of the immigrant into bareness is manifested in the ways in which private information from prospective immigrants is mined through a technology of introspection and scrapping of data. This by any other term is a form of shaming, punishment, and disciplining of Kenyan immigrants meant to reduce and simplify them into readable or intelligible data in turn meant to determine their humanity and manufactured citizenship.

The study participants who were lucky enough to endure the grueling process of immigration in Canadian embassies in Kenya also faced the challenge of having to leave behind their family for a couple of years. This presented a challenge to them in Canada since they had to go back and forth (read this as spatial liminality) trying to prepare immigration papers for their immediate family living in Kenya. Participant 2 noted:

> I applied for a visa and got it without any issue. I came here as a student and even so it was good because moving here was exciting but on getting here that is when the reality sunk on me and I realised that am starting all again from scratch. I came here first by my self. I sponsored them and that was close to seven years down the line. I kept going back and forth. There were some financial challenges and I was working here and supporting family and paying the bills here.

The going back and forth is a testament of an African body that is supposedly returned (read this as a form of shaming, disciplining, and deportation of Africa to remain in its mapped space). This act of return/deportation was also manifested by the ways in which Kenyan men had to start life afresh after coming to Canada.

According to Participant 3,

> However, even with the admission, the challenge was to bring the family, because I have a wife and a small daughter. It was such a great challenge to get them the papers especially specific appointment and interviews with the high commission. I had to leave my family behind. When you look at all this thing, as an African man you are leaving your family behind you. You feel like you have to make a very strategic choice. If you don't leave

you will miss out a lot. You also need to come and fix the systems like the house and know where you will sleep.

In another quotation that supports Participant 3, Participant 2 provided the reason for delays in reuniting African families:

> There is suspicion and insecurity around your marriage and many people have lost their families because of separation. That brings in the question of immigration. While Canada claims to take pride in reuniting families, on the other side they take responsibility on separation of families because the immigration system takes longer to reunite.

From these quotations, the immigration process is built on a framework that imagines Africans (read Africa) as untrustworthy, and they have to undergo a rigorous processing to determine whether they are worthy of Canadian charity to immigrate. This act marks Kenyan immigrants as welfare and immigration cheats who should be watched over, as they can prey on the Canadian system. This race-based immigration assertion sanctions and authorizes an overly rationalized form of processing Kenyan immigrants with a plan to remain and ground (a form of child disciplining and punishment) them on the shores even when they cross over to Canada.

This technique of grounding children is meant to help them deal with their emotional mental health issues, more so their anxiety. According to The Pragmatic Parent (n.d.) website, adults have words that they can use to express their emotions while children lack the same. It goes without saying that the grounding of the African immigrant is supposed to help them deal with their emotional instinctual self since they are coming from a space so determined as having childlike behavior. It also goes to show that Africans are assumed as not intelligible beings and lack the language to express their anxiety. It also expresses the fact that the Western mind predetermines Africans and Africa as an emotional and psychologically broken and in need of grounding.

The kind and number of questions Africans are asked in the immigration process are so personal and private. This works in similar ways with the welfare system in Canada, where all those who are on government support are constantly seen as welfare frauds (Moffatt, 1999) who should be suspected, inspected, and watched over. The act of watching over is a form of power modalities meant to locate the cheat as the alien, violent other whose life must be reduced and streamlined to the bare minimum for them to be considered as welfare receivers.

According to Participant 3, the model of questioning and the set of questions purposefully sought to mark immigrants (read this as a form of calculated shaming) as unworthy subjects; he says:

> The challenges of coming here through a student visa means you have to jumps so many handles. The application required writeups and submitting host of documents that you would need to go and get some background checks, getting a visa from the embassy so that they can approve your documents seemed, process of getting an appointment means you have to go to the bank to get a bank statement, you have to have money in the account, to show them that you are in a position to take care of yourself. At the same time you need recommendation letters from peers. So if you look at all those things combined, it means that you are leaving Kenya to come and visit this country, they ask you so many question so that financially you are exposed. It is documented that this is your financial position. Something you did not have to reveal when you were in Kenya. Nobody would ask your statement so that you can access your education.

While the immigration process made it difficult to for some to access the Canadian educational dream, getting a job in Canada even with the right experience was another problem Kenyan immigrants faced. The process of accreditation marked and accented Kenyan education as not "experienced" and rational enough to be applied in Canada (read this as Kenyan education has an accent that cannot be applied in Canada). Participant 7 had this to say on accreditation:

> I came here with my family. To come here, jobwise was very complicated because I was working with an international company, my manager when I broke the news, we discussed and I said I know a bit of some people here. The goal for me was to start networking. When I came here I had already started the interview with my company here in telecommunication. It made sense to use the same skills here. But again I went through it and for some reasons this did not mature up even today I don't know why. But at some point I contacted the agency and they said that here you know there is an international labour policy that you cannot move from one market to the other because of non competitive. But again that was one way of dismissing my experience.

It was also noted that Kenyan men who wanted to go back to school would face racial deportation based on their accent. As Participant 4 shared:

> I was a student then. In school I was not talking. I did not have that confidence. The thing I hated most is when people do not understand what I have just said. I had to relearn English. You know the funniest thing—the English you are taught in Kenya is not the English that people are taught here. For example in Kenya when you were learning English, were you ever taught silent words? For example the word "work" we were told letter "r" is silent in Kenya. But here the "r" is active. Now go ask for work using the Kenyan silent word and tell me whether you will get it. That affected me in the classroom because I couldn't talk. Once I understood what was going on, it made it easier.

Participants often were asked where their accent came from. That helped mark them out of the education world and finally casted them out as alien and deportable beings. According to Participant 3,

> Here I am the only Black man in our class. Our class is composed of 22 students and I am the only Black person there. So it is very clear to you. Like you look at a parking lot and there are 10 cars; nine are white and one is red. It stands out. But maybe the question would be. Does that red car know that it stands out? For my case you will know that you are the only one because there is something inherent in all of us because we want to know who is next to me or who is in my class. When you look around and ask from which country and they say Canada, Turkey. Then you realize that I am the only one from Africa. All of them are White apart from me who is Black. In the office I am also the only Black person.

Universities used Kenyan students as a multicultural or diversity tool meant to create an impression of being progressive and welcoming to difference. According to Participant 8:

> Because you are so unique, it is easy to mingle because everyone is looking for the diversity. You fill the quota of diversity in town, in friends' circles, the university. So, you get invited to very many things because you are the diversity sort of. It was very boring. I used to work on summer. The job was being a tour guide and because I was an elite student, when I walk to the administrator's office they already know me. They make things up for you. I was also in the poster board for the university. They

also hired me for their brochures for their diversity quotas because the university could not present itself as just a White and Asian university in their student recruitment because they go to other countries to recruit.

Such students would appear in the university pamphlets as an impression of a multicultural university. This by any measure collapsed diversity into the African students, leaving them to carry the weight of a White university. It rendered diversity policy into a commodity (African student) that could be sold on the market. This would attract other students who would mark and elevate the status of a White university in the world market.

This in a nutshell provided a framework that fetishizes Africa as in need of help while simultaneously creating the space for marketing the university to the world. Such practices of inclusion of Africa to the world were simultaneously the same processes that disappeared them. Such African disappearance authorized by the university rendered African students as a commodity that could be sold in the marketplace, which returns (read deportation) them into their objectified self. This form of marketization of Africa in the marketplace reminds us of the very form of commercialization of Black bodies by slave owners.

3 Philosophical Reflexivity and Analysis

> The colonized is elevated above his jungle status in proportion to his adoption of the mother country's cultural standards. He becomes whiter as he renounces his Blackness, his jungle.
> FANON, 1967, p. 18

What do these findings have to do with Africa and its presence in the beyond (read the world)? How would the experience of a Kenyan student help us imagine research? In short, how has Africa been accented in research practice and what lesson do we learn in terms of applying an afro-pessimist methodology that celebrates an accented Africa as a center of knowledge production? These and many other questions help open Africa to new orientations that are beyond its conceptualization as a dark spot or a stain where there is neither life nor knowledge. This chapter argues that for Africa to rewrite this colonial history, a great philosophical disorientation is necessary. This chapter engages with the realities, values, and ways of life that shape how we look and imagine Africa both at home and beyond. The plan is to work around and within transcultural/national identities and politics while researching beyond the cultural component and sensitivity that remain colonial and that objectifies and interns Africa in terms of recording and documentation (a major element in immigration policy). This chapter also looks at African-based culturally competent research practices as reductionist in the ways that they reduce Africa into objects that are then sold into the marketplace. A look at participants' comments on university and the politics of multiculturalism helps shed light on the intricacies of Canadian universities as centers of knowledge production and culturally competent spaces while simultaneously concealing their role in the objectification, grounding, and quantification of Africa as a product for sale in the market.

Speaking of the ways in which cultural competency patronizes Black bodies, Fanon (1967) says:

> "Oh, I know the blacks. They must be spoken to kindly; talk to them about their country; it's all in knowing how to talk to them. For instance." I am not at all exaggerating: A white man addressing a Negro behaves exactly like an adult with a child and starts smirking, whispering, patronizing, cozening.
>
> p. 31

To speak of a culturally proficient research practice is to look at the ways in which Africa is seen as a place for data provision and the West as a place for production and rationalization of those emotional and childish data. According to participants' comments, African students are employed as tools to reflect (be reminded of the colonial *kipande* system) multicultural university, making them labor for the same while concealing the implication of unequal university spaces. This colonial narrative continues to shape Africa/ns as a space in need of the West while simultaneously affirming the West as self-sustaining. Such a paternalistic orientation and imagination sees Africa as stuck in a state of nature that is brutish and nasty (read Hobbes and state of nature that is perpetually in a state of war) and in need of Western research for it to develop. The world/research is therefore supposed to visit or enter Africa to bring a form of civilization. This form of civilizational narrative continues to impact Africa in terms of social death perpetrated by researchers who continue to misrepresent Africa as backward and childlike and in need of Western alms/methods of development for its survival.

For researchers to imagine Africa differently, a form of philosophical death of research and researchers is of fundamental importance. Philosophical death is necessary for research and researchers to start a critical reflexive journey of imagining how they are implicated in the social death and internment of

Africa and Africans. In other words, such forms of social death are generated in the method/methodologies that continue to mark Africa and Africans as social excess and remains and that need social simplification and reductionism for them to be considered human. Philosophical death therefore means a break away from such colonial contraction and construction to start embracing the fact that Africa is also a producer of knowledge. For research to meet such a death, it will mean recognizing itself as not the universal knower but rather a learner. Research and researchers must symbolically die to acknowledge both the histories of colonialism that continue to cause immeasurable trauma on Africa and Africans, as well as the place of research in such atrocities.

This will mean that researchers cease to understand and begin to imagine Africa. For some time now, researchers seek to simplify and reduce Africa into a commodity that can be understood in terms that are neo-liberal market oriented. An afro-pessimist researcher will have to look in the pupils of Africa and disappear in them (read this as decolonial praxis of disappearance steeped in philosophical death praxis) in ways that are psychic. This will mean researchers becoming vulnerable in terms of losing their place as the experts and embody a space of not knowing but rather engaging with Africa. The researcher will have to create genuine allyship with Africa to allow Africa to speak in ways that are contextual and relevant to African realities, histories, and values. To that end, afro-pessimist methodologies remind us of the role of Indigenous perspectives that are outside a fixed philosophical orientation.

In a society that is quickly becoming accelerated and transformed spatially and technologically, it's timely that we reform and refocus our imagination and understanding of Africans beyond Africa. This by any stretch of the imagination calls for a reconceptualization of Africa beyond the static colonial mapping inscribed through a geographical beacon meant to localize and fix Africa into a singular point of context, history, and culture. Afro-pessimist method/ologies call for freeing Africa from its ontological position as colonial hostage and imagining Africa as having multiple complex histories and contexts. Such multiplicities are a necessary mix to dismantle the social prisons that continue to view and ground Africa as backward and stagnated in its growth. The breakaway/out process of Africa from its colonial past will help answer some of the racial issues faced by African bodies when they are crossing or have crossed over into the Western hemisphere. To that end, to rethink of Africa beyond Africa is an ethical global demand necessary to imagine how Africans in diaspora come to be viewed as deportable bodies and how such a viewpoint can be misread in ways that bring social change in the imagination of Africa and Africans in the West. African beyond African—or what many would refer to as afro-pessimism orientation/methodologies—will help to open critically reflexive dialogues on the fluidity of Africa in global conversations.

This chapter looks at the issues facing Africa and African diasporas as pegged in this parochial and colonial entertainment and enterprise of imagining Africa as a location perpetually and perceptually held in the past. The chapter also attempts to look at the reason why Africans in diaspora are imagined as inhabiting one country, which makes it possible to collapse African life into one prison of imagination, which has both material and symbolic consequences in terms of social life. This helps to explain why Africa/ns are never at home but rather are held hostage both psychically and physically. To speak of Africa beyond Africa is to imagine of the ways through which Africa can engage globally with other continents in ways that are fair, fluid, and ethical.

To imagine Africa beyond Africa calls for substantive freedom of Africa and Africans' social collapsing into a prison of Africa where their movements are conscripted and denied. This act of opening Africa to the world allows one to look critically at the ways in which Africa cannot speak of itself but rather must wait for others to tell its story. To speak of Africa beyond Africa is to come to terms with the fact that Africa does really have a mouth and a face that is beyond colonial representation of a muted Africa. Africa has many voices in terms of its cultures, contexts, and histories and the expressions are necessary ethical foundations of an African social matrix that cannot be regulated through research. Such an epistemological orientation will open multiple narratives and imagination of telling and speaking Africa beyond the fixes and static ontological elaboration that is manufactured for Africa. In this sense, this chapter calls for imagining Africa both through a complicated and matrixed ontological, methodological, axiological perspective. Such a philosophical orientation is a necessary ethical demand in a society that is ever fluid, technological, and moving.

Africa must move beyond its colonial international boundaries for it to be counted as cosmopolitan. This social-based African movement must break away from the fixed colonial definition that misrepresents Africa as lying somewhere outside what may be termed as true world. To argue for such a pluralistic social movement of Africa beyond colonial beacons (read prisons), Africa must engage with its immediate and historical challenges that look at it as a child that needs to be saved from itself. I argue that such misrepresentation of Africa as child has been sustained by research and has both figurative and substantive consequences for Africans living abroad and at home. An afro-pessimist methodology breaks this recycled representation of Africa as dependent and consumer of Western alms to start imagining Africa as producer of knowledge. It also looks at Africa's development as steeped in African-based research that is contextual and matrixed in African histories and values. Such values and context celebrate the child in Africa rather than erasing the same through a rationalized and Western model of knowledge production.

Africa continues to be represented as an imperfection and a place where rawness and crudity is the way of life. To speak of an afro-pessimist perspective is to sit in comfort of such imperfection. This chapter argues that such imperfection is an ontological and ethical requirement for research. Afro-pessimism as a methodology of imperfection always fails us when we try to order, regulate, and organize Africa (read research on Africa/ns) into colonial ensembles that can be understood. Africa and Africans cannot be understood but rather imagined and acknowledged as speaking subjects. To understand Africa and Africans reduces and simplifies their ways of life and commits the ontological social death.

The pedagogical and ethical changes to imperfection require us to fail and embrace failure as part of knowledge production. Otherwise, how would we know except through failure? Failure becomes a necessary tool of knowing and embracing the imperfect Africa/n. This perspective of failure and imperfection helps us work and imagine the world as a perfect imperfection that fails us wherever we try to understand it. This is what Levinas (1979) calls an ethical demand of understanding the face of the other who happens to swallow or imprison us even before we get to know them. As researchers, we are always late whenever we try to understand the other (read collapse the other as social death). Foucault (1985, 1986a, 1986b,1997a), writing on ethics of care and knowing the self, argues that care is violent whenever we try to give metrics of understanding those we come close to. According to Fleck et al. (2011),

> In a hermeneutic approach the researcher recognizes that truth lies hidden, revealing itself as appearances, or things that announce insights. Further, our interpretation of what seems to be might not be how it is at all (Heidegger, 1962/1995). The gaze is directed "towards the regions where meaning originates, wells up, percolates through the porous membranes of past sedimentations –and then infused us, permeates us, infects us, touches us, stirs us, exercises a formative effect" (van Manen, 2007, p. 11). There is no one "saying" that can capture all that is understood. Words themselves limit and distort complex meaning (Gadamer, 1982). The way to understanding is through a kind of thinking Heidegger describes as "meditative."
> p. 16

As afro-pessimist researchers and practitioners, it is imperative that we learn not to reduce the other but rather imagine them, because by doing so you disappear in them as they appear in your psyche in ways that help trouble the truth you have been told about them. The other is an ethical demand to come to terms with social and political massacres researchers continue to mete in/on Africa. The African eye is a necessary ethical requirement for researchers to critically reflect on their participation in the continuous perfection of Africa (read this is killing the child in Africa), which has led to an atrocious social death of African bodies both in Africa and beyond. To look through and in the African eye helps introspect the self in ways that open historical colonial injustices on Africa/n space and bodies and how those atrocities continue unimpeded and unmitigated. Research and researchers should mitigate such atrocities in ways that are contextual and African centered. An African-centered mitigation should not be inward and lagging in simple and singular identity politics but also open to the African matrix in terms of gender, race, sexualities, and other markers of oppression. In a way, when talking of failure and imperfection, a researcher is reminded to deny the cure technologies that instrumentalize Africa to perfect its image to the world. Such forms of instrumentalization have both social and psychic effects in terms of how we look at and imagine Africa, one being that the continent requires alms from the West to appear in the world.

In a nutshell, to become afro-pessimist researchers and practitioners, we need to grieve the loss of Africa in the current geopolitical environment that tries to perfect the continent and simultaneously inter it. As research/practitioners, our work is not to save Africa but rather to listen to the multiple voices and speeches emanating from its peoples and the philosophies that continue to shape the lives of so many Africans both on and beyond the continent. This means that many researchers will have to face a philosophical death, in that they must disappear (read become vulnerable) from their expertise and learn to actively listen more. The researcher who dies philosophically will have to become the graveyard through which Africa can be buried and resurrected to speak in a diversity of tongues and accents.

4   Concluding Remarks

This chapter argues that Africans and Africa collectively are an accented space meant to be fixed and grounded in its pastness through a process of return and deportation. Such a form of social elimination can only be read through the everyday experiences of Africans in diaspora. For Africa to break away from social, economic, and political internment, it needs to work together with Africans in diaspora beyond everyday monetary remittances. This chapter also called for a break from the social prison of an Africa that accommodates the world rather than being in ways that are African centered. This calls for an orientation that sees Africa beyond Africa, which means breaking African national borders to allow meaningful social, political, and economic international/glocal connections. While there have been post-independence international coalitions calls, it seems to me that they have collapsed because their methodologies remain colonial and tied to national prisons.

An afro-pessimist call for international breakaway is based on African identity politics, in that Africa will need to engage with the difficult piece of diversities of identities within it in terms of cultural values. This mean embracing cultural difference as an important cornerstone of African people. This will mean working internationally beyond a singularized Africa (Africa as Black) and embracing racial configuration—reimagining Africa as a rainbow space with cacophonies of colors that are necessary for a beautiful Africa. Researchers therefore will need to work with these colorful noises as a necessary method/ology for social justice. Rather than silencing such voices on the altar of quantification, it is necessary to embrace such noises that speak of the local contextual differences. Researchers will need to work with African emotions, some of which are connected to colonial and imperial oppression that is historical. Such emotional noises emanate from a place of colonial trauma and help the healing of African psychic life. They are an expression of grief following the historical collapsing of Africa into national silos that continue to impact Africa in terms of everyday experience in diaspora. An afro-pessimist research methodology works with such forms of grief to imagine Africa rather than understand it. Africa must break away from social objectification and start imagining itself as a fluid and an open space of social, economic, and political engagement. This international African perspective should not shy away from everyday lateral conflicts between them. These conflicts should help start off negotiations of bringing Africa and Africans together.

Afro-pessimist methodologies in practice and research call for a reimagination of how we look at Africa from a philosophical viewpoint. This will mean disorienting colonial thought and representation of Africa as merely consumers of knowledge rather than producers of the same. Such a colonial representation makes Africa a receiver of alms rather than the producer of knowledge, helping affirm the West as a self-sufficient and rational space. To that end, afro-pessimist methodologies help researchers and practitioners question the ways research practices continue to freeze, conserve, preserve, and noun Africa into epistemological, ontological, axiological, and methodological containers, silos, or prisons in the name of African nations meant to control its progress beyond such colonial mapping. Research is greatly implicated in such forms of social and political grounding, incarceration, interment, and deportation of Africa and African intra-nationally and internationally.

References

Bolt, J., & Gardner, L. (2020). How Africans shaped British colonial institutions: Evidence from local taxation. *The Journal of Economic History, 80*(4), 1189–1223. https://doi.org/10.1017/S0022050720000455.

Cappelen, C., & Sorens, J. (2018). Pre-colonial centralisation, traditional indirect rule, and state capacity in Africa. *Commonwealth and Comparative Politics, 56*(2), 195–215. https://doi.org/10.1080/14662043.2017.1404666.

Fanon, F. (1967). *Black Skin, White Masks* (C. M. Markmann, Trans.). Grove Press. (Original work published 1952.).

Fleck, K., Smythe, E. A., & Hitchen, J. M. (2011). Hermeneutics of self as a research approach. *International Journal of Qualitative Methods, 10*(1), 14–29. https://doi.org/10.1177%2F160940691101000102.

Foucault, M. (1980). *Power/Knowledge: Selected Interviews and Other Writings, 1972–1977* (C. Gordon, Trans.). Pantheon.

Foucault, Michel (1985). *The Uses of Pleasure*. London: Penguin.

Foucault, Michel (1986a). *The Care of the Self*. London: Penguin.

Foucault, Michel (1986b). *Dream and Existence: Michel Foucault and Ludwig Bingswanger*. Seattle: Review of Existential Psychology and Psychiatry.

Foucault, Michel (1997a). Technologies of the Self. In *Ethics: Essential Works*, vol. 1. P. Rabinow (ed.), 223–252. London: Penguin.

Lévinas, E. (1979). *Totality and Infinity: an Essay on Exteriority*. Dordrecht: M. Nijhoff Publishers.

Mbembe, A. (1992). Provisional notes on the postcolony. *Africa: Journal of the International African Institute, 62*(1), 3–37. https://doi.org/10.2307/1160062.

Mbembe, A. (2001). *On the Postcolony*. University of California Press.

Mbembe, A. (2017). *Critique of Black Reason* (L. Dubois, Trans.). Duke University Press.

McNamee, L. (2019). Indirect colonial rule and the salience of ethnicity. *World Development, 122*, 142–156. https://doi.org/10.1016/j.worlddev.2019.05.017.

Moffatt, K. (1999). Surveillance and Government of the Welfare Recipient. In A. Chambon, L. Epstein, & A. Irving (Eds.), *Reading Foucault for Social Work* (pp. 219–245). Columbia University Press.

Müller-Crepon, C. (2020). Continuity or change? (In)direct rule in British and French colonial Africa. *International Organization*, *74*(4), 707–741. https://doi.org/10.1017/S0020818320000211.

Parsons, T. (2011). Local responses to the ethnic geography of colonialism in the Gusii highlands of British-ruled Kenya. *Ethnohistory*, *58*(3), 491–523. https://doi.org/10.1215/00141801-1263866.

The Pragmatic Parent. (n.d.). *5 Grounding Techniques for Kids with Anxiety and Big Worries*. https://www.thepragmaticparent.com/grounding-techniques-for-anxiety-kids/.

Wehbi, S. (2017). The Use of Photography in Anti-oppressive Research. In H. Parada & S. Wehbi (Eds.), *Reimagining Anti-oppression Social Work Research* (pp. 39–46). Canadian Scholars' Press.

Wilderson, F. B., III. (2017). Blacks and the master/slave relation. In *Afro-pessimism: an Introduction* (pp. 15–30). https://rackedanddispatched.noblogs.org/files/2017/01/Afro-Pessimism2.pdf.

CHAPTER 7

Markets Logics in Research Process and the Denigration of Black Bodies

Dionisio Nyaga

> All of these forms of taking life or letting life die are not just concrete examples of how the metric of grievability works; they wield the power to determine and distribute the grievability and value of lives. These are the concrete operations of the metric itself, its technologies, its points of application. And in these instances, we see the convergence of the biopolitical logic of the historic-racial schema with the phantasmagoric inversions that occlude the social bond.
> BUTLER, 2020, p. 121

∴

I am writing this chapter around a time when the world is still engaged with the death of many Black men on North American street under police chokehold; where appeals by Black men to police officers to be let loose to breath has been dismissed and has become a common feature in those violent encounters. Butler (2020) agonizing on the racial phantasmagoria behind the death of Eric Gurner says that:

> a person, such as Eric Garner in the United States in 2014, is put into a police choke hold, and then audibly announces he cannot breathe and visibly can be seen to be unable to breathe, and it is registered by everyone at the scene that he will not survive the prolongation of that police choke hold, which then, after the announcement, strengthens to become a stranglehold, strangulation, murder. Does the police officer who strengthens the hold to the point of death imagine that the person about to die is actually about to attack, or that their own life is endangered? Or is it simply that this life is one that can be snuffed out because it is not considered a life, never was a life, does not fit the norm of life that belongs to the racial schema; hence, because it does not register as a grievable life, a life worth preserving?
> p. 117

With the death of George Floyd under the same "I cannot breathe" circumstances, this chapter looks at how the chokehold works to imprint a gendered form of colonial practice that marks Black bodies as life less, emotional, and dispensable while simultaneously confirming the white police officer (also read researcher) the quintessential public body/savior. Such ways of thinking and imaginings has become normalized in research where Black death is a necessary evil for the exultation of the white research subject.

The levels of police profiling of Black youth is yet another form of earmarking Black bodies for public punishment, display and consumption. I argue that such acts of social elimination and death are an ongoing historical act of registration and management of Black life that marks such bodies as social public excesses that needed to be dispensed to purify and clean the city. Research has participated in such forms of social elimination of Black bodies justifying such practices and policies as necessary for the existence of a peaceful and neat city. To un-map such practices, knowledge producers need understand that what we attest in north American street in terms of Black death has been an ongoing psychic practice made physical by the everyday practice of Black extinction.

Research as a process of producing knowledge is colonial and is implicated in the historical violence meted on Indigenous communities (Dei, 2013; Reye Cruz, 2008; Smith, 2021). According to Smith, (2021), the term research is associated with negative histories of violence among Indigenous communities. Dei (2013) makes a clear connection between colonialism and research and the effect that has among racialized and people of African descent. Such forms of colonial violence suctioned by and through research is made possible through the imperial neoliberal corporate logics (Nyaga, 2021; Torres & Nyaga, 2021) that reduces, simplifies, quantifies, and enumerates Black and Indigenous communities into products (read objects) for sale in the marketplace. Such a process of reductionism, rationalism and simplification is arguably a form of social death, in that it works towards removing emotions, relationships and histories from Black and Indigenous bodies in the name of making them human and saving them from nature (read this as state of nature and war). Consequently, research becomes the very process of improving and inviting the nature (read this as Black and Indigenous bodies) into the world of human civilization. Such forms of improvement of nature becomes the very process through which Black bodies are disappeared and dispossessed of their voices. Subsequently, the process of producing knowledge become the very process of burying the Black social excess or superfluous population under the guise of civilization. Such forms of epistemological processing of Black bodies that is grounded on colonial violence and Black social expendability, simplification, quantification, and rationalization of Black bodies and that serve and increasing appetite for corporate residual value is unethical at best. To that end, research continue to work in ways that reaffirm the excessive dumping and concealing of Black lives (read this as emotion/nature) in ways that authorizes, confirms, normalizes neoliberal markets logics (Nyaga, 2021). In a nutshell, research more of a process of mining nature (read this as Black) for the purpose of profit making.

Such a line of thinking about neoliberal research markets and Black lives helps imagine the ways in which Black bodies are regularly regulated and returned (read this in line with rationalization of emotions (Black) as a form of deportation, incarcerated or social death) while being reminded of their non-being through the acts and practices of registration and management of Black bodies as superfluous social excesses that needs to be rationalized for them to have a life (read as white life). What that means is that the processes of registration and management (read this as analysis as a research process) works in ways that understands (reduces through analysis) Black bodies as lifeless beings that needs to be saved from their emotions and state of nature through a process of colonial civilization. The very process of civilization or exiting Black life from nature; through the registration and management of Black lives becomes the very process of squeezing out Black breath through chokehold which is manifested by calls from Black bodies to be allowed to breath. The death of George Floyd and many other Black bodies in the hands of policemen is a reminder of the ways in which research informs policy and how the same justified the killing of Black bodies through stranglehold. The process of registration and management of Black data is simultaneously the very process through which researchers participate in putting their knee on the necks of Black bodies and squeezing life out of them. As such, research as a process of management of Black miasma (data) continue to commit genocidal practices that I argue are unethical and that there is a dire need to do research with Black communities differently.

1   Research Process and Social Elimination of Blackness

Management, codification, and registration of Black lives into objects or codes point to one among the many ways that research squeezes out Black breath (life) while seemingly looking like a charitable act of giving life to Black bodies. To give Black a life (white life) assumes that Black life is not life enough but rather a form of existence that is outside human life. That means that Black is not human and has no life and that to do research on Black bodies is in and of itself a form of social generosity or messianic savior ship to an already non-existing non-being. It is in the liminality and partialism of 'give and take away' life to Black other, that Black bodies are spatially collapsed, incinerated and disappeared while confirming western research/er as the savior. The partialism in in neoliberal registration, codification, and management of Black life in data management becomes the chokehold that evaporates Black lives in simple, continuous, unverifiable, and consistent ways, and therefore making knowledge production an act of social elimination of Black degenerate others in ways that are unaccountable and inhumane. The registration and management of Black data is a common research feature and works in ways that collapses Black stories into numbers that can then be conserved and preserved for public consumption.

I argue that such neoliberal market practices and logic of registration and managements of Black data/narratives are forms of Black colonial chokehold that precede what we come to witness later in the form of Black incarceration, deportation, and profiling in education, policing, and welfare systems. This chapter, therefore, calls for an engagement with the psychic forms of registration and management of Black lives/data for us to understand the colonial and police chokeholds on Black bodies in Northern American cities.

This chapter, therefore, seeks to make public the concealed colonial tactics and mechanism that work together in complex ways to mark Black lives as expendable, dispensable and life lifeless. I look at the psyche of research practice and process to start to agonize and imagine other research process and practices that are hidden from public view and conversations and how such epistemological concealment disappears, chock and bury Black bodies. In a nutshell, this chapter is a psychic examination of research methods and methodologies to jumpstart a discussion on how we can work to revolutionize research in ethical and non-violent ways. My wager is that prior to witnessing this public spectacle in the form of Black chokehold, a lot has been happening behind the curtain and works in ways that prepare and organizes the ultimate visible chokehold; and that for us to understand the spectacle, we need to unmask and unregister the research (read psychic).

I argue that the birth registration of Black body is simultaneously its ultimate management of its death. Since research process is quintessentially a form of registration and management of species, it goes without saying that research is implicated in the social death of Black bodies.

To make real this claim, I look at interview schedules as one of the examples of registration and management of Black bodies in ways that incarcerate and imprison them into tick-boxes, subsequently rendering them objectionable, unimaginable, and disposable. The art of squeezing Black data into tick boxes takes out its emotions (read as breath) therefore committing epistemological genocide. This means that data collection becomes the very process of eradicating Black histories and existence in ways that are violent. The process of data collection subsumes Black death as a necessary epistemological require therefore forgoing the ethical demand to sustain Black lives. That means that Black and Blackness is timeless and has no history to tell, rather it must be told and written by the researcher on its (read this as state of thinging Blackness) behalf.

This chapter looks at research as representational process of the timeless and spaceless Black to start asking how knowledge production simultaneously become production of Black death.

The processing neoliberal colonial logics of the white registration and management of Black other works simultaneously as an elimination of Blackness (Black actions and emotion) in ways that squeeze life out of Black bodies. I seek to argue that the process is rife with violence and death of the human. Such violence starts from the field when we as researchers decide which questions will be asked and which form of conversation will not be allowed in the interview. That is an epistemological violence that is organized in the kind of interview questions and sampling processes we undertake when preparing to do research. This chapter recognizes that interviews are a process of standardizing the kind of conversation that will be allowed in production of knowledge. The very process of standardization (read classification and the practice of prison complex) is a reminder of the ways in which information is organized into smaller prison cubicles called questions. This form of organization is in and of itself militaristic in terms of determining what is to be considered the answer and what is to be deported and casted out.

In a nutshell, the very process of data collection becomes the process of deporting the deplorable other. I argue that we are stories and without stories we cease to exist. Our existence as Black bodies that are gendered, raced, and classed cannot be standardized. The process of standardization in research expressed in interviewing is the very process of stealing our Blackness by rationalizing our existence. That process of funneling our stories through the interview schedules fixes, imprison, nouns, and stratifies Blackness into Black cells and their emotional assumed as unnecessary in knowledge production. This helps explain why Black is considered violent and angry and is expected to act human by taming its anger; a process that explains the levels of mental health challenges facing Black communities as they try to look less violent in white spaces.

It is equally imperative to also engage with how the process of sampling as equally an expression of anti-Blackness. As argued before, the process of determining who is going to be interviewed is the same process of determining who can be trusted to give an authentic story of Black and Blackness. This determination of Black representation is rife with what Pon, (2009) calls ontology of forgetting; in that while participant in a study may be Black, there is no one standard story line that can be taken as true stories for all Black bodies. Such a reductionist and simplistic research practice is white and is implicated in anti-Blackness. While we may be Black, the act of Black representation is political and must be critically and ethically imagined when doing sampling to determine who is going to participate and who is left out of this representational politics. Black and Blackness is complex and brings with it multiple histories which cannot be reduced into one Black participant and assumed as representation all Blacks. Such a form of sampling makes the Black representative place enormous labor on the Black participant, returning us to the plantation story. That form of return is in and of itself a form of deportation to that past which I argue is a form of shaming and punishment. I also argue that to identify one Black body as the only trusted participant renders other Black stories out of shape and that they can shape up through this appointed Black. In the process, the researcher creates a standard of measure in the Black other to which all others Black stories must exist. In the process of doing that, the Black representative must act and perform Black in ways that are comfortable to the white researcher, thereby rendering your research white and out of touch with Black lives. The same process of identification could also be a process of pathologizing other Black stories and lives as not Black enough therefore requiring salvation from their darkness. This and many other limitations of sampling speak of how, in rights to Black representation, the very process of Black disappearance and sanctioned violence against Black lives can also exist.

A third research process that would explain this art of white neoliberal registration and management of Black life in research is the ways in which we analyze Black stories through quantitative tools such as "Statistical Package for the Social Sciences" or "SPSS" in ways that are assumed to clean, sanitize or civilize the Black data (read this as Black miasma) in ways meant to forget Black ontologies and as such this chapter marks such forms of processing as colonial and anti-Black. It is these quantitative models of processing that simultaneously disappear, nullifies and forget Black lives in ways that are violent and colonial. The expulsion of Black emotions(miasma) in the processing of data is a process of an epistemological strangulation of Black values, histories and realities meant to confirm and glorify science as the only way to civilization. It is now clear that western science is simultaneously an epistemic process of denigrating those others that are deemed lesser beings and whose life if lost would not be considered valuable.

2   Black Methodological Conception

In a nutshell, my claims are that research should be organized in ways that help account for those others who have been discounted as voiceless. I argue that such forms of Black epistemological death is unethical and requires that research engage more with Black data in ways that are steeped in Black realities, histories and values. It should be noted that while we can use such rational western models in knowledge production, we equally need to make them Black in ways that are beyond color coating progressive research methodologies and instead be made to speak in diverse Black accents that are complex and interlocked. To argue for beyond color coating politics of knowledge production is to affirm the need for culturally informed research that looks at Black beyond Black. This will mean that researchers will need to look at Black and Blackness as an intersected and interlocked realities that works beyond what we imagine as physical color. This means that Black should be seen as rainbow, in that to read Black and Blackness is to accept the fact that Black is established by many colors that are nameable and others that have no names and yet they exist and live a life that is Black. This philosophical underpinning of research with Blackness means that researchers will need to celebrate and embrace the art of getting lost in jungle of rainbow colors. It also means that while some forms of Black and Blackness are legible and imaginable, others will remain hidden and yet existing and tell their stories. This means that any researcher who engages with Black communities will have to lose themselves (read this as epistemological humility) to start imagining rather than understanding (read this as reductionism and simplification of western science) Black life. Research among and with Black communities should be a process of loss of self and grieving Black death in research. To think of research as a process of Black grief is to start to imagine how research can account for the loss of Black bodies in policy and on the city streets in North America and elsewhere in the world.

The psychic analysis in research offers a broader picture of imagining Black life beyond what we see and start engaging with that which we cannot see. Through such a psychic analysis, we can relate and connect one anti-Black racism to another in ways that help account those atrocities. The act of relating and connecting one struggle to another helps in accounting, remembering, and grieving those Black bodies that have been lost and whose loss is never considered a loss (Butler, 2006; 2020). As researchers working with Black communities, we need to agonize, account for the loss, grief, and remember Black life in ways that are psychic and therefore ethical. Black life is a culmination of multiple forms of chokeholds performed and made real through research and practice and for which this chapter seeks to open such death registers (Black scars and traumas) and to start imagining the ways in which Black life matter in knowledge production. I argue that to opens Black psychic registers calls for an engagement with Black histories (note the plural), values, and ethical conversations about Black lives.

3   Welcome to the Jungle of Black Messiness

While there are historical records and documentation of how slaves were sold and exchanged in the markets (McKittrick, 2020: Johnson 1999), it is important as researcher that we do not reduce or quantify such Black experiences into a single neat story. Black is never a neat ontology but rather occupies a reality that is messy, and which invites researchers to work with the jungle that is Black in ways that never arrive or seeks to understand Black and Blackness.

I argue that for interviewing to be Black and transformative in terms then it will have to open the gates to a discussion of Black anger in ways that are context oriented rather than standardized test expressed as interview schedules. Interviews or the process of data collection will have to cease to be white and engage with diversities of Black stories without necessarily conscripting or imprisoning Black stories. This process of Black interviewing will have to engage with multiple diverse Black stories as knowledge grounded in their ontological backgrounds that have multiple histories. To deny the existence of this multiplicities of Black ontologies is in and itself a form of Anti-Blackness in data collection and a form of Black imprisonment, deportation, and incarceration Black stories.

With these critically reflexive perspectives of engaging with sampling and interviewing one is left to ask and agonize with the how infusing Black rights and lives in research. Such a process of knowledge production steeped in Blackness should consider Black lives as complex and complicated and that it cannot be reduced or simplified into interview questions. This will mean the interview questions and its colonial method/ology will have to disappear for them to come to terms with the histories of atrocities meted on Black bodies by researchers. To disappear means that research will have to exist outside it white and whiteness and embrace Black philosophies in terms of ontologies, epistemologies, methodologies, and axiology. These forms of philosophies will have to breathe life to an already disappeared white research in ways that looks and engage with Black stories within their context and complex histories. This means that those Black stories given by participants will have to be considered as knowledge practiced diversely. According to Bannerji (2000):

> For an individual, her knowledge, in the immediate sense (which we call 'experience'), is local and partial. But none the less it is neither false nor fantastic if recognized as such. It is more than the raw data of physical reflexes and feelings. It is the originating point of knowledge, the door to our social subjectivity.
>
> p. 12

The process of sampling will also have to engage with the complex and multiplied realities of Black life in ways that does not append a form of manufactured rights to one Black life and assume that it is a representation of other Black lives. This means that Black representation method/ologies steeped in Black lives will have to be considered on research process. This will mean disappearing sampling methods in ways that allow multiple representations to breathe life in research. Such a form of identification should not be narrowing of Black life but rather widening Black and Blackness in ways that allow Black to speak in its multiplicities. This representation should also prepare the researcher to identify ways in which they can engage with Black participants without necessarily leaving Black load on Black shoulders. White researchers should take a step to form an alliance with Black community not just for research's sake but for transforming society in ways that are Black. Such an alliance should be transformational both to the researcher and participant in terms of their physical and psyche lives. In a nutshell, sampling should be an engagement with Black psychic lives in ways that open avenue of appreciating the multiplicities of Black lives. All this aspect to Black lives should be considered when doing sampling.

4   Conclusion

> The silence, or rather the prudence, with which the unitary theories avoid the genealogy of knowledges might therefore be a good reason to continue to pursue it.
>
> FOUCAULT, 1980, p. 87

Research as a process of producing knowledge needs to work in ways that account and grieve Black trauma without necessary measuring such grief (read this as inconsolable mourning). The ways of accounting such historical traumas should be Blackened without reducing them in Black. In short, research and the ethics that guide the process of producing knowledge needs to verb Black and Blackness without necessarily nouning the process of Black grief. For a while, research has masqueraded as culturally competent or sensitive practice and therefore ethical but on the centrally it continues to manifest its racist practices in Black communities. These forms of research and ethical performances fail to engage with histories of atrocities meted on Black communities and instead collapses Black bodies into tools that are assumed as culturally important therefore reproducing Black trauma. Research that assumes as ethical becomes the very practice of constituting and retooling black bodies for sale in the marketplace. This chapter, therefore, calls for critically reflexive research exercises that looks at Black bodies as not just cultural tools and instruments but rather as beings that have spirits.

This chapter engages with these colonial atrocities to argue that for research to be just, humane, and geared towards transformative change, it needs to break from its knowledge fixation and embrace Black ethics as a necessary demand in research process. This will mean that knowledge production will have to break from its institutional industrial and corporate wall and embrace communities' values, histories, and context as a way of decolonizing what we know and how we come to know what we know. This means that research will need to engage with it historical violence against Black communities in ways that are outside corporate profit maxim. To do that, research need to disappear and be buried in graveyards to come face to face with its implication in term of the continued death of Black bodies. To claim that research needs to disappear is to argue for a critically reflexive research process that looks at knowledge from a place that is ethical and humane.

Such a critically reflexive research process calls for reformulation of the philosophical assumptions that guide research such that those truths that continue to be buried and marked as irrational acquire an ontological and epistemological space to speak their truths in ways that are contextual and historically oriented. Such an ethical process of knowledge insurrection is a necessary demand for decolonizing research since it does not only dig deep (read archeology and truth making) but engage and displace that which has been dug in ways that are transformational and transgressive (genealogy) (Foucault, 1980). To do this, research will need to be political. This will mean that knowledge production will need to engage with ethical demands that pay attention to histories, context, and values of communities that we study. The fact that we study communities comes with its own ethical dilemma, in that we can never understand communities (read reduce or quantify) but rather imagine who they are.

It is important that we resurrect such Black histories and ways of life in ways that speak of the present economic environments that continue to corporatize and rationalize Black stories for sale to the highest bidder. Mercer (1994) says:

> Far from summoning history as though it were a given body of knowledge passively waiting to be depicted or narrated, it is the opacity of the ongoing relation between past and present that...
>
> p.42

researchers need to throw themselves into. To do this, we recall and remember diversities of Black stories without pasting (read this as process of deportation and incarceration of Black and Blackness) them. We need to ask methodological questions about such resurrections so that we steep them with Black realities and values informed by histories of colonial oppressions on Black lives. Such resurrections must be messy (read this as critical reflexivity), complex, and outside colonial spatial time. This is a necessary philosophical demand; for it fails to fall prey to the singularization of Black and Blackness and instead works toward verbing (Walcott, 2003) and deinstitutionalizing Black histories.

References

Butler, J. (2006). *Precarious Life: the Powers of Mourning and Violence*. Verso.

Butler, J. (2020). *The Force of Nonviolence: an Ethico-political Bind*. Verso.

Dei, G. S. (2013). Critical perspectives on indigenous research. *Socialist Studies* (St. Albert), 9(1). https://doi.org/10.18740/S47G64.

Foucault, M. (1980). *Power/Knowledge: Selected Interviews and Other Writings, 1972–1977*. New York, NY: Pantheon.

Johnson, W. (1999). *Soul by Soul: Life inside the Antebellum Slave Market*. Cambridge: Harvard University Press.

McKittrick, K. (2020). "Demonic grounds: Sylvia Wynter," excerpt from demonic grounds (2006). *Journal of Transnational American Studies*, 11(2). https://doi.org/10.5070/T8112051014.

Mercer, K. (1994). *Welcome to the Jungle: New Positions in Black Cultural Studies*. Routledge.

Nyaga, D. (2021). Critical Research Methodologies. In *Critical Research Methodologies*. Leiden, The Netherlands: Brill. https://doi.org.ezproxy.lib.ryerson.ca/10.1163/9789004445567_003.

Pon, G. (2009). Cultural competency as new racism: an ontology of forgetting. *Journal of Progressive Human Services*, 20(1), 59–71.

Reyes Cruz, M. (2008). What if I just cite Grasiela: Working toward decolonizing knowledge through a critical ethnography. *Qualitative Inquiry*, 14(4), 651–658.

Smith, L. T. (2021). *Decolonizing Methodologies: Research and Indigenous Peoples* (Third ed.). Zed Books.

Torres, R., & Nyaga, D. (2021). Research as an Inconsolable Mourning. In *Critical Research Methodologies*. Leiden, The Netherlands: Brill. https://doi.org.ezproxy.lib.ryerson.ca/10.1163/9789004445567_009.

Walcott, R. (2003). *Black Like Who? Writing Black Canada*. Toronto, ON: Insomniac Press.

PART 3

Critical Reflexive Research Methods

CHAPTER 8

Teaching to the Tensions
Pushing the Boundaries of Qualitative Social Work Research

Susan Preston, Susan Silver and Purnima George

As three faculty members in a social work program in Canada, we have engaged with research in many ways. In this chapter, we discuss the ways in which we have engaged in the pedagogy of research, reflecting on our experiences of teaching qualitative research with undergraduate social work students. In particular, we take pause to consider how qualitative research, long heralded as an emancipatory form of knowledge production, has nonetheless continued to perpetuate the inequities, power differences, and marginalization oft attributed specifically to quantitative research. We each bring our own histories and current work into this chapter, recalling our unique experiences, and seeking what is common for reimagining the pedagogy and substance of teaching qualitative research.

While social work began to more fully embrace research in the latter part of the 20th century (Reid, 2001), it has been our observation, shared by others, that "many social workers still do not recognise the potential of research, nor its value for them as practitioners" (Alston & Bowles, 2019, ii). The shift towards evidence-based practice may have infused a strong interest in research in social work, but this engagement continues to be flawed in consistent and appropriate application (Proctor & Rosen, 2008). Evidence-based practice also has been soundly critiqued in social work scholarship for decades, including arguments that, among other concerns, it negates the relationship focus of practice, ignores context, and reproduces whiteness (Nevo & Slomin-Nevo, 2011; Shaw, 2005; Webb, 2001; Yee, 2017). The resistance to research by many social workers, combined with the eschewing of evidence-based practice, is often founded on the argument that conventional research and evidence-based practice are both predicated on positivist categorizations and predictions, that problematically deny the uniqueness of human experiences. Yet this critique need not negate the value of research for and by social workers.

Qualitative research has held promise for social work, grounded in the everyday lives of people, focused on the rich details of experiences, specific to individual and community contexts. Counter to the critique that quantitative research both objectifies and essentializes human experience, often without attention to systemic impacts on individual lives, qualitative research is posited as a more caring, subjective approach to understanding human experience, attentive to the impact of societal structures. In this way, qualitative research is often trumpeted as a socially just approach to knowledge production, as a transformative and liberatory research practice (Johnson & Parry, 2016; Lyons et al., 2013). Aligned with a phronetical view of our world that acknowledges and interrupts power (Petersen & Olson, 2015), qualitative research is championed as a panacea for research that both exposes and resists marginalization and oppression.

It is from this position that we initially developed the qualitative research course we teach in our Bachelor of Social Work (BSW) program. We focused on the value of qualitative research, noting its importance alongside, not subordinate to, quantitative research. We stressed the value-laden approach that acknowledged distinctive experiences over what is common, and attended to the many models that assess the rigor of qualitative inquiry (Lincoln & Guba, 1985; Padgett, 2016; Sandelowski, 1993). We talked about the importance of relationship in the research process, and heralded narratives as rich reflections of human experiences.

Over time, we began to realize that our course was problematic. It was not sufficiently attentive to engaging in critical reflexive research, dehegominzing knowledge production, and centring the voices from communities over the voice of researchers. As qualitative inquiry in social work evolved, our course too had to evolve. At the same time, we recognized that some of our course content contradicted our school's anti-oppression focused curriculum, insufficiently attentive to power in both research relationships and processes. We knew our course needed to change, that we had to interrupt the epistemic imperialism inherent in conventional qualitative research, and reimagine qualitative research, and the teaching of it, in new ways.

Scholarship about teaching research is vast, but the tome specific to social work, and precisely to qualitative research is limited. There is an acknowledgement that social work students often are resistant to research courses, alongside being anxious about the content and their success in the course (Adam et al., 2004; Maschi et al., 2013). It also has been recognized that pedagogical practices need to align with the epistemological foundation of qualitative research, thus resisting the banking model of teaching, and instead embracing a reflexive and visceral engagement with the material (Lincoln, 1998; Stark & Watson, 1999). O'Connor and O'Neill (2004) challenge us that although the goals of qualitative research might foster anti-oppressive practice, realizing its potential requires more than just developing a knowledge base; it also requires integrating a different way of 'being' as a researcher and social worker.

"The classroom experience, and the experience of learning about qualitative research, becomes a model for integrating this understanding" (O'Connor & O'Neill, 2004, p. 23) and alongside our own reflections, these challenges have guided our course evolutions.

1 Re-teaching Qualitative Research: Our Stories

What follows are narrative accounts of our own experiences, as social work research educators, in our journey to revisioning our school's undergraduate qualitative research course. We each share stories about critical moments, in our own research practice and/or in our teaching practice, that caused pause in our work, and resulted in significant changes in the course over time. We intentionally share our stories individually, to situate our own experiences, before drawing together the commonness of our reflections.

Susan S. takes up issues of representation and researcher power in her narrative. She discusses ways to disrupt conventional qualitative knowledge producers and methods of knowledge production. Susan P. addresses power and representation by examining the interconnection between research and activism, as well as resisting white/colonial knowledge production, drawn from both her research experiences and teaching practices. Purnima presents the connection between community practice/activism and issues of relationality, reciprocity, and dehegemonization in research. She shares a story of community-based participatory research, noting how she uses this, and other stories, in her teaching. We conclude the chapter with 'lessons learned', which we hope will provide mindful support to graduate students and early-career faculty members as they engage with qualitative research practices.

2 Susan S.: Searching for Stories that Transform Knowledge

2.1 *My Goals and Approach when Teaching Research*
I have been teaching social work research courses at the graduate and undergraduate levels for over 25 years. Some may think that the substantive nature of research doesn't change over time, as evidenced by textbooks that have remained very similar through their various editions. However, I have come to understand research as dynamic, and as a historically, culturally, and politically situated form of inquiry (Strega, 2005). Our teaching team takes the position that research is not an objective, apolitical and ahistorical process of discovery, but instead accords epistemic privilege (Kovach, 2005) on certain methods

and universal truths. I thus focus my teaching on building an understanding of research as situated, exposing and disrupting the hegemony of truth and method. I unveil the obscure ways that power relations are structured and embedded in the research process, and how conventional research produces knowledge in service to white supremacy, colonialism, and racism (Baskin, 2005; Mohanty, 2002; Smith, 2012). Thus, whether students will be reviewing research studies, participating in research studies, or conducting research studies, it is critically important that they understand how dominance is reified in the research process. Recognizing that conventional Western research is fundamentally a political act of domination, is a first step in reclaiming research as a tool for social change and social justice.

When teaching research, we distinguish between quantitative and qualitative research methods. We discuss that quantitative research methods are informed by a positivist paradigm and are primarily used for prediction and control of the natural world and individual behaviour (Neuman, 2013). Their search for the discovery of universal truths, in a "scientific" manner that is claimed to be neutral and unbiased. While these claims have long been refuted, the "scientific method" continues to be the standard against which other types of research are judged.

Qualitative methods, particularly those informed by an interpretive paradigm, while more narrative and meaning-seeking, may appear less oppressive on the surface, and thus appeal to those committed to unsettling dominance in the research process. However, without critical attention to the power structure framing and operating in the qualitative research process, and the ways in which the interpretive paradigm is mapped onto positivism, we will undoubtedly reproduce dominant understandings, not unsimilar to those of quantitative studies.

As a means of challenging the embedded and ubiquitous power of positivism, the research course has evolved over time to reflect and integrate epistemologies and methodologies that resist this dominance and offer ways of decolonizing knowledge production (Silver, 2017), honoring the voices and communities that have been ignored, erased, and misrepresented. Engaging with issues of representation, subjectivity and positionality have led us to disrupt dominant understandings of what counts as legitimate knowledge and who are credible knowledge producers. In this manner, research becomes an act of resistance (Brown & Strega, 2005) that can lead to transformative and liberatory possibilities. My experience is that as our course has become more critical and radical, student interest and engagement has increased. Students begin to discover and appreciate the parallels between "practise" and "research" and recognise that research is indeed a vital form of critical social work practice.

However, we recognize that it would be a disservice to our students if we did not teach conventional quantitative and qualitative methods, as these are still most supported by funders and journals. Consequently, as we teach traditional research methodologies, we also explore the ways in which these can be implemented in less oppressive ways. For example, when exploring phenomenology and lived experience, I bring in narrative-based interviewing principles (Chase, 2003), recognizing the power of the story. By asking questions that invite participants to tell their stories from their own positionality, "we learn how people as individuals and as groups make sense of their experiences and construct meanings and selves" (Chase, 2003, p. 80). Consequently, learning how to ask questions and how to listen become powerful ways of gaining a deeper and more complex understanding, and thus limiting, not eliminating, the degree of researcher interpretation and representation.

2.2 Critical Teaching Moments – Representation and Social Media

Considerations of the researcher as the expert, and thus imbued with the power and authority to interpret and represent the "other", are central and paramount to the course. Through acts of interpretation and representation within the research process, we make visible the "other" and their world. Thus, social change requires us to change the ways in which we make reality visible (Flaherty, 2002). Quijano (2000) alerts us to the considerable consequences of misrepresentations and "partial and distorted" understandings (p. 556). When the researcher is positioned as the "expert" and as the standpoint that makes the "other" visible, research not only perpetuates dominance, but is itself an act of domination. Thus, our challenge in the research course is teaching how we can disrupt acts of domination that create and control what we know and how we know it.

As I struggle with this challenge, I am increasingly drawn to social media platforms, such as YouTube and Instagram, that provide a space for self-publishing first-person digital narratives. As a space for knowledge creation, these platforms provide spaces for sharing voices, experiences and perspectives that are most valued, yet often unheard, muted, or discounted.

These emergent social media technologies thus make possible the decentralized production of knowledge, with the capacity to disrupt conventional knowledge producers and knowledge production. When working with MSW students on their major research papers, or with students in the undergraduate qualitative research course, I position social media and other cultural texts as credible sources of data for their qualitative research projects. Many of my

MSW students have indeed used forms of social media, such as YouTube videos and blogs, as data in their major research papers.

2.3   Narratives in the Public Domain

YouTube is a public platform and as such, videos that do not require any sign-in or membership to view are considered in the public domain and with no expectation of the privacy of their content. However, I remind my students that while institutional ethics approval is not necessary, nor is consent required, as critical researchers we are not exempt from the many ethical issues that arise from accessing publicly available data. We discuss the tensions of working with public narratives and the need to consistently reflect on the power dynamics at play. For example, how does the researcher engage with issues of representation when there is no opportunity for a participant check-in or validation. Further, how does one use YouTube videos that were included in the analysis and then subsequently taken down by the uploader during the course of the research. Situations of this nature blur the private-public dichotomy and raise additional ethical dilemmas including informed consent and minimizing harm (Legewie & Nassauer, 2018; Patterson, 2018).

I have often used first-person digital "patient" narratives as examples of how these can be used to unsettle dominance and foreground the voices of those that are deemed not credible knowledge producers (Devan, 2021). Our common understandings of various illnesses and diseases are fundamentally medical representations that essentialize and categorise states, degrees, and experiences of illness. In attempts at studying the social implications of diseases, researchers have tended to use surveys and standardized tests to evaluate quality of life, diets, medications and other treatments (Ashton & Beattie, 2019; Aumayer, 2015; Hindryckx et al., 2018; Lönnfors, 2014). Thus, the patient experience continues to be framed and mediated through a medical lens. While not to minimize the importance of medical knowledge, what is generally missing and made invisible are the day-to-day realities of the illness that include the complexities and unique challenges that defy medical classification (Defenbaugh, 2008). Using social media to self-publish, "patients" can determine which aspects of their experiences they wish to share and bring new awareness to the lived experiences of a chronic illness.

Along with the possibilities gained by using social media, we must also be critical of these technologies, and their connection and embeddedness within dominant social and political discourses (Kellner & Kim, 2010). In class, we discuss how hegemonic knowledge is reflected and reproduced in cultural and social texts. We take up these tensions recognizing that while these new technologies provide opportunities for new understandings to emerge, they are also mapped onto or are in conversation with the dominant discourse. The research classroom thus becomes a place where we explore new ways of knowing and understanding, while also acquiring the necessary critical skills that prepare us to be vigilant of the lurking dominant narratives, whether medical, social, cultural, political, that mediate both what we produce and how our realities are constructed.

Consequently, our role as critical qualitative researchers and academics is to understand the layers of representation that operate in the research process, including the researcher's power and the power of the dominate narrative. Through making visible and peeling away these often taken for granted operations of dominance, the emergence of transformative stories and voices become possible.

3 Susan P: the Details Matter: Reconceptualizing Qualitative Research

3.1 *My Passion for Research*

I am a graduate of our university's BSW program, and I recall taking the undergraduate research course as a student. I was a mature student, and Susan S. was a young professor who taught that research course. Research was the course everyone dreaded, and I recall sitting in the back corner, hoping I would never be called upon to answer a question. Well, Susan S. clearly is an incredible teacher – because that is where my first interest in academic research began.

However, my passion for research generally arose many years prior, when I was working as a counsellor in a community-based criminal justice program for youth and young adults. It was a flexible, easy-going workplace, where creativity was welcomed. I started questioning what was and was not working in our services, and was provided the opportunity to do some surveys with clients and look over some of our records of client demographics. I started compiling some information about what I learned from the survey and from reviewing case files, and shared what I learned with the Executive Director. Some of that information was then used to tinker with a few of our programs. I did not realize it at the time, but I was conducting my first social services research study.

That first study was rudimentary and flawed, but I often reflect back on it and wonder if that was in fact the first stirring of an interest in research, which was then fueled by completing my BSW research course with Susan S.

These two stories are a way to lead into my passion for research and for teaching research. When I began teaching research in 2003, my focus was on making sure students got the technical information that formed the substance of the course. I was not deeply engaged as a reflexive researcher (Fook, 2011, 1996; Probst, 2015; Probst & Berenson, 2014) or instructor; I was more interested in helping students to understand the "how" of conducting research. Thinking back on those moments, I was early in my career as a university instructor, and I took comfort in the tangible concreteness of the content; I felt confident in teaching the "facts" of research design. However, over time, I encountered several critical moments that influenced my practice as a researcher and as a faculty member teaching research.

3.2   My 'Aha' Moments

As I became more confident with the technical content of the research course, I began to find my own voice in the course. It was challenging as a new faculty member, knowing that I was teaching the course that most students "loved to hate", that they were mostly reluctant and disinterested in the content (Dodd & Epstein, 2012; Epstein, 1987; Harder, 2010). I quickly learned that most students focused on "getting through the course", that their intention was to memorize and get a passing grade, not to learn and understand. This was my first 'aha' moment, when I embraced the idea that my main goal as a research instructor was to demystify research (Appleton et al., 2016; Udall, 2019). I began to change my approach to introducing course material, by making connections between the course content and everyday living. Some students began to participate more in class, and seemed to have more of an interest in the content.

My next 'aha' moment was thinking about making the link between research and practice. There has been a long-standing divide between social work practice and social work research, perhaps rooted in the relative newness of social work-specific research (Kirk & Reid, 2002). I made connections between research and practice (Osmond & O'Connor, 2006) in three ways, introducing the ideas of (a) using research to inform practice, (b) practitioners conducting research, and (c) research as a form of practice. Similar to making connections to everyday living, these practice-focused connections further engaged students.

Around the same time that I was making these changes in my approach to teaching research, our school developed an anti-oppression vision/mission, and slowly began several curriculum reviews. This was my third and most compelling 'aha' moment, which played out in two phases. In the first phase, our research teaching team brought a stronger critical lens to the quantitative research course, wherein we began critiquing positivism and the value-neutral objectivity nature of this approach to knowledge production. The second phase, more related to this book, occurred when our teaching team focused that critical lens (Kincheloe & McLaren, 2011) more fully on the qualitative research course.

Qualitative research often is positioned as the softer side of scientific inquiry, something that can augment the gold standard of quantitative research. In teaching qualitative research, I have observed students feeling more comfortable with the content than in quantitative research. Qualitative research can be championed as an approach that incorporates and appreciates the subjective, values, contextual differences and uniqueness, and more (Padgett, 2016; Shaw & Holland, 2014). It may be perceived by some as the more critical form of research, and has become more pronounced and respected within scholarly circles in the 21st century (Bansal & Corley, 2011).

This assumed criticality of qualitative research also aligns it with social justice (Denzin, 2009; Johnson & Parry, 2016). It is seen as more appropriate for culturally diverse communities (Lyons et al., 2013), focused on centring participant voices/experiences (Guishard et al., 2018), with particular methodologies being reconstructed along social justice lines (Charmaz, 2005; Humphries, 2008; Madison, 2011). However, as our school continued to deepen and expand its anti-oppression concentration, other 'aha' moments emerged for our team.

For me, two moments stand out in my own process of reflecting on research and teaching, and changing my practices: (a) exploring the connection between research and activism, and (b) reimagining ways of knowing/forms of knowledge production. Below I discuss both of these experiences.

Irwin (2020) has argued that social work, including social work education, is sliding away from activism and social justice action, instead sliding into managerialism within neoliberalism. Additionally, similar to the siloing of research and practice (Teater, 2017), we sometimes see a siloing of practice and activism (Mattocks, 2018), and rarely see a connection between research and activism. I wanted to bring these together, to connect the ways in which justice, equity, and anti-oppression are embedded in our curriculum, to be more present in the research course. Kende (2016) notes the importance of both conducting research about activism and using research as a form of/within activism, providing a platform to engage in these ideas in class.

It has been my experience, both in my own work and in my observations about students and social workers, that activism is often spurred by a passion about an issue; in turn, the activist actions often reflect that passion, through attending protests, posting on social media, and more. What I find helpful in the research course is to harness this passion, and encourage students to consider the connection between research and activism.

I begin by noting that research is a powerful tool that can produce data supporting the arguments being made in the activist actions. In other words, research about the social issue can then be used to make the advocacy and arguments stronger when engaging in social action about the issue. This idea is not new to human services (Wheelock, 1993), and though not prominent, it is slowly rising in the research scholarship, from general ideas (Efroymson, 2006), to those more specific and related to social work, such as perspectives from bioethics (Scully, 2019), medicine (Terry et al., 2007), mental health (Greenwood et al., 2013), and psychology (Alexander & Allo, 2021). At the same time, I share examples from my own practice history, where I have used research to gather knowledge in an effort to advance social justice, whether that be in organizations or with government policy and/or programs. It is at this point that students start to see the connection between their anti-oppression/social justice intentions and the value of research. This approach also then aligns with shifting trends in research that interrupt notions of the researcher as expert, and instead centre the voices of participants and communities in determining what matters to them (St. Denis, 2004), what research questions are asked and what answers are questioned (Wilson, 2008), and how research is conducted, and by whom, in line with community-based participatory research (Branom, 2012; Minkler & Wallerstein, 2008).

Alongside this discussion, I also talk about the efficacy of advocacy efforts. I encourage students to consider what advocacy approaches are most effective in what circumstances, regarding what social issues. Often students struggle to think about how they would know what efforts are effective, and I suggest that there is research about effective social actions that can be useful when designing an advocacy campaign. Research in this area is more pronounced than what is noted above, perhaps connected to the surge in civic engagement scholarship over the past several decades (Woodford & Preston, 2013). Research about activism includes scholarship related to activism generally (Atkinson, 2017), and more specifically, motivation to engage/take action (e.g., Kende et al., 2017), strategies to integrate activism into clinical practice (e.g., Lee et al., 2013), and effective social actions for change (e.g., Cullerton et al., 2018). At the same time, I talk about my own social action activities, and what I have found to be effective and ineffective, thus also giving voice to individual lived experiences. Again, students begin to realize that research can help them consider how to best design social action campaigns to be the most effective. This exploration has equally been useful in my own advocacy practices.

While reinforcing the links between activism and research has been useful in terms of engaging students and making connections to community-informed research, efforts to shift the way I teach through reimagining ways of knowing/forms of knowledge production has been, and continues to be, a deeper journey. In my early days as a faculty member and researcher, I drew on my conventional western training in research methods, focusing on the linearity of the research process, using peer-reviewed research studies to inform my work, and positioning myself as a neutral outsider when gathering data. Yet all of these practices felt inconsistent with my own social work practice histories and my own evolving knowledge within anti-oppression and social justice scholarship.

One example is connected to the use of literature reviews as part of a research process. I recall the expectations from my early research training, that required all literature review sources to be empirically-based and peer-reviewed, from academic journals, which continues as the gold standard today (Fink, 2019; Galvan & Galvan, 2017). However, this approach aligns neither with newer trends in qualitative research that centre lived experiences, nor with our school's anti-oppression framework that seeks to maximize the voices of marginalized communities. Over time, and informed initially by Reyes Cruz (2008), I began to question the privileging of conventional research for knowledge production, recognizing, among other things, the ways in which academic literature reproduces whiteness (Buggs et al., 2020). Without negating the value of conventional empirical inquiry, I began to seek out "non-academic" knowledge to inform my own research, and began bringing those ideas into the classroom.

This approach fell in line with many relevant aspects of social work. First, there is an ethical expectation that social workers will use research to inform their practice (CASW, 2005). However, many social workers do not have access to academic journals that exist mostly in university libraries. This conundrum was addressed early in the days of evidence-based practice ideas, with Berman's (1995) call for using "grey documentation" to compensate for minimal access to research literature, but was not developed much beyond that point. Additionally, this approach still held academic literature as primary. Drawing initially from the ideas of grey literature (Rothstein & Hopewell, 2009), I began to seek knowledge from government documents, organization reports, and media sources. However, over time I expanded my use of "non-academic" sources, to include blogs, videos, and social media postings. In these ways, I was seeking knowledge beyond the scope of conventional research, and thus exposing myself to a vaster and more varied canon of knowledge – all of which improved my capacity to develop and conduct meaningful and authentic research.

I brought these ideas into the classroom, arguing that drawing knowledge from sources beyond conventional research was a way to interrupt dominant privilege reproduction in academic literature, while also centring community voices and those whose lived experiences might not ever be reflected in academic sources. There was, and continues to be, a tension when navigating an evaluation of the credibility of these sources, but as with other trends in qualitative research, these tensions will be resolved over time.

At the same time, I positioned this approach as one way to dehegemonize (Gegeo & Watson Gegeo, 2001) white dominant knowledge. Most students embraced this approach, and welcomed the opportunity to expand their knowledge sources beyond academic literature while also resisting the reproduction and privileging of white dominant knowledge.

3.3 Reflections

Similar to what Susan S. noted, we take an approach of teaching conventional methods, while also critiquing them. For me, this involves introducing the general idea of each class' content, while at the same time noting its flaws and considering how it can be "done differently", founded on principles of social justice and anti-oppression. There is not a lot of literature that specifically addresses anti-oppression principles and research, so I often will refer students to early work by Strier (2007), followed by Rogers (2012), introducing the idea of bringing anti-oppression into research, and use my own co-authored work on integrating anti-oppression principles with phenomenology (Preston & Redgrift, 2017) as an example of how to dehegemonize conventional qualitative research methodologies, towards more socially just practices.

My examples here draw from many moments in my research teaching practice where I have intentionally stopped, reflected, challenged my "ways of doing/ways of knowing", and have then sought ways to shift my approach. While these examples are varied, what is common across them is thinking about ways to make research more meaningfully relevant to social work students, and to work with students to reimagine more socially-just ways to engage with research.

4 Purnima: Realigning Research for Disrupting Hegemony, Seeking Epistemic Justice, and Emancipation

4.1 My Passion for Teaching Research

My passion for teaching research comes from the experience of utilizing research within my community work when pavement dwellers (people living on sidewalks) were unlawfully evicted and deported by the State government (George, 2018). The findings of our research study were used by the Supreme Court of India to provide a ground-breaking judgement in favour of pavement dwellers that challenged the action of the State. This experience has taught me that research is a political activity geared towards accomplishing social work's social justice and social change mission. Over the years, I have converged my passions for community work/activism and research through community-based research, which opens up the possibility of working with communities to dehegemonize research and develop ways of researching congruent with communities' ways of knowing (Chilisa, 2012). Such work contributes to challenging the reproduction of neo-colonial and hegemonic ways of research. Dehegemonization in this chapter stands for delegitimizing the cultural authority and their ways of normalizing dominant forms of knowledge production (Gegeo & Watson Gegeo, 2001). The possibilities of sharing examples of my research and inspiring students keep me interested in teaching the research courses.

4.2 Critical Moment That Influenced My Teaching

In my teaching experience over the years, I have realized that most social work students take research *only* because it is a mandatory course. They believe that research is unnecessary for practice and needed to get through the course. Research does not change the social realities of communities, and research skills are required only for higher education in social work. Additionally, both research courses are content-heavy with unexciting information, and students find it challenging to engage with the complexities of the content. In my strivings to address these barriers, I have also sought feedback from students on what makes their learning about research more accessible and exciting. Over the years, many students have told me that they find my examples (they have called them stories) very interesting. It helps them understand and remember the content well. This feedback has profoundly influenced how I teach. Below is an example I share with students on how I bring together my knowledge of community practice/activism, critical, anti-oppressive research and research epistemology and operationalize them to address issues of power, relationality, researcher accountability, reciprocity, misrepresentation, and dehegemonization.

4.3 The Research Context

The research context was an agency serving older adults in Toronto that had received funding for research that explored abuse by older adults. Two geographic communities located close to the agency (one of these was a "high priority neighbourhood") were selected for the following reasons: a) the older adults were racialized and from two South Asian countries; b) most of them had a precarious immigration status of being a "refugee" or "sponsored"; and c) they lived in households that provided bare minimum for survival as their children faced the brunt of labour market discrimination (Reh'ma Community

Services, 2010). These vulnerabilities revealed that their challenges were connected with the systemic violence the families were experiencing. However, they get positioned as the racialized other in society with supposedly different/ inferior cultures (Said, 1995). Such framing of their situation (Hunter, 2002) prompted us to utilize the Community Action (CA) framework to facilitate community engagement and action on research findings (St. Dennis, 2004).

Keeping with CA and AO perspectives (Potts & Brown, 2015; St. Dennis, 2004), importance was given to facilitating community engagement (Tanabe et al., 2017). Even though of South Asian origin, I was critically aware of my privileges (Humphrey, 2007; Langhout, 2006) and decided to decentre myself and relocate decision-making power with the community (Fitzgerald, 2004; Kovach, 2005). A Community Advisory and Action Committee (CAAC) (comprising older adult men and women residents of both communities, community leaders, religious leaders and community partner agencies) was formed to provide sanction and overall direction. Also, a Research Team (RT) (comprising residents, agency volunteers, staff members, and myself) was formed for each community to develop their recruitment, data collection, analysis and dissemination strategies (Gray & Schubert, 2010; Maiter et al., 2008). The RT considered the following context-specific factors and guiding principles while developing the research design.

Context-specific factors such as recruiting older adults from places of religious (Mosques) and social gatherings (weekly meeting groups), principles of organizing meetings within the communities and supporting local businesses and entrepreneurs throughout our research guided our work. The RT considered ways of reciprocating through in-kind support for the "gift of data" members offered (Potts & Brown, 2015; Maiter et al., 2008) and demonstrated accountability by continuing work with members beyond research (Potts & Brown, 2015; Wilson, 2008). Creating a trusting and safe environment for eliciting "real" data/hidden script (Chavez et al., 2008; Siddle-Walker, 1996) by extending data collection over a period allowing for time to establish sufficient rapport and trust along with facilitating communication (Chilisa, 2012) through collecting data in the languages spoken by members, were other factors that informed our data collection methods. Striving to include the most marginalized in the data collection (Potts & Brown, 2015; Tanabe et al., 2017) and addressing the gender-based practices of the communities, we designed separate data collection sessions for men and women (Sorrenson & Kalman, 2018). Additionally, recognizing that the "subjugation of local knowledge formations is further entrenched along the lines of race, ethnicity, social class, age and gender" (Chilisa, 2012, p. 76), we were challenged to address such dehegemonization and develop data collection, analysis and dissemination methods that honoured communities' ways of knowing and sharing (Gegeo & Watson-Gegeo, 2001; Greenwood & Levin, 2004). The example given below presents our operationalization of this concept.

4.4 Implementing "Baithak"

Data was collected in one of the communities through a method we named "Baithak," a meeting place where village/town meetings are held in the country of origin of that community. We chose this name to recognize their historical and cultural context, expecting it might also kindle their interest to engage. Like the name, the structure of "Baithaks" reflected the community's cultural and religious values and practices (Gegeo & Watson Gegeo, 2001).

The "Baithaks" were conducted as dialogues (Chilisa, 2012; Pe Pua, 1989) in the languages community members spoke, and to avoid any suspicion and fear, the sessions were not recorded. They were held on a scheduled day and time every week for over two hours, with a built-in time for members to network with each other. The "Baithak" sessions followed an organic rhythm with informal but purposeful conversations (Pe Pua, 1989).

The first "Baithak's" focus was on establishing rapport, getting to know members, and learning about their families (Gutierrez, 2003; Reitsma-Street & Brown, 2004; St. Denis, 2004). It took two "Baithaks" for members to be comfortable. Gradually, as members became comfortable, in the third "Baithak," members shared their challenges as "sponsored" immigrants offering a general critique of the policy without going deeper into *their* situation. We knew that these were only the public transcripts (Chavez et al., 2008), and members seemingly needed more time to share their personal stories. Along with these conversations, the members also asked for clarifications on policies, information on services, support for filling out forms or requested that we accompany them to government offices to complete immigration-related formalities. The agency staff agreed to provide support outside the "Baithak" (Powell & Takayoshi, 2003). In the following weeks, as the members gained greater trust in us and felt safe in the company of others, the discussion moved from a generic critique of policies to sharing the heart-wrenching challenges of the negative impact of immigration status on their personal lives. This was a turning point in the "Baithak" as personal became political (Stone & Priestly, 1996), shame was transformed into a common problem, casual acquaintances with other older adults into alliances and "Baithak," into a forum for addressing their concerns (Fine, 2006). These discussions continued in the following "Baithaks," leading to the development of an action plan marking the end of our data collection phase. To continue work in the communities, the agency hired a new staff member from the same country, who had community activism experience and resided in the neighbourhood to work with older adults from both communities.

It is noteworthy to share that while the data collection was going on, a "Baithak" session happened to be on a significant religious day when members fasted during the daytime and broke their fast in the evening. The members and the RT decided not to cancel the "Baithak." As a mark of honouring this religious practice, the "Baithak" was scheduled for a longer time with time for prayer and food. The agency made arrangements for individual prayer carpets and traditional cultural food for breaking the fast. This "Baithak" was appreciated by all members, deepened the existing relationships, and laid a strong foundation for data analysis, dissemination and future work in both communities (Wilson, 2008).

The stance of dehegemonization informed the research's meaning-making (data analysis) and knowledge-sharing (dissemination) stages. Since the data was not recorded, the agency staff, volunteers and I met after every "Baithak" to jot down ideas and keywords expressed by members during the session. This exact process was followed for the data collected from both communities. All the ideas and keywords were compiled, translated and transcribed for thematic analysis. The themes were taken back to the older adults in both communities to ensure that the findings represented what they wanted to convey (Madison, 2011). In the weeks that followed, the RT and community members who participated in data collection in both communities brainstormed on strategies for disseminating findings that would attract the attention of community residents and partners and motivate members to take action on the findings. Members from both communities decided to disseminate findings through art forms popular within their culture. Two different dissemination methods, a skit and poetry presentations, were planned with separate dissemination events for each community (George, 2017). Both events were very well attended by community residents, partner agencies, CCAC, and local politicians. Additionally, I prepared a research report for the funder that I decided not to publish for my academic career (Reh'ma Community Services, 2010).

4.5   *Tensions and Critical Reflections*
Below I outline some tensions experienced within this research process.
- Timelines – Like most community-based research, even this research demanded more time. The agency had to renegotiate the timelines with the funder and successfully obtained an extension.
- Role of historical political factors in shaping inter-community relationships – It took us the entire research timespan to bring together both communities because the historical political relations between the two countries

affected their relationships in Canada. The RT had to consciously work in both communities to shift these understandings and illuminate how both communities were constructed as homogenous (of South Asian origin), decontextualized (from their history and politics), racialized and therefore, marginalized.
- Researcher positionality – I am from a South Asian country other than the countries that both of my communities came from; my country's relations with those countries are vastly different. Before I started working in these communities, I had to clarify my positionality as a researcher in the Canadian context, specifically with one of the communities.
- The researcher role – Even though the decision-making got relocated with the communities, I still had to do much brainstorming and hold discussions with different individuals and groups in the communities, including the program coordinator, agency staff and volunteers, and RT. The program coordinator and I still carried the overall responsibility of logistics, keeping the project moving, and submitting the report to the funder (Rutman, Hubberstay, Barlow, & Brown, 2005). This meant that I had to be critically self-reflexive throughout the research (Herising, 2005).

The example I have shared above, and the emergent tensions, are key points in my teaching. One can romanticize community-based participatory research without acknowledging the challenges within. When using these experiences in my teaching, I share the benefits and acknowledge the tensions, all within the frame of encouraging students to see the value and importance of doing qualitative research differently as part of their social justice commitment.

5 Lessons Learned

Having discussed our individual stories, we now turn to what we can draw from across those narratives, to consider what lessons we have learned, with the hope that sharing our reflections will be helpful to others.

Dehegemonization and utilizing communities' ways of knowing and sharing are strengths to be brought forward in critical qualitative research. The use of culturally appropriate data collection, analysis, and dissemination benefits the research process significantly. It can sustain participant interest and enhance participation from communities. Drawing on Purnima's example, even though the nature of membership for the "Baithak" was open, there was no drop in attendance. Gradually, more older adults started attending. Older adults felt heard, and most of them living in isolation came out networked with others. They felt that their voices were heard, and they found a forum to articulate, share and find resources to address some of their challenges and thereby gained agency. The dissemination event (presenting the findings through a skit) was a great success. The event inspired the community partners to provide support in addressing the issues of older adults leading to a substantial mobilization of resources from all over the GTA.

Establishment of credibility and trust is key to meaningful research engagement with communities. Purmina's example talked about continuing work in the community helps to facilitate building the agency's and the researcher's credibility and trust among community members. In her example, the work continued with older adults in both communities. After two years of work, the members named food insecurity as a critical issue impacting them and expressed a desire to address it. Based on the stigma attached to poverty and food insecurity, they were not ready to take up this issue earlier.

Establishing relevance and interest related to research is critical for engaging students if we hope to imagine future social workers being more involved in research. However, as Susan P.'s reflections demonstrate, we have to find ways to engage students that are aligned with anti-oppression and social justice principles, while also connecting to what matters to them, what ignites their passion. Sharing examples of our own research experiences provide an opportunity to students to see that research is not solely about producing science-driven knowledge but also about developing socially relevant knowledge (Gray & Schubert, 2010) focused on social justice.

While new and creative sources of qualitative data are made possible, such as Susan S.'s examples using social media such as YouTube, as researchers and as academics teaching research, we must be very mindful of how hegemonic knowledge is reproduced in the research process and how we unintentionally contribute to its reproduction. Our research courses provide a space in which to reveal, resist and reimagine research as an act of transformation.

Students see the prospect that it is possible to disrupt the hegemony of eurocentrism in knowledge production and take a stance of "intellectual sovereignty" (Warrior, as cited in Ladson-Billings, 2000, p. 405), a position free from the tyranny and oppression of the dominant discourse while undertaking research. They also begin to realize that even though not following the beaten and mainstream path of research is challenging and calls for much investment of time, operationalizing dehegemonization and utilizing culturally appropriate ways of researching have a much deeper significance in the way and through which historically marginalized communities resist hegemony and intellectual subjugation of their ways of knowing and sharing. These realizations and critical reflections on tensions and accomplishments become important lessons for students through the research journey that they carry along with them.

References

Adam, N., Zosky, D. L. & Unrau, Y. A. (2004). Improving the research climate in social work curricula: Clarifying learning expectations across BSW and MSW research courses. *Journal of Teaching in Social Work, 24*(3), 1–18.

Alexander, A. A., & Allo, H. (2021). Building a climate for advocacy training in professional psychology. *The Counseling Psychologist, 49*(7), 1070–1089.

Alston, M., & Bowles, W. (2019). *Research for Social Workers: an Introduction to Methods.* Routledge.

Appleton, C., Rankine, M., & Hare, J. (2016). Research pods: Breaking down barriers, demystifying research for social work students and practitioners in the practice setting. *Advances in Social Work and Welfare Education, 18*(2), 108–123.

Ashton, J. J., Gavin, J., & Beattie, R. M. (2019). Exclusive enteral nutrition in Crohn's disease: Evidence and practicalities. *Clinical Nutrition, 38*(1), 80–89.

Atkinson, J. D. (2017). *Journey into Social Activism: Qualitative Approaches.* Fordham University Press.

Aumayer, H., Grigat, D., Ghosh, S., & Kaplan, G., Dieleman, L., Wine, E., Fedorak, R., Fernandes, A., & Panaccione, R. (2015). Living with inflammatory bowel disease: A Crohn's and colitis Canada survey. *Canadian Journal of Gastroenterology and Hepatology, 29*(2), 77–84.

Bansal, P., & Corley, K. (2011). The coming of age for qualitative research: Embracing the diversity of qualitative methods. *Academy of Management Journal, 54*(2), 233–237.

Baskin, C. (2005). Gathering stories: Aboriginal research methodologies. *Canadian Social Work Review, 22*(2), 171–189.

Berman, Y. (1995). Knowledge transfer in social work: the role of grey documentation. *The International Information and Library Review, 27*(2), 143–154.

Branom, C. (2012). Community-based participatory research as a social work research and intervention approach. *Journal of Community Practice, 20*(3), 260–273.

Brown, L., & Strega, S. (2005). Introduction: Transgressive possibilities. In L. Brown & S. Strega (Eds.), *Research as resistance: Critical, Indigenous and anti-oppressive approaches* (pp. 1–17). Canadian Scholars' Press.

Buggs, S. G., Sims, J. P., & Kramer, R. (2020). Rejecting white distraction: A critique of the white logic and white methods in academic publishing. *Ethnic and Racial Studies, 43*(8), 1384–1392.

Canadian Association of Social Workers (CASW). (2005). *Code of Ethics.* CASW.

Charmaz, K. (2005). Grounded Theory in the 21st Century: A Qualitative Method for Advancing Social Justice Research. In N. K. Denzin & Y. S. Lincoln (Eds.), *The Sage Handbook of Qualitative Research* (3rd ed., pp. 507–535). Sage Publications Ltd.

Chase, S. (2003). Learning to Listen: Narrative Principles in a Qualitative Research Methods Course. In R. Josselson, A. Lieblich, & P. McAdams (Eds.), *Up Close and*

Personal: the Teaching and Learning of Narrative Research (pp. 79–99). American Psychological Association.

Chavez, V., Duran, B., Baker, Q.E., Avila, M.M., & Wallerstein, N. (2008). The Dance of Race and Privilege in Community-based Participatory Research. In M. Minkler & N. Wallerstein (Eds.), *Community Based Participatory Research for Health: from Process to Outcomes* (2nd ed., pp. 91–106). Jossey-Bass.

Chilisa, B. (2012). Decolonizing thse Interview Method. In *Indigenous Research Methodologies* (pp. 203–224). SAGE.

Chilisa, B. (2012). Whose Reality Counts? Research Methods in Question. In *Indigenous Research Methodologies* (pp. 73–96). SAGE.

Cullerton, K., Donnet, T., Lee, A., & Gallegos, D. (2018). Effective advocacy strategies for influencing government nutrition policy: A conceptual model. *International Journal of Behavioral Nutrition and Physical Activity, 15*(1), 1–11.

Defenbaugh, N. L. (2008). "Under erasure": The absent ill body in doctor – patient dialogue. *Qualitative Inquiry, 14*(8), 1402–1424.

Denzin, N. K. (2009). *Qualitative Inquiry and Social Justice: Toward a Politics of Hope*. Left Coast Press.

Devan, H., Elphick-laveta, T., Lynch, M., MacDonell, K., Marshall, D., Tuhi, L., & Grainger, R. (2021). "Power of Storytelling": A content analysis of chronic pain narratives on YouTube. *Canadian Journal of Pain, 5*(1), 117–129.

Dodd, S. J., & Epstein, I. (2012). *Practice-based Research in Social Work: A Guide for Reluctant Researchers*. Routledge.

Efroymson, D. (2006). Using media and research for advocacy: Low cost ways to increase success. *HealthBridge*. https://healthbridge.ca/dist/library/Using_Media_and_Research_for_Advocacy_low_cost_ways_to_increase_success_June_2006.pdf.

Epstein, I. (1987). Pedagogy of the preturbed: Teaching research to the reluctants. *Journal of Teaching in Social Work, 1*(1), 71–89.

Fine, M. (2006). Intimate details: Participatory action research in prison. *Action Research, 4*(3), 253–269.

Fink, A. (2019). *Conducting Research Literature Reviews: From the Internet to Paper*. Sage Publications.

Fitzgerald, J. (2004). Powerful voices and powerful stories: Reflections on the challenges and dynamics of intercultural research. *Journal of Intercultural Studies, 25*(3), 233–245.

Flaherty, M., Denzin, N., Manning, K., & Snow, A. (2002). Review symposium: Crisis in representation. *Journal of Contemporary Ethnography, 31*(4), 478–516.

Fook, J. (1996). *The Reflective Researcher: Social Workers' Theories of Practice Research*. Allen & Unwin.

Fook, J. (2011). Developing Critical Reflection as a Research Method. In *Creative Spaces for Qualitative Researching* (pp. 55–64). Sense Publishers.

Galvan, J. L., & Galvan, M. C. (2017). *Writing Literature Reviews: a Guide for Students of the Social and Behavioral Sciences*. Routledge.

Gegeo, D. & Watson-Gegeo, K. (2001). "How we know": Kwara'ae rural villagers doing indigenous epistemology. *The Contemporary Pacific, 13*(1), 55–88.

George, P. (2017). Critical Arts-based Research: An Effective Strategy for Knowledge Mobilization and Community Activism. In H. Parada & S. Wehbi (Eds). *Reimagining Anti-oppression Social Work Research* (pp. 57–69). Canadian Scholars' Press.

George, P. (2018). Moving beyond Education to Addressing Injustice: Case of Critical Engagement of College of Social Work with Eviction and Deportation of Pavement Dwellers in Mumbai. In P. George, G. Balakrishnan, V. Anand, & F. Chaze (Eds.), *Community Practices in India: Lessons from the Grassroots* (pp.144–154). Cambridge Scholar Publishing.

Gray, M. & Schubert, L. (2010). Turning base metal into gold: Transmuting art, practice, research and experience into knowledge. *British Journal of Social Work, 40*, 2308–2325.

Greenwood, D. J. & Levin, M. (2004). Local knowledge, Cogenerative Research, and Narrativity. In W. Carroll (Ed.) *Critical Strategies for Social Research* (pp.281–291). Canadian Scholars' Press.

Greenwood, R. M., Stefancic, A., & Tsemberis, S. (2013). Pathways Housing First for homeless persons with psychiatric disabilities: Program innovation, research, and advocacy. *Journal of Social Issues, 69*(4), 645–663.

Guishard, M. A., Halkovic, A., Galletta, A., & Li, P. (2018). Toward epistemological ethics: Centering communities and social justice in qualitative research. *Forum Qualitative Sozialforschung/Forum: Qualitative Social Research, 19*(3), 1–24.

Gutierrez, L. (2003). Participatory and Stakeholder Research. In E. Freeman (Ed.). *Encyclopaedia of Social Work, Supplement*. NASW Press.

Harder, J. (2010). Overcoming MSW students' reluctance to engage in research. *Journal of Teaching in Social Work, 30*(2), 195–209.

Herising, F. (2005). Interrupting Positions: Critical Thresholds and Queer Pro/Positions. In L. Brown & S. Strega (Eds.), *Research as Resistance: Critical, Indigenous and Anti-Oppressive Approaches* (pp. 127–152). Canadian Scholars' Press.

Hindryckx P, Vande Casteele N, Novak G, Khanna R, D'Haens G, Sandborn WJ, Danese S, Jairath V, & Feagan BG. (2018). The expanding therapeutic armamentarium for inflammatory bowel disease: How to choose the right drug[s] for our patients? *Journal of Crohns Colitis, 12*(1), 105–119.

Humphries, B. (2008). *Social Work Research for Social Justice*. Palgrave Macmillan.

Humphrey, C. (2007). Insider-outsider: Activating the hyphen. *Action Research, 5*(1), 11–26.

Hunter, M. (2002). Rethinking epistemology, methodology, and racism: Or, is white sociology really dead? *Race and Society, 5*(2) 119–138.

Irwin, J. (2020). Activism and social work. *Social Work and Policy Studies: Social Justice, Practice and Theory, 3*(2). https://openjournals.library.sydney.edu.au/index.php/SWPS/article/viewFile/14305/12962.

Johnson, C., & Parry, D. (2016). Contextualizing Qualitative Research for Social justice. In C. Johnson & D. Parry (Eds.), *Fostering Social Justice through Qualitative Inquiry: a Methodological Guide* (pp. 11–22). Routledge.

Kellner, D., & Kim, G. (2010). YouTube, critical pedagogy, and media activism. *Review of Education, Pedagogy, and Cultural Studies, 32*(10), 3–36.

Kende, A. (2016). Separating social science research on activism from social science as activism. *Journal of Social Issues, 72*(2), 399–412.

Kende, A., Lantos, N. A., Belinszky, A., Csaba, S., & Lukács, Z. A. (2017). The politicized motivations of volunteers in the refugee crisis: Intergroup helping as the means to achieve social change. *Journal of Social and Political Psychology, 5*(1), 260–281.

Kincheloe, J. L., & McLaren, P. (2011). Rethinking Critical Theory and Qualitative Research. In *Key Works in Critical Pedagogy* (pp. 285–326). Brill Sense.

Kirk, S., & Reid, W. (2002). *Science and Social Work: a Critical Appraisal.* Columbia University Press.

Kovach, M. (2005). Emerging from the Margins: Indigenous Methodologies. In L. Brown & S. Strega (Eds.), *Research as Resistance: Critical, Indigenous and Anti-oppressive Approaches* (pp. 19–36). Canadian Scholars' Press.

Ladson-Billings, G. (2000). Racialized Discourses and Ethnic Epistemologies. In N. Denzin & Y. Lincoln (Eds.). *The Sage Handbook of Qualitative Research* (2nd ed., pp. 257–277). Sage.

Langhout, R. D. (2006). Where am I? Locating myself and its implications for collaborative research. *American Journal of Community Psychology, 37*, 267–274.

Lee, M. A., Smith, T. J., & Henry, R. G. (2013). Power politics: Advocacy to activism in social justice counseling. *Journal for Social Action in Counseling and Psychology, 5*(3), 70–94.

Legewie, N., & Nassauer, A. (2018). YouTube, Google, Facebook: 21st century online video research and research ethics. *Forum, Qualitative Social Research, 19*(3).

Lincoln, Y. S. (1998). The ethics of teaching in qualitative research. *Qualitative Inquiry, 4* (3), 315–327.

Lincoln, Y. S., & Guba, E. G. (1985). *Naturalistic Inquiry.* Sage.

Lönnfors, S., Vermeire, S., & Avedano, L. (2014). IBD and health-related quality of life – Discovering the true impact. *Journal of Crohn's and Colitis, 8*(10), 1281–1286.

Lyons, H. Z., Bike, D. H., Ojeda, L., Johnson, A., Rosales, R., & Flores, L. Y. (2013). Qualitative research as social justice practice with culturally diverse populations. *Journal for Social Action in Counseling and Psychology, 5*(2), 10–25.

Madison, D. S. (2011). *Critical Ethnography: Method, Ethics, and Performance.* Sage.

Maiter, S., Simich, L., Jacobson, N. & Wise, J. (2008) Reciprocity: An ethic for community-based participatory action research. *Action Research*, 6(3), 305–325.

Maschi, T., Wells, M., Yoder Slater, G., MacMillan, T., & Ristow, J. (2013). Social work students' research-related anxiety and self-efficacy: Research instructors' perceptions and teaching innovations. *Social Work Education*, 32(6), 800–817.

Mattocks, N. O. (2018). Social action among social work practitioners: Examining the micro–macro divide. *Social Work*, 63(1), 7–16.

Minkler, M. and Wallerstein, N. (2008). Introduction to CBPR: New Issues and Emphases. In M. Minkler & N. Wallerstein (Eds.), *Community-Based Participatory Research for Health* (2nd ed., pp. 5–23). Jossey-Bass.

Mohanty, C. (2002). "Under Western Eyes" revisited: Feminist solidarity through anti-capitalist struggles. *Journal of Women in Culture and Society*, 28(2), 499–535.

Neuman, W.L. (2013). The meanings of methodology. In *Social research methods: Qualitative and quantitative approaches* (7th ed., pp. 91–124). Allyn & Bacon.

Nevo, I., & Slonim-Nevo, V. (2011). The myth of evidence-based practice: Towards evidence-informed practice. *British Journal of Social Work*, 41(6), 1176–1197.

O'Connor, D. L., & O'Neill, B. J. (2004). Toward social justice: Teaching qualitative research. *Journal of Teaching in Social Work*, 24(3–4), 19–33.

Osmond, J., & O'Connor, I. (2006). Use of theory and research in social work practice: Implications for knowledge-based practice. *Australian Social Work*, 59(1), 5–19.

Padgett, D. (2016). *Qualitative Methods in Social Work Research* (3rd ed.). Sage.

Patterson, A. N. (2018). YouTube generated video clips as qualitative research data: One researcher's reflections on the process. *Qualitative Inquiry*, 24(10), 759–767.

Pe-Pua, R. (1989). Pagtatanong-tanong: A cross-cultural research method. *International Journal of Intercultural Relations*, 13, 147–163.

Petersén, A. C., & Olsson, J. I. (2015). Calling evidence-based practice into question: Acknowledging phronetic knowledge in social work. *British Journal of Social Work*, 45(5), 1581–1597.

Potts, K. L. & Brown, L. (2015), Becoming an Anti-oppressive Researcher. In S. Strega & L. Brown (Eds.), *Research as resistance: Revisiting Critical, Indigenous and Anti-oppressive Approaches* (2nd ed., pp. 17–42). Canadian Scholars' Press.

Powell & Takayoshi (2003). Accepting roles created for us: The ethics of reciprocity. *College Composition and Communication*, 54(3), 394–422.

Preston, S., & Redgrift, L. (2017). Phenomenology as Social Work Inquiry: Parallels and Divergences with Anti-oppressive Research. In H. Parada & S. Wehbi (Eds.) *Reimagining Anti-oppression Social Work Research* (pp. 87–98). Canadian Scholars Press.

Probst, B. (2015). The eye regards itself: Benefits and challenges of reflexivity in qualitative social work research. *Social Work Research*, 39(1), 37–48.

Probst, B., & Berenson, L. (2014). The double arrow: How qualitative social work researchers use reflexivity. *Qualitative Social Work, 13*(6), 813–827.

Proctor, E. K., & Rosen, A. (2008). From knowledge production to implementation: Research challenges and imperatives. *Research on Social Work Practice, 18*(4), 285–291.

Quijano, A. (2000). Coloniality of power and eurocentrism in Latin America. *International Sociology, 15*(2), 215–232.

Reh'ma Community Services (2010). George, P., Munawar, A., Qazi, M. & Delarosa, E. *From Silence to Resistance: Racialized Immigrant Seniors Reclaiming Space*. A community action research conducted by REH'MA Community Services, Toronto.

Reid, W. J. (2001). The role of science in social work: The perennial debate. *Journal of Social Work, 1*(3), 273–293.

Reitsma-Street, M. & Brown, L. (2004). Community Action Research. In W. Carroll (Ed.) *Critical Strategies for Social Research*, (pp. 303–319). Canadian Scholars' Press.

Reyes Cruz, M. (2008). What if I just cite Graciela? Working toward decolonizing knowledge through a critical ethnography. *Qualitative Inquiry, 14*(4), 651–658.

Rogers, J. (2012). Anti-oppressive social work research: Reflections on power in the creation of knowledge. *Social Work Education, 31*(7), 866–879.

Rothstein, H. R., & Hopewell, S. (2009). Grey Literature. In H. Cooper, L. Hedges, & J. Valentine (Eds.), *The Handbook of Research Synthesis and Meta-analysis* (2nd ed., pp. 103–125). Russell Sage Foundation.

Rutman, D., Hubberstay, C., Barlow, A. & Brown E. (2005). Supporting Young People's Transitions from Care: Reflections on doing Participatory Action Research with Youth from Care. In L. Brown & S. Strega (Eds.), *Research as Resistance: Revisiting Critical, Indigenous and Anti-oppressive Approaches* (pp. 153–179). Canadian Scholars' Press.

Said, E.W. (1995). *Orientalism* (pp. 1–30). Penguin Books.

Sandelowski M. (1993). Rigor or rigor mortis: The problem of rigor in qualitative research revisited. *Advances in Nursing Science, 16*(2), 1–8.

Scully, J. L. (2019). The responsibilities of the engaged bioethicist: Scholar, advocate, activist. *Bioethics, 33*(8), 872–880.

Shaw, I. (2005). Practitioner research: Evidence or critique? *British Journal of Social Work, 35*(8), 1231–1248.

Shaw, I. G. R., & Holland, S. (2014). *Doing Qualitative Research in Social Work*. Sage.

Siddle-Walker, V. (1996). *Their Highest Potential: An African American School Community in the Segregated South*. University of North Carolina Press.

Silver, S. (2017). Decolonizing a Graduate Research Course ... Moving Away from Innocence and Ignorance. In H. Parada, & S. Wehbi, S. (Eds.), *Re-imagining Anti-oppression Social Work: Reflecting on Research* (pp. 113–123). Canadian Scholars Press.

Smith, L. T. (2012). *Decolonizing methodologies: Research and Indigenous peoples* (2nd ed.). Zed Books.

Sorensson, E. & Kalman, H. (2018). Care and concern in the research process: Meeting ethical and epistemological challenges through multiple engagements and dialogue. *Qualitative Research, 18*(6), 706–721.

St. Denis, V. (2004). Community-based Participatory Research: Aspects of the Concept Relevant for Practice. In W. K. Carroll (Ed.), *Critical Strategies for Social Research* (pp. 292–303). Canadian Scholars' Press Inc.

Stark, S., & Watson, K. (1999). Passionate pleas for "Passion Please": Teaching for qualitative research. *Qualitative Health Research, 9* (6), 719–730.

Stone, E. & Priestley, M. (1996). Parasites, pawns and partners: Disability research and the role of non-disabled researcher. *British Journal of Sociology, 47*(4), 699–716.

Strega, S. (2005). The view from the post-structural margins: Epistemology and methodology reconsidered. In L. Brown & S. Strega (Eds.), *Research as resistance: Critical, Indigenous, & anti-oppressive approaches* (pp. 199–236). Canadian Scholars' Press.

Strier, R. (2007). Anti-oppressive research in social work: A preliminary definition. *British Journal of Social Work, 37*(5), 857–871.

Tanabe, M., Pearce, E., & Krause, S. K. (2017). "Nothing about us, without us": Conducting participatory action research among and with persons with disabilities in humanitarian settings. *Action Research, 16*(3), 280–298.

Teater, B. (2017). Social work research and its relevance to practice: "The gap between research and practice continues to be wide". *Journal of Social Service Research, 43*(5), 547–565.

Terry, S. F., Terry, P. F., Rauen, K. A., Uitto, J., & Bercovitch, L. G. (2007). Advocacy groups as research organizations: the PXE International example. *Nature Reviews Genetics, 8*(2), 157–164.

Udall, J. (2019). Demystifying Social Research Methods. In *Demystifying Architectural Research* (pp. 43–50). RIBA Publishing.

Webb, S. (2001). Some consideration on the validity of evidence-based practice in social work. *British Journal of Social Work, 31*(1), 57–79.

Wheelock, A. (1993). Building common ground: Combining research and advocacy. *Equity and Choice, 10*(1), 62–64.

Wilson, S. (2008). *Research Is Ceremony: Indigenous Research Methods*. Fernwood Publishing.

Woodford, M. R., & Preston, S. (2013). Strengthening citizen participation in public policy-making: A Canadian perspective. *Parliamentary Affairs, 66*(2), 345–363.

Yee, J.Y. (2017). Carrying out Research on Whiteness, White Supremacy, and Racialization Processes in Social Service Agencies. In H. Parada & S. Wehbi (Eds.), *Re-imagining Anti-oppressive Social Work Research* (pp. 59–68). Canadian Scholars' Press.

CHAPTER 9

Qualitative Research as Resistance

The Use of Vignettes to Support Situated Knowledge and the Deconstruction of Colonial Policies

Laura Wyper

1   Introduction

My qualitative PhD research was prompted by my observations at the adult education Literacy and Basic Skills (LBS) site where I worked related to provincial policy changes and a move to outcomes-based reporting (Wyper, 2018, 2019; Elias et al., 2021). At the site where I worked there were student demographic changes happening related to decreased access to service for English as a second language learners, seniors, and developmentally delayed adults. From my perspective these changes were forms of marginalization related to racism/linguistic racism, ageism and ableism as access to services and the ability to participate (or not in these cases) was decreasing. I questioned whether the observations I made in relation to the implementation of the policy changes at this site would relate to other LBS sites and LBS communities across Ontario (Wyper, 2018, 2019). The changes I was seeing related to the new LBS policy had me thinking about many different aspects of power, alluded to by Niyozov and Tarc (2015) that are not only issues within education but within societies generally, including who has power and gets to define things, what this has meant historically in Canada as a settler state, who then gets access, how access increases or decreases opportunity and thus participation in society, and the implications of these factors. These concepts had me questioning the ways practitioners might understand these changes, how they were combining theory with practice (praxis), and if they were gatekeeping in various ways that would lead to more or less access and opportunity (Wyper, 2018; Elias et al., 2021).

This was my starting point, but given my proximity to this work, I needed to understand the larger provincial picture through the responses from research participants. This would allow me to gain the advantage of other rural, northern or southern practitioners perspectives, and it would add further understanding to the richness and plurality of our regional and situational differences and the impacts of the policy changes to LBS services in Ontario.

In other words, I wanted to examine the LBS policy changes in relation to Ball's (1993) first and second order effects to see whether other LBS practitioners and program coordinators were experiencing similar situations, and how they were managing the policy changes. This reasoning was based on the understanding that bringing, in this case, the challenges of policy changes to light and naming potential problems, in terms of the marginalizations that may be happening, can lead to change. Lederach (2006) discusses this idea with respect to conflict transformation as an ability to respond to conflict and to see it as an opportunity to open a space and initiate a process that allows communication to come about (p. 27; In Wyper, 2018). As such this research was a form of resistance to, activism with, and giving voice to practitioners in the field regarding the impacts the new policy changes were having on students. It would also bring to light the types of responses they were enacting related to these policy changes which we could all then share in our attempts to mitigate marginalizations if they were happening.

2 Resistance as Research: Anticolonialism, Decolonialism, and Anti-oppression

As both an LBS practitioner and then Program Coordinator over a period of ten years, and someone who works from an anti-colonial, decolonial, and anti-oppressive practice lens, I had the lived and theoretical experience to ground myself in this research, and to reimagine how we and why we do research. Carpenter and Mojab (2013) note that "feminist critiques of social organization and their visions of resistance to subordination and domination emerged concurrently with anti-colonial and anti-capitalist work, particularly the ongoing critique of the social relations of reproduction" (p. 164; In Wyper, 2018). Many authors note this centering as insiders/outsiders, where these relations can then be analyzed and critiqued, at both personal and political levels (Doucet and Mauthner, 2006; Hesse-Biber, 2012; In Wyper, 2018). I also really valued situated knowledge and contested "universalist forms of knowledge and rather [recognized] the embodied, varied and localized experiences and insights" (Haraway, 1991, p. 5; In Amauchi et al., 2022; In Wyper, 2018) from each of the participants.

As noted by Spring (2008), postcolonial analysis addresses dominant forms of knowing which result from economic and political power, and how Western ideology has had global impacts. These impacts are not because it is correct but rather due to the hegemonic way it conceptualizes power both politically and economically, and the cascading effects like marginalization, it has for many left outside those circles of power (p. 336; In Wyper, 2018). This type of marginalization was my concern in that those most affected by the policy changes I was seeing were older, disabled, or people who did not have English as a first language. Such hegemony is dangerous, exploitative for most populations in that it marginalizes those it can not or does not see as useful for its own economic gain, and is destructive for the planet (Spring, 2008) as driven by these anthropocentric, androcentric, and ethnocentric ideologies (Martusewicz et al., 2011). Gonzalez (2015) also proposes that anti-colonialism can be thought of as any movement that opposes forms of colonialism or imperialism (Wyper, 2018).

Anti-colonialism and postcolonialism attempt to deconstruct colonial truths and its "thought is about discoursing on difference, power, racial and social oppressions as well as the silences" (Dei and Kempf, 2006, p.9; In Wyper, 2018). Transformative and reconstructivist pedagogies would see "defeating colonial power [... as recognizing ...] this power, how it is structured into an integrated system, and to begin to disrupt it through knowledge of how the system works. With this knowledge the system can be challenged and dismantled." (Iseke-Barnes, 2008, p. 124; Wyper, 2018). Through deconstructions and reconstructions of power, anti-colonial and postcolonial work can become decolonizing work (Wyper, 2018).

Decolonizing, once viewed as sovereignty work of Nations is now viewed, in some spaces, to include "a long-term process involving the bureaucratic, cultural, linguistic and psychological divesting of colonial power" (Smith, 1999, p.98, as cited in Iseke-Barnes, 2008, p. 123; In Wyper, 2018). According to Mignola (2011) decolonial space-making is a way of building alternatives to colonial space, mindsets, worldviews, and discourse as an "epistemic disobedience" (p. 45; In Wyper, 2018). Decolonial thinking thus brings in other frames of reference that are "nonlinear, situated and non-Eurocentric" (Cupples and Glynn, 2014, p. 59; In Wyper, 2018).

The focus on policy resistance in organizational studies historically was based on decreasing resistance and continuing the status quo, which is obviously based in colonial power structures that intend to keep the accumulation of wealth, power, decision making and resource allocation in the hands of a few. This concept of organizational resistance can be due to a misalignment between the culture of the agency and the new policy, and can be seen as explicit resistance, resulting in management decisions that oppose the policy directives being presented (Lombardo and Mergaert, 2013, p. 301; In Wyper, 2018). I was directly opposed to the policy changes as the effects I was seeing was an increased marginalization of vulnerable adult education populations. This new policy was a direct contradiction to the institutional culture where

I worked as our focus was meeting the needs of adults that came to us needing literacy services. We did not value some community members less than others, as neoliberal ideology would have us do, but rather were adamant about serving those who were most vulnerable, advocated for sites to remain open, and creatively changed programming in our attempts to mitigate the policy changes while still keeping within the bounds of the changes. My research was trying to make sense of what was happening, how widespread it was, and what others were doing in the face of the changes.

Recently literature on resistance to policy implementation has questioned this original response that attempts to mitigate resistance itself and acknowledges that our more pluralistic responses are largely based on our worldviews, ways of being, knowing and doing, and as such can be a healthy response that meets local needs in more responsive ways (Wyper, 2018). This is where policy resistance and research as resistance intersect. Looking at how we respond to policy and how we resist (or not) was an interesting aspect of the research I undertook, and was a part of my own resistance to policy itself; thus, my own research was a part of my resistance as I was searching for other resistors and their strategies to combat the second order effects of the policy changes. According to Sekou (2014), such individuals "operate from a social justice framework that insists community organizing can radicalize public institutions and make them more accountable to marginalized groups" (p. 182; In Wyper, 2018). As such, this resistance should be viewed as change that can move an agency towards more equitable service provision that supports social justice rather than perpetuating historical abuses of power (Wyper, 2018). Issues of equity in education are systemic in provinces and territories across Canada (Lange et al., 2015). Globally, neoliberalism is being critiqued in terms of the continuation of historical colonial power structures (Agnotti, 2012; Block et al., 2012; Carney, 2011–2012; Sage, 2014; Starkey, 2012; In Wyper, 2018), which then also is seen as part of New Program Management (NPM), both of which then perpetuate inequity in education as well (Dunleavy et al., 2005; Haque, n.d.; Hennessy and Sawchuk, 2003; Lapsley, 2009; Ryan et al., 2017; Siltala, 2013; Van der Sluis et al., 2017; In Wyper, 2018).

The ways administrators and practitioners respond, react and/or resist neoliberal and NPM types of policy change at individual or institutional levels can have cascading effects for everyone involved. This means it will affect the kind of access made available at their particular sites and ultimately equity of access to education. Practitioner responses risk perpetuating colonial power structures if they enact inequities, oppressions and marginalizations. Comparatively, practitioner and administrator responses can be anti-colonial or decolonial responses if they deconstruct governmental policy, and increase access and equity for citizens (Wyper 2018, p.8, 2019, p.34).

3 Research Questions and Methodology

I developed my research questions (below) by drawing on my own concerns as a long-time practitioner and then program coordinator (administrator).

3.1 *Overarching Research Questions*

1. What changes in practices have administrators/practitioners at LBS sites observed and how do they believe these changes are related to changes in provincial LBS policies?
2. How have the demographics of the students served changed? Are some subgroups of students served more or less frequently than before?
3. What strategies are staff at LBS sites using to resist and/or mitigate the changes?
   WYPER, 2018, p.45, 2019, p.35

This study was a qualitative research methodology that used open-ended vignettes in interviews in order to understand the effects of LBS policy changes on practices in the province of Ontario (Wyper, 2018, 2019).

The use of these scenarios or vignettes allowed for exploration of what could be sensitive topics, while also having the potential for a wide variety of practitioner responses. The idea was to talk about the scenario, as a beginning "icebreaker" perspective, to allow the interviewees to move naturally through a process of explaining what happens at their sites to reveal their general attitudes and beliefs (Barter and Renold, 1999; In Wyper, 2018). A vignette approach, rather than a yes and no answer approach, was an ethically important approach as it created space for the very epistemic disobedience Mignolla (2011) discusses. This approach allowed for a discussion not only of what was happening but also the situated 'why' by interviewees, and was an opening for any other emergent issues their specific site was facing. For example, after interviewees described what they anticipated would happen to a student in a particular vignette scenario, they might tell me of other scenarios that I was not seeing but they were in their specific context. In cases where the interviewee indicated that they "did not serve" the type of student described in the scenario I offered, I could then ask further questions that would allow me to better understand their situational community context, such as "Are there other agencies that you are aware of which might provide service for these individuals?" I could follow up by asking for more detail, such as "Are students likely to encounter wait lists for services at the other agency that you are aware of?" I saw my research participants as holders of place-based, or context specific situational knowledge that expanded my experience and informed my theoretical perspective. This allowed me to incorporate my experiences as a practitioner and an administrator into an evidence-based sample of the picture of LBS organizations and programs in Ontario. (Wyper, 2018, 2019).

3.2   *Site Sampling and Reasoning*

The research participants were LBS practitioners and/or LBS administrators and were chosen from both groups as a way to hopefully mobilize "the living knowledge of people connected to each other and their environment and weaves a collective understanding of ways to act for the common good" (Chevalier and Buckles, 2013, p. 3; In Wyper, 2018). LBS sites were found across four streams and three sectors in Ontario. According to the Cathexis (2016) report for the Ministry of Advanced Education and Skill Development (MAESD), there were approximately 274 service delivery sites serving over 37,000 learners in classroom settings. In 2014–2015 there were approximately 33,000 Anglophone stream learners, 3,000 Francophone learners, 1,200 Aboriginal learners, and just over 300 Deaf stream learners physically present at LBS sites. The report also noted that, in 2014–2015, colleges in Ontario served 15,570 learners, community agencies served 11,439 learners, and school boards served 10,043 learners (pp. 8–10; In Wyper, 2018, 2019; Elias et al., 2021).

I originally chose site administrators and practitioners from both Northern and Southern Ontario on the basis of sampling across LBS streams (Francophone, Deaf, Aboriginal, and English), and sectors (College, School Board, Community-based). Because some streams did not occur in all sectors, an equivalency of voice and representation within the sectors of which they are part was a goal. First Nations LBS sites are rarely seen within the College or School Board sectors, unless they were co-located, for example, and thus I needed to strategically ensure that there was similar representation by that stream. I sampled from six Community-based First Nations LBS agencies to ensure equivalency of voice as those in other streams, and in an effort to deconstruct whose voice is normally heard in the neoliberal and hegemonic power imbalance I was simultaneously critiquing. I also wanted to ensure that voices in both areas of the province (north and south) were accounted for due to the regional differences that could make programming responses to policy very different and based on place-based needs. For this reason, at times alternate sites of similar stream and sector were found if the original sites I'd approached did not want to participate to have that balance of voices from across the province (Wyper, 2018, 2019). If I were to do this same research now, I would have actually used a snowball sampling method that would link resistors through word of mouth. We all had our smaller networks within the larger provincial network and many practitioners were talking about the policy changes among themselves. A snowball sampling method would have focused my research more on the types of resistance happening than it currently did, while also still confirming that certain demographics within the larger adult education population were in fact being marginalized. Snowball sampling to increase the voice of resistors would have also potentially led to an increase in mitigation strategies that could be shared across the province with other practitioners.

Given the range of possible organizational structures I ended up interviewing 22 site administrators and/or practitioners who represented the 24 sites I had originally wanted to sample. These 22 participants oversaw approximately 50 sites across the province given the way that individuals often have more than one site they are responsible for (Wyper, 2018, 2019). As noted above, this was ethically differentiated in this way to ensure equivalency of voice across streams and regions of the province given our pluralistic and place-based needs and to ensure the voices not usually heard would be counted.

In terms of the Cathexis report on number of students served I would argue that these numbers did not necessarily form a true picture, as they may not have counted students who were served historically, up until 2012, who found themselves outside the mandate or in the process of being displaced from centres for various reasons given the terms of the new policy. The number and characteristics of these learners are at the very heart of the layered research question: who is really being served? who was being served and is no longer eligible, and which learners are still being served but in smaller numbers. This data is largely hidden. The "lost" learners are not easily counted in a quantitative approach, are an example of the marginalizations neoliberal policy enact, and that methods like quantitative research can both knowingly and unknowingly enable. To avoid this type of perpetuation of erasure not only of people themselves, but of them through the methods of research we use, I had to rely on the recollections and the accumulated knowledge of practitioners in the field. My approach and valuing of practitioner experience was similar to Weaver's (2016) notion that through "bottom-up approaches that advocate for the participation of community partners, knowledge is co-generated to address the root causes of issues that affect the community" (p. 3; In Amauchi et al., 2022). Although we may never know what the total numbers of displaced persons are from these services due to the policy changes, the use of qualitative methods in this way allows insight into which groups are experiencing displacement at some sites, even if the method cannot track actual numbers lost. I also would argue that it is not "about numbers" in any case— everyone who faces displacement from participation in services is being marginalized, and is important (Wyper, 2018, 2019).

This largely unseen phenomenon of displacement is one of the most important reasons motivating this research study. It also gave voice to practitioners, their recent experiences, frustrations, concerns, and strategies as they related to the LBS funding changes, even as sites attempt to balance their statistical measures and their community's needs in their bid to secure their site's future funding within this new mandate (Wyper, 2018). Related to displacements, some LBS staff did not have the pre- and post-comparative analysis available to them due to being relatively new instructors, but some nonetheless saw shifts that had been happening slowly over the last few years since policy changes happened, and again it was this situated knowledge, even without the historical continuity before 2012 that told the stories of their sites. We all knew the names of the learners we were no longer able to serve, or were now 'creatively' continuing to serve (Wyper, 2018).

Further to practitioner historical knowledge, site staffing could range from one person who does it all, from administration to instruction, to large sites where a LBS manager may or may not even be on site even if they are working with LBS classroom instructors. Because programming happens across various sectors, these administrative and instructional roles would also look different in community-based centres compared to the more hierarchical structures often found in college and school board service providers. College and school board LBS programs could be housed within larger adult education departments and be accountable to the institutional chain of command; staff at these larger institutions may have done some intake data management on student files but may not have been responsible for financial reporting. Community-based centres on the other hand could have been accountable to Boards of Directors or Band Offices. In all cases LBS programs may have been running as an isolated and fragment cell within a larger structure, or as a stand-alone independent agency (Wyper, 2018). These structures were important to understand related to the potential 'creative compliance' that was happening or decisions related to gatekeeping that could have been made beyond the LBS centres or staff's decision making authority. These factors were a part of the additional follow up questions I would often ask to better understand the individual situated context of each site, the participants experiences, and their responses.

3.3 Data Analysis

I manually coded all data using thematic tables along the lines proposed by Creswell (1994) and McDavid et al., (2013). As I was the only one analyzing the data, the possibility of inconsistencies in coding was minimized (Wyper, 2018). After transcription, a copy of each participant's responses was sent back to them to edit, add to, or clarify in any way. Although this data analysis method could be viewed as a limitation due to the inability to assess inter-coder reliability, I would argue that my insider/outsider duality was a contextual strength as I also had situated knowledge not only as a practitioner in the field but as discussed by Gherardi (2008) I was situated in the dynamics of interaction in which "knowing in practice articulates the emergent – in situ – nature of knowledge from interactions" (p.7). As mentioned earlier, the intentional use of vignettes was meant to increase open-ended participant-researcher interactions that allowed for further exploration of meaning prior to even beginning coding and thematic categorization. It was this relational piece in the work that added a depth of context and meaning for me as the researcher, and of research results I would argue.

When I began coding, I started with the basic responses for each scenario, looking at the primary question of whether students were being served, not served, or referred elsewhere. I then coded each site according to other key words and overriding themes. Although wording could be stated differently, if the overarching theme was noted across a third or more of the interview responses, I added it to the final dissertation and used specific participant quotes related to each theme in my thesis to embody the passion and concern I had heard in their voices. These themes were interpreted, through descriptions and explanations by participants, and then used to identify chapter themes—to do with creative compliance, resistance, capacity, student demographics, community need, the idea of what literacy education is, and gatekeeping that was decreasing access (Wyper, 2018, 2019).

4 Discussion

4.1 Ethical Considerations

There was a thread of secrecy that needed to be applied to my research to ensure any negative or retributive consequences for either the agencies or the individual practitioners participating in this study was avoided. As LBS agencies and practitioners were funded by the Ministry of Advanced Education and Skill Development (MAESD), either directly as service providers or indirectly as employees of these agencies, the research needed to ensure confidentiality in order to avoid this. This became a sensitive issue when reporting findings as, even with confidentiality, some sites would have been identifiable. Thus, to ensure both confidentiality and anonymity, in some instances sites needed to be incorporated into the larger thematic findings. This was unfortunate in many instances as a more specific analysis could have added richness to the research results. In other instances the type of agency, programming, or the gender, race or social location of practitioners also had to be hidden to add a layer of confidentiality and anonymity for sites. Although in some instances social location may explain practitioner praxis, related to privilege for instance, this is not always the case due to cycles of socialization (Harro, 2010a), cycles of liberation (Harro, 2010b), internalized oppressions and other intergenerational issues linked to colonialism, power, privilege, and oppression; therefore, as the correlation between social location and practitioner praxis was not a focus of the study, I leave it to a future study to ask these questions specifically (Wyper, 2018).

As the researcher, I was also at some risk because I could not conduct the research anonymously, but it was essential to ensure confidentiality for my participants. I took care to conduct this research outside the hours of paid work, as an academic researcher and PhD student outside the boundaries of my employment. My position would theoretically have allowed me access, by way of my government username and password, to materials that would not normally be accessible to a researcher given confidentiality restrictions on government data. However, I understood clearly that any use of non-public materials for the purposes of my research would be both a breach of my terms of employment and my confidentiality commitment to the District School Board and the MAESD. This meant that I only used data that could be gleaned from publically accessible websites, from interviewee responses, and from documents that anyone registering for an LBS class would be able to see (Wyper, 2018).

5   Conclusions

Ball (2014) directs our attention to where policy is made and where relationships and networks emerge in the process of creating new forms of governance. He characterizes this networking as an example of the interconnectivity of ideas, people, and politics, both globally and locally. Joshee (2014) looks at policy webs, while Patria (2013, p. 151) sees research, education and campaign strategies as a grassroots way of finding spaces to make change. These tenets can be applied to the LBS research I undertook as an attempt to better build interconnectivity and encourage space making (Ball, 2014; Joshee, 2014; Patria, 2013; Phoenix, 2014; In Wyper, 2018) processes that are important to practitioners in the field. It is in this interconnectivity of LBS organizations, and through a shared understanding of our situations that both creative compliance, resistance and mitigations of policy change can happen (Wyper, 2018).

My hope was that this form of qualitative research would challenge LBS policies. In some small ways it has through the work of Elias et al. (2021), in relation to the further critique of adult education in Canada. It also demonstrates the importance of our work as researchers, practitioners and activists in the field as we can engage in deconstructivist work and resistance to colonial policy by way of "'deep democracy', characterized by 'internal criticism and debate, horizontal exchange and learning, and vertical collaborations and partnerships'" (Appadurai, 2002, p. 46, cited in Bifulco, 2013, p. 183; In Wyper, 2018).

References

Amauchi, J. F. F., Gauthier, M., Ghezeljeh, A., Giatti, L. L. L., Keats, K., Sholanke, D., Zachari, D., Gutberlet, J. (2022). The power of community-based participatory research: Ethical and effective ways of researching. *Community Development, 53*(10), 3–20. https://doi.org/10.1080/15575330.2021.1936102.

Angotti, T. (2012). The urban-rural divide and food sovereignty in India. *Journal of Developing Societies, 28*(4), 379–402.

Appadurai, A. (2002). Deep democracy: urban governmentality and the horizons of politics. *Public Culture, 14*(1), pp. 21–47. https://doi.org/10.1215/08992363-14-1-21.

Ball, S. (1993). What is policy? Text, trajectories and toolboxes. *Discourse: Studies in the Cultural Politics of Education, 13*(2), 10–17.

Ball, S. (2014). *Towards Global Education Policy*. Retrieved from Lecture Notes Online Website: http://unimelb.adobeconnect.com/p6hau2zz1y4/ CIE 1006: Democracy, Human Rights and Democratic Education in an Era of Globalization (Democratic Education & Globalization), Session 9. OISE. Toronto, ON.

Barter, C., & Renold, E. (1999). The use of vignettes in qualitative research. *Social Research Update,* issues 25. http://sru.soc.surrey.ac.uk/SRU25.html.

Bifulco, L. (2013). Citizen participation, agency and voice. *European Journal of Social Theory, 16*(2), 174–187.

Block, D.R., Chavez, N., Allen, E., & Ramirez, D. (2012). Food sovereignty, urban food access, and food activism: contemplating the connections through examples from Chicago. *Agriculture and Human Values, 29*, 203–215.

Carney, M. (Winter 2011–2012). "Food security" and "food sovereignty": What frameworks are best suited for social equity in food systems? *Journal of Agriculture, Food Systems, and Community Development, 2*(2), 71–87.

Carpenter, S., & Mojab, S. (2013). What is "Critical" about Critical Adult Education? In, Nesbit, T., Brigham, S.M., Taber, N., and Gibb, T. (Eds.), (2013). *Building on Critical Traditions: Adult Education and Learning in Canada* (pp. 160–172). Toronto: Thompson Educational Publishing, Inc.

Cathexis Consulting Inc. (2016). *Evaluation of the Literacy and Basic Skills (LBS) Program: Final Report.* http://www.tcu.gov.on.ca/eng/eopg/publications/lbs-eval-report-2016-en.pdf.

Chevalier, J.M., & Buckles, D.J. (2013). *Handbook for Participatory Action Research, Planning and Evaluation.* SAS2 Dialogue. Ottawa. https://www.uwlanc.org/sites/uwlanc.org/files/Planning%20and%20Evaluation.pdf.

Creswell, J.W. (1994). *Research Design: Qualitative and Quantitative Approaches.* London: Sage Publications.

Cupples, J., & Glynn, K. (2014). Indigenizing and decolonizing higher education on Nicaragua's Atlantic Coast. *Singapore Journal of Tropical Geography, 35*(1), 56–71.

Dei, G.J.S., and Kempf, A. (Eds.), (2006). *Anti-Colonialism and Education: the Politics of Resistance.* Toronto, ON: Sense Publishing.

Doucet, A., & Mauthner, N.S. (2006). Feminist methodologies and epistemology. *21st Century Sociology, Volume 2* (p.36–42). Sage Publications. http://www.andreadoucet.com/wp-content/uploads/2010/11/Doucet-Mauthner-2005-Feminist-Methodologies-and-Epistemologies.pdf.

Dunleavy, P., Margetts, H., Bastow, S. & Tinkler, J. (2005). New public management is dead --long live digital-era governance. *Journal of Public Administration Research and Theory, 16*, 467–494.

Elias, P., Luk, A., Perry, J., Qureshi, N., Wyper, L. (2021). Adult Literacy Policy and Practitioners: Sites of Contradiction and Resistance. In Brigham, S.M., McGray, R., Jubas, K. (Eds.). *Adult Education and Learning in Canada: Advancing a Critical Legacy* (2021). Canadian Association for the Study of Adult Education (CASAE).

Gherardi, S. (2008). Situated knowledge and situated action: What do practice-based studies Promise? *The Sage Handbook of New Approaches to Organization Studies.* pp. 516–527. https://www.researchgate.net/publication/292654065_Situated_knowledge_and_situated_action_What_do_practice-based_studies_promise.

Gonzalez, R. (2015). Anti-colonialism. *Citelighter.* [Video File]. http://www.citelighter.com/political-science/comparative-politics/knowledgecards/anti-colonialism.

Haque, M.S. (n.d.). New public management: origins, dimensions, and critical applications. *UNESCO– EOLSS Sample Chapters Public Administration and Public Policy, (1)*1–8. http://www.eolss.net/Sample-Chapters/C14/E1-34-04-01.pdf.

Haraway, D. (1991). *Simians, Cyborgs and Women: the Reinvention of Nature*. London: Free Association Books.

Harro, B. (2010a). The Cycle of Socialization. In Adams, M., Blumenfeld, W.J., Castaneda, C., Hackman, H.W., Peters, M.L., and Zuniga, X. (Eds.), (2010). *Readings for Diversity and Social Justice* (2nd ed.), pp. 45–51. New York: Routledge, Taylor & Francis Group.

Harro, B. (2010b). The Cycle of Liberation. In Adams, M., Blumenfeld, W.J., Castaneda, C., Hackman, H.W., Peters, M.L., and Zuniga, X. (Eds.), (2010). *Readings for Diversity and Social Justice* (2nd ed.), pp. 52–58. New York: Routledge, Taylor & Francis Group.

Hennessy, T., & Sawchuk, P. (2003). Worker response to technological change in the Canadian public sector: Issues of learning and labour process. *Journal of Workplace Learning, 15*(7/8), 28–43.

Hesse-Biber, S.N. (2012). *Handbook of Feminist Research: Theory and Praxis* (2nd ed.). Boston College: Sage Publications Inc. https://www.sagepub.com/sites/default/files/upm-binaries/43563_1.pdf.

Iseke-Barnes, J.M. (2008). Pedagogies for decolonizing. *Canadian Journal of Native Education, 31*(1), 123–148.

Joshee, R. (2014). *Policy Webs: Democratic Approaches to Policy and Education, Diversity, Social Justice; Course Summing-Up*. Lecture. CIE 1006: Democracy, Human Rights and Democratic Education in an Era of Globalization (Democratic Education & Globalization), Session 7. OISE. Toronto, ON.

Lange, E.A., Chovanec, D.M., Cardinal, T., Kajner, T., & Acuna, N.S. (2015). Wounded learners: Symbolic violence, educational justice, and re-engagement of low-income adults. *The Canadian Journal for the Study of Adult Education, 27*(3), 83–104.

Lapsley, I. (2009). New public management: the cruelest invention of the human spirit? *ABACUS: a Journal of Accounting, Finance and Business Studies, 45*(1), 1–21.

Lederach, J. P. (2006). Defining conflict transformation. *Peacework, 33*(368), 26–27.

Lombardo, E., & Mergaert, L. (2013). Gender mainstreaming and resistance to gender training: a framework for studying implementation. *Nordic Journal of Feminist and Gender Research, 21*(4), 296–311.

Martusewicz, R. A., Edmundson, J., & Lupinacci, J. (2011). *EcoJustice Education: Towards Diverse, Democratic, and Sustainable Communities*. New York: Routledge Taylor & Francis Group.

McDavid, J.C., Huse, I., & Hawthorn, L.R.L. (2013). *Program Evaluation and Performance Measurement: an Introduction to Practice*. Los Angeles: SAGE Publications, Inc.

Mignolo, W.D. (2011). Epistemic disobedience and the decolonial option: a manifesto. Transmodernity. *Journal of Peripheral Cultural Production of the Luso-Hispanic World, 1*(2), 45–66. http://escholarship.org/uc/item/62j3w283#page-3.

Niyozov, S., & Tarc, P. (Eds). (2015). Working with, against, and despite global 'best practices': Educational conversations around the globe. *A RICE / CIDEC compendium*.

RICE CIDEC Symposium at OISE, University of Toronto 2104. https://www.oise.utoronto.ca/cidec/UserFiles/File/Website/Compendium_GBP_Final_Jan_2016.pdf.

Patria, H.D. (2013). Uncultivated biodiversity in women's hands: How to create food sovereignty. *Asian Journal of Women's Studies, 19*(2), 148–161.

Phoenix, A. (2014). *Exercising Global Citizenship in the Family – the Case of Language Brokering*. http://unimelb.adobeconnect.com/p484l1kylfh/ CIE 1006: Democracy, Human Rights and Democratic Education in an Era of Globalization (Democratic Education & Globalization), Session 10. OISE. Toronto, ON.

Ryan, S., Connell, J., & Burgess, J. (2017). Casual academics: a new public management paradox. *Labour and Industry: a Journal of the Social and Economic Relations of Work, 27*(1), 56–72.

Sage, C. (2014). The transition movement and food sovereignty: from local resilience to global engagement in food system transformation. *Journal of Consumer Culture, 14*(2), 254–275.

Sekou, F. (2014). Race, class, and community organizing in support of economic justice initiatives in the twenty-first century. *Community Development Journal, 49*(2), 181–197.

Siltala, J. (2013). New public management: the evidence-based worst practice? *Administration and Society, 45*(4), 468–493.

Smith, L. T. (1999). *Decolonizing Methodologies: Research and Indigenous Peoples*. London: Zed Books.

Spring, J. (2008). Research on globalization and education. *Review of Educational Research, 78*(2), 330–363.

Starkey, H. (2012). Human rights, cosmopolitanism and utopias: implications for citizenship education. *Cambridge Journal of Education, 42*(1), 21–35.

Van der Sluis, M.E., Reezigt, G.J., & Borghans, L. (2017). Implementing new public management in educational policy. *Educational Policy, 31*(3), 303–329.

Wyper, L. (2018). *Neoliberal Conceptual Framing and the 'Disappearing' of Marginalized Adults from the Basic Adult Education Learning Landscape in Ontario*. [Unpublished PhD dissertation]. University of Toronto. https://tspace.library.utoronto.ca/bitstream/1807/87302/3/Wyper_Laura_E_201803_PhD_thesis.pdf.

Wyper, L. (2019). What is basic adult education? And who gets to learn? *Access Learning Careers and Identities*. ESREA./Rennes 2 University.

CHAPTER 10

Remembering in Research

Doing Research in Asian Communities

Rose Ann Torres

1   Introduction

Research is a collection and analysis of data (Bryman & Bell, 2019; Padgett, 2017; Torres, 2021; Torres & Nyaga, 2021). Simply put, it is a method we use to know everything about what we want to accomplish, and the reason why we can forecast what will happen in the future. Research allows us to make estimates based on the data we gathered through the studies we conducted. It helps us regulate mechanisms that make people thrive or struggle. It determines whether we can create a policy or not. It dictates the nature of the policy that will be used in health, education, financial, and other sectors to regulate the population.

Research has been used to collect information from different individuals and communities. These individuals often are racialized and Indigenous people. What is interesting is that researchers seemingly are intrigued by the notion of using racialized and Indigenous peoples as a subject of study. Yet, researchers' fascination with racialized and Indigenous peoples can wind up as a way to address issues in communities or to recolonize the very same communities. These communities are subjected to researchers' demands to get information (referred to also as data, material, evidence, facts, statistics, figures, etc.). The question is: Do we continue allowing this to happen to marginalized communities? We need to reimagine how research is conducted in Asian communities in way that community members are respected, valued, and loved. We need to ask ourselves about the allure and attraction that motivates researchers to use racialized and Indigenous participants in their studies. What is it in the lives of racialized and Indigenous persons that researchers always want to know? And why do they want to know? What compels researchers to use racialized and Indigenous populations as a subject of study? And why is remembering an ethical prerogative of the research process?

As an Asian educator, my focus is understanding how we do research in the Asian communities through remembering (Keightley, 2010; Kenten, 2010; Kuhn, 2005). Some may argue that the different approaches of qualitative methodology—such as narrative inquiry, ethnography, grounded theory, phenomenology, and case studies—are appropriate enough to conduct research; however, in this chapter, I am not focusing on any of these approaches. Instead, I would like to explore how remembering must be included in the process of research. Therefore, what I am going to outline in this chapter are the different ways to remember when we conduct research. But I must note at the outset that this is not the only way of doing research; instead, it is a way in which we can begin to think how we can conduct research within and without the Asian communities from anti-racist, critical race feminist, and anti-oppressive approaches.

2   Who Am I in Relation to Research?

I was introduced to research in a university setting. I considered research as one of the most challenging aspects of postsecondary education because I thought I was expected to follow rules and regulations. I was very confused because I could not relate on a personal level to any such rules and regulations; they were far removed from who I was—and who I am. It was hard for me to conceptualize a statement of the problem (and all the other parts of a research proposal) because I was expected to adhere to a certain format, methodology, and structure to construct a statement. This was a very alienating experience for me. The lived realities of the community that I wanted to know more about could not be made to "fit" into a structure that ultimately would alter (if not completely eradicate) their story. The methodology that I was told to follow was completely contradictory to what I saw in the community that I grew up with. The format that I was instructed to follow to construct a statement of the problem made me feel far removed from my own community. It was a painful process for me to comply with the rules of thesis writing that were not connected to or informed by the very community upon which my research was based.

Thinking of my university experience, I feel some embarrassment as I reflect on the people who were involved in my research. My experience was not helpful in building a relationship with the community: I did not get a chance to build that relationship, and I did not know how to build relationships. It was not part of my research course. I also did not ask how to do so. I was not informed in class that I should build relationships. Doing research becomes a necessary process to gain something out of the pain of the other. The research process is commodified and one-sided; the researcher asks questions, and the participant responds. I see this kind of research process as being problematic because it does not involve any deeper engagement about the topic; it's all about finishing the research. The finished product is a form of reward to some and detrimental to others.

This way of doing research has nothing to do with transforming or bettering society. It is about making sure that the systems that either dominate or privilege us remain intact. It is a way of feeding the system that privileges some and subordinates others. It is about forgetting the other while researcher "gets the prize"—a reward that is meant to remember the researcher and disremember the participants. This kind of research is a manifestation of how coloniality is entrenched through the rules, regulations, and practices embodied in the *how* of doing research. I wondered what I could do to address the colonial research methodology that continues to denigrate and undermine study participants, especially the Indigenous and marginalized communities in Canada. I decided not to remain in my comfortable vantage point while they who participate in our research suffer the consequences.

3   Understanding the Histories and Manifestation of Colonization in Canada

We cannot claim that we do exhaustive research if it does not include the histories of colonization and "resistance" (Lo, 2008). However, it is important to know the difference between knowing and understanding history. *Knowing* history is about having the knowledge but not doing anything about it; *understanding* history is about wanting to know about the history and wanting to change its trajectory—a trajectory that looks at the details of colonization and how it continues to manifest in our everyday lives. It comes with an intent of understanding how history affects the present time and having the interest of interrogating whiteness and white supremacy.

This methodology of remembering the history is very important to consider when conducting research so we understand how issues we experience come into being. One of my Filipino students in the university shared with me her experience of going to counselling in Canada. She expected to receive support from the counsellor but instead ended up feeling stigmatized. When I asked her what could have been done differently during the counselling process, she informed me that the counsellor should have focused on the root cause of the issues that lead her to seek help, instead of being offered advice that was not useful to her. This scenario helps us to rethink the methodology that we use in our research. While the scenario pertains to the field of counselling, it is closely aligned with research practice: Before delving into the solution, we need to explore the root cause of a problem.

In this same way, although the research topic may be about a contemporary issue that involves perceptions of Asians, we cannot disconnect the topic from the history of colonization that in turn informs how contemporary issues exist. Rules and regulations are grounded upon the legacy of colonization. Even the ways in which we research are colonial in nature. "This present ontology of liberal democratic nation-states such as the United States and Canada involves forgetting the history of white supremacy, racism, and Western imperial projects that proved central to the states' formation and ascendancy" (Pon, 2009, p. 66). The ontology of forgetting the history of colonization is a manifestation of a racist society; it is about shifting the gaze to Indigenous and racialized people so that they are to be blamed for their experiences of different layers of oppression. When individuals continue to be blamed for their own hardships, the sense of culpability embeds deeply in their psyche—so much so that they now believe that such oppression is their own fault.

This tactic of domination is important from the perspective of the oppressors because it epitomizes the way they now control, divide, and ultimately annihilate the oppressed. For example, in one of the studies that I conducted in the Filipino community in Toronto, I asked respondents for their views on the issue of racism. I expected that they would tell me about their experiences with racism but instead they told me how thankful they were to be in Canada, how Canada is a very "nice place," and that the Canadian government is so generous. This kind of answer reflects how the system uses money, services, welfare assistance, and so on to imprint itself into the psyche of an individual. It is a form of training the mind of the oppressed to forget the history of colonization in which we otherwise could discern patterns of domination against Indigenous and racialized people. Regardless of the topic we are researching, we need to include a discussion of colonization as a way to remind us that whatever is going on now is connected to the history of colonization. For example, current policies used to regulate us are connected to those that were founded upon colonization. Pon et al. (2011) for instance note that:

> Racism and sexism were evident in Section 10 of [Canada's Immigration Act of 1923] that stipulated that applicants for a certificate of citizenship who were not fluent in English or French required a residency period of 20 years. Those fluent in French and English were required to have only five years of residency. But non-white immigrant women were the most likely of applicants not to be fluent in French or English. In this way the Act maintained and reproduced systemic racism and sexism.
>
> p. 390

As researchers, I believe it is necessary to address the history of colonization in our engagement with study participants, something that I (mistakenly) had overlooked in my previous study among the Filipino community in Canada. We cannot discuss racism without having a critical engagement about the history of colonization and white supremacy. And so, what happened in my field research study was that I informed them about my study, and with so much excitement, I asked them about racism. Yet because I asked my participants about racism without having explained to them the meaning of race and racism, or illustrating how race has been used to divide and categorize Asians, then I could not expect a critical answer. It is not because the participants do not already "know" about race and racism; rather the onus is on researchers to engage with participants by telling them what we think about an important topic (in this case, racism) rather than putting all the responsibility on them. If I had taken the responsibility and shared what I know about the colonial history of Canada, my participants' responses likely would have been different. Through this, the conversation could have been focused about Indigenous people in Canada, and how colonization impacted their lives. I also could have asked them about the history of the so-called head tax in Canada, and if they had not heard of it, it would have been a good opportunity for me to share with them what I know. In this way they could have seen that their experiences are connected to the legacy of colonization.

Researchers have the ethical responsibility to begin a conversation with participants in a manner that the latter could have an opportunity to lead the conversation as well. The problem that we are having in the process of collecting data is that researchers impose a hierarchy of order of how to do things. For example, the current model tends to expect participants to ask any questions for clarification—questions they may not even know to ask! What if we reverse or dismantle the order of how to do things in research? What if we forget the order and let the discussion flow? What would that look like? This will give the participants the opportunity to remember the history of colonization and to connect their experience to with that of colonization.

According to Gupta et al. (2014), "in the context of [a] particular focus on professional immigrant women from India and China, there is the added challenge of taking into account capitalist relations in their originating countries that are imposed upon and interact with pre-capitalist, colonial, post-colonial and socialist formations" (p. 58). The discussion of history helps us all to understand the social formations that manifest because of the everyday experiences of an individual through the system of domination—an experience that has been influenced by different forms of ongoing colonization. In doing research, it is important to understand how these different social formations came into being. We need to (re)construct a new way of doing research. Community engagement should occur only when the communities themselves are the ones who tell us how we should go about engaging with them. Much research has been undertaken under the guise of community engagement, but we must ask ourselves: What kind of engagement does a community allow us to do when universities lead the research? What perspectives are being adopted in terms of the meaning of engagement? Who determines the different forms of engagement? If engagement is defined based on colonial interpretations and models of reciprocity, how do we use this in the communities? How do we do engage minoritized communities when the call is from and helmed by a university researcher? Who made the decision in terms of the process of community engagement? What are the ethical issues that we need to pay attention to when we engage in the community? How do we define ethics? And who established such definitions in the first place?

Frantz Fanon encapsulates the experience of racialized people in a Western country:

> I had to meet the white man's eyes. An unfamiliar weight burdened me. In the white world the man of Color encounters difficulties in the development of his bodily schema. ... I was battered down by tom-toms, cannibalism, intellectual deficiency, fetishism, racial defects. ... I took myself far off from own presence. ... What else could it be for me but an amputation, an excision, a hemorrhage that spattered my whole body with black blood?.
>
> As cited in BHABBA, 2004, p. 60

The feeling of amputation is symbolic, in that individuals who forget (or have never been introduced to) the history of colonization can experience psychic amputation. When we talk about amputation, we are focusing about ejection or exclusion from or discrimination by the dominant segment of the population based on racialization. The Indigenous Peoples in Canada have experienced such psychic (not to mention cultural and geographic) amputation through the country's residential school system (Barkan, 2003; Bombay et al., 2011, 2012, 2014). We become numb to such injustice and atrocity, and because of our numbness, we tend to accept racism as the status quo—that it's okay. We consider it as an individual's fault. While I acknowledge that individuals all may have some responsibility in their acceptance or rejection of their own oppression, we must not forget that the system is implicated in the oppression of people, and that each person experiences oppression differently based on race, class, gender, and other forms of differences.

Researchers must find a way to have a discussion on how racism manifests in different ways. It can manifest through the research method of collecting data if we are not critical in the *how* of doing research. For example, if we ask questions in our research that have no explanation, why ask such questions? There is a need to explain and have a dialogue with the participants about the questions being asked in the research process. This way the participants can perhaps identify ways they have been racialized. Research goals should always be aligned with the communities' goals. If the goals of the communities are to subvert issues that have been "amputating" them, then researchers should ask the communities about ways to address such issues. How do we do this in our research? Simply put, the study participants should have a say in the process of research.

George (2017) states that "Critical and anti-oppressive social work research is premised on the notion that research has political purpose and has the potential to galvanize communities for addressing societal injustices inequities" (p. 29). This can only be achieved when we approach research from the participants' perspectives. Western researchers need to reject the notion of doing research from a colonial perspective. Indigenous people have been calling out researchers to do research from their own perspectives (Smith, 1999). The research must respect the existence of different communities and refrain from collecting data only for the vested interest of the researcher (Smith, 1999). If we collect data from this point of view, then we miss some of the nuances of issues we want to explore.

There should be a wider conversation of how to go about doing research in the communities, with individuals who are in vulnerable positions. They are in vulnerable positions because of the process of ongoing colonization in different aspects of our society. What I have in mind when we do research is the discourse of whiteness in research. How does whiteness manifest in research? What is whiteness or white supremacy? According to Yee (2015), "Whiteness can be viewed as the normalization of helping those who are marginalized via a set of practices and techniques that, in the end, maintains the status quo of privileging white people and failing to recognize systemic and structural inequalities" (p. 569). It manifests through the process of doing research within Indigenous and marginalized communities that purports to assist them but still uses methodologies that maintain the same power imbalance to marginalize them (Smith, 1999)—research that never intended to question the systemic and structural inequalities that underpin research. It is research that takes information from the participants and never acknowledges the true owner of knowledge (Torres & Nyaga, 2021). It is research that privileges one knowledge over the other. It is research that objectifies the participants. It is research that (un)intentionally maintains participants' position as the oppressed rather than shedding light on the truth. It is research that reiterates that the subjects do not have culture (Torres, 2017) and they do not have the capacity to resolve the challenges they face. Research that commodifies those lives of Indigenous and marginalized groups. Whiteness and white supremacy can easily co-opt research, more so when the methodology is coming from a colonialist perspective. More pointedly, researchers' use of certain methods without critically assessing how they have been applied in the communities is dangerous.

4   Communities' Histories Are Fluid

There are many Asian communities in Canada. Making assumptions about a community without understanding how it evolved based on external circumstances may give our study misleading results. Colonization has been embedded in every aspect of our lives. In other words, we have been internalizing colonization without even knowing it. We need to be critically reflexive in ways that we look at the very simple struggles that we face in connection to the global struggles that we collectively experience. Still, while we may collectively share life's struggles, it does not mean that we experience them in similar ways. Race, class, gender, sexuality, and other intersecting and interlocking markers of identity need to be considered when we talk about collective struggles. Therefore, although it is important to know the histories of the individuals and communities that we seek to investigate, we must be aware of who is telling the story of such history. There are many books written about histories of the world, communities, peoples, cultures, and practices. If these histories have been written to propagate one discourse, then we have a reason to questions such written materials.

Bhabha (2004) states that:

> Our existence today is marked by a tenebrous sense of survival, living on the borderlines of the "present," for which there seems to be no proper name other than the current and controversial shiftiness of the prefix "post": post modernism, post colonialism, post feminism. ... The "beyond" is neither a new horizon, nor a leaving behind nor of the past. ... Beginning and endings may be the sustaining myths of the middle years; but in the fin de siècle, we find ourselves in the moment of transit where space and time cross to produce complex figures of difference and identity, past and present, inside and outside, inclusion and exclusion.
>
> p. 2

Bhabha explains clearly how our existence in our communities is complex and shifting. We cannot ascertain any single, definitive description about these communities. For example, if we make an assumption that a community of Filipinos who live in Toronto's Jane and Finch neighborhood all benefit from social welfare, we must first ask: What is social welfare? Indeed, why is it that a government provides this kind of service? Why are certain groups of racialized people involved in social welfare programs? Has social welfare been used to sustain the ongoing struggles of these communities? How is social welfare implicated in the making of the "other"? And who exactly deems the other as being the other? These are some of the questions that can help us to better understand the relationship between Canada and the racialized community. These kinds of questions help us realize the implications of the institutional powers (the "system") in relation to the experiences of Asians in Canada.

A convenient description of one's community can result in non-existence. As there are different communities, so too are there many different experiences in each community, including in terms of how community members negotiate their positions in Canada. These forms of negotiations stem from their ability to see beyond their existence. Like in my research that I conducted in the Filipino community, their ways of breaking down the issues that they experience in their communities are so deep. When I say deep, I mean how they explained to me the hidden meanings of each of their experiences. They connect the dots and give meanings to each of these dots. To describe them collectively as meek or subservient is not a correct interpretation of who they are.

We should not forget, for example, the aforementioned head tax, nor Japanese interment, nor the Komagata Maru incident when we look at the struggles of Asians in Canada. According to Pon (2009), "rushing to practice is often related to a refusal to engage with learning about social violence, such as colonialism, racism, and slavery, which can cause intense difficulty for learners" (p. 21). Such knowledge is difficult for learners because learning about racism often entails the challenging work of self-knowledge, including acknowledging how we are all implicated in contradictory relationships of oppression. The danger of doing so in research is that we tend to place the blame on marginalized participants rather than on the systems and institutions that are the root cause of their oppression.

5 Asian Communities and the Discourse of Class

As Reay (1998) reminds us, "what it means to be middle or working class, black or white, female or male shifts and changes, not only from one historical era to another, but for individuals over time as they negotiate the social world" (p. 266). Class struggles cannot be disconnected from participants' experiences. This is to acknowledge that we all have different experiences, predicated on different locations, spaces, boundaries, and imaginations. In doing research, all these things need to be considered. Males, females, LGBTQ+, girls, boys, the young and the old all may have different levels of class, and class is not merely about the financial and social resources we have but also the emotion that we put into everything that we do. We cannot quantify the definition of class, because if this is how we define class it eliminates others who never acquire resources because of their race or other forms of categorization, but they work so hard. Gupta et al. (2014) argue for a different conceptualization of class, stating

> that the shift from "traits" to relations allows us to think about class as a process—a journey that individuals undertake, not only within a particular society, but as they move between and across national boundaries and borders. This conceptualization allows us to render a more dynamic analysis of class, not only as a set of fixed positions, but as performance; that is, in order for class to be visible in the social world, it has to be enacted by people on a continuous basis through their daily lives as they interact with each other and reproduce their livelihood.
> p. 57

Gupta et al.'s definition of class helps us to understand how we need to consider it in the research process. This quote also suggests that there is a need to redefine class beyond having material things.

Nonetheless, Canada has marginalized Indigenous and racialized communities who do not possess the Canadian education and experience. We need to reimagine class in a different way that encompasses sacrifices, desires, and struggles. When I say sacrifices, I refer to individuals who work hard but are not recognized because they have not obtained the necessary qualifications that have been prescribed to them. This qualification is a colonial tool meant to disregard the contributions of Indigenous and people of colour. For example, most of the Filipino caregivers in Canada are Filipino women (Nyaga & Torres, 2017) who have a university degree, yet these caregivers often receive less than the minimum wage and must work long hours without being paid overtime rates. When you look at this kind of work, a caregiver is an essential worker who is tasked with a family's well-being, including the preparation of food, making sure the house is clean, as well as intensive personal, bodily care for persons who are unable to do so independently. In other words, they take care of families' physical, emotional, social, and spiritual well-being. Their presence is a significant contribution to their employer because they do the work that sustains the family. For example, they may tutor their employer's children, although such responsibility is not considered as part of their salaried work because it's not part of the contract; many of them are deemed to be nannies who are not supposed to think—they are not considered to be thinking beings. This very act of not considering Filipino caregivers as thinking beings is a manifestation of racism. However, Filipino caregivers fight back! They fight back from a non-violent perspective, using love as a way to counter racism.

Thus, how do we capture this meaning of class that clearly defines the work of the women? If we do research and blindly use the methods that have been set up to consider the linear meaning of class and dismiss other ways of doing work, then we end setting a path to failure and oppression for participants like the caregivers in my study. What we need to remember in the doing of research is to look at class from the ontology of the participants and not the textbook that has been drafted by those who have been given the opportunity to produce knowledge. What if we forget the methods of research and allow the participants to speak of their lived realities? I argue that if we adopt such an equitable approach to research, we may be able to see them not just as participants but as knowledge co-creators. Indigenous healers have been sharing their knowledge of healing but because of their class, they are not considered as people who can put forth valid ideas in the broader system of science and medicine. There is thus a need to reimagine class beyond materiality (Reay, 1998). In this we can adapt other ways of knowing.

6 We Must Remember That They Speak Different Languages

In doing research it is important to consider the participants' languages. To know the language of the participants is to understand their way of life—their customs, traditions, desires, memories, pains, and sufferings. All these things are connected to their languages. Most of the time, researchers focus on how they can gather information, with little time to more deeply understand participants' language. Western-based researchers often use English when conducting their studies and will employ translators during interviews or transcriptions if their participants cannot speak English. This is the simplest way of collecting data. But the question remains: Is research all about collecting data haphazardly and forgetting the realities of the participants? Are we seeing the participants as data only? What happens to their desire—their desire to give more meaningful information—which can only be garnered when participants have the opportunity to speak in their language and about their language? Language is a powerful tool in fighting against oppression, particularly among oppressed Asians. According to Gupta et al. (2014),

> the lack of English language proficiency (especially among Chinese immigrants) and Canadian experience (for women from both China and India) are by now standard rationales for excluding immigrants from high ranking positions. They are thus forced to take up entry level jobs that are poorly remunerated compared to their white Canadian counterparts with similar or identical qualifications and work experience.
>
> p. 67

Gupta et al. succinctly explain how language has been used as a tool to discriminate against immigrants. How do we then use language in our research that will not discriminate against participants? How do we then incorporate participants' language in our research? Language is an expression of everything.

7 We Must Understand That the Newcomer Is Socially Constructed

Pon (2009) states that "the modernist notions of newcomers and Canadian culture are central aspects of the process of othering. The concept of the newcomer and Canadian culture reify the former as 'other'" (p. 68). In this way the newcomer is socially constructed as being different from Canadians and belonging outside of the nation-state. According to this logic, the newcomer and the Canadian culture are mutually exclusive and binary categories. As researchers, we must understand that the notion of newcomer is socially constructed because otherwise we end up dismissing the impact of colonization. It is one of the ways of claiming that racialized people do not know about Canada. Such an approach is very insidious because it can be used to justify why minoritized populations are living in poverty. They cannot question anything because they are newcomers; the dominant society has full control of their lives—the way they think, how they feel, how they react, how they move about in social environments, what they eat, and so many other things that are beyond their control. This is a mechanism to divide their lives into multiple parts, a psychic fragmentation through which they cannot reconcile why they are doing what they are doing.

As researchers, it is important that we clearly understand the notion that newcomers are socially constructed for the purpose of racializing (i.e., "othering") people who come from another country (Thobani, 2007). It is way of muting somebody so that this raced, gendered, and classed society can continue to execute violence (Razack, 2005). So, when newcomers can no longer imagine themselves, they can be easily sucked in by society. When a researcher is not aware of how this socially constructed notion of newcomer works, then research becomes violent. Violent because we are taking information from the people who are now fully controlled by the system without their permission. We are extracting information from the people who are so called newcomers without their consent.

8   We Must Remember That They Have Histories of Resistance

In every struggle and challenge faced by marginalized communities, there are different forms of resiliency and agency (Torres, 2021). For example, Filipino communities have founded different social organizations that allow them to work collectively in navigating the different challenges they face. They also use such venues to address the issues they face in their communities. For example, during the COVID-19 pandemic, an Ottawa-based Filipino organization was able to get a funding to bring together Filipinos to talk about resiliency both during and beyond the pandemic (Damasco & Torres, 2021). In every community, they are doing something to address the challenges that they encounter. In doing research, it is important to include information corresponding to how marginalized communities are responding to the challenges that they face. We must understand that when investigate the struggles of our participants, we must simultaneously focus of their different forms of resistance. Focusing solely on their challenges and overlooking their forms of resistance essentially symbolizes (and perpetuates) the systems that dominate such marginalized communities. It shows that we are not ready to engage in the *how* of addressing problems. We thus must remind ourselves that such communities have agency and resiliency.

9   Conclusion

This chapter discusses different ways to do research in the Asian communities. I argue that we must remember the history of colonization, because it will help us understand and engage with problem of anti-Asian racism. I also discuss the reasons why we need to be aware that there are many Asian communities in Canada, communities with diverse experiences in terms of anti-Asian racism, sexism, classism, and other forms of oppression. I also discussed the importance of understanding their language. Language is so important in different Asian communities. Our language means lives. We can only engage critically and ethically with the participants when we understand and speak their language. One of my students said that language is where we can find healing. I wholeheartedly agree with my student that language is powerful; it connects us to where we belong.

I also explored the discourse of newcomer as socially constructed. The construction of the word "newcomer" is not innocuous as it may appear. It is political and it determines the way of life of the other. It is a question of citizenship—that even when newcomers obtain formal citizenship through registration, they often are not perceived as true "citizen" because they were "newcomers" to start with. It a political discourse that eliminates some and privileges others. This newcomer becomes even more problematic when we now include the discussion of race, class, gender, and other forms of categories. As researcher, we are ethically obligated to know how such discourse affects Asian research participants. And finally, I included a discussion of resistance. I argued that we cannot keep exploring the pain of Asian participants without exploring how they have resisted the tribulations they encounter. I also maintained that in every form of colonization facing Indigenous and racialized groups like Asian communities, they fight back.

These are some of the topics we cannot forget no matter what research methodologies we use, be they quantitative or qualitive approaches. For scholars whose research interest is Asian communities, it is important to incorporate history, culture, and forms of resistance, among considerations. I argue that to ethically embark on research within the Asian communities we must consider the participants' race, gender, class, and other forms of categorization that serve only to (re)produce imbalances of power within and beyond these communities. We must not only focus on their struggles but also understand that their dilemma is not of their creation; it is connected to the systems and institutions founded upon the legacy of colonization.

References

Barkan, E. (2003). Genocides of Indigenous Peoples: Rhetoric of Human Rights. In R. Gellately & B. Kiernan (Eds.), *The Specter of Genocide: Mass Murder in Historical Perspective* (pp. 117–140). Cambridge University Press. https://doi.org/10.1017/CBO9780511819674.006.

Bhabba, H. K. (2004). *The Location of Culture*. Routledge.

Bombay, A., Matheson, K., & Anisman, H. (2011). The impact of stressors on second generation Indian residential school survivors. *Transcultural Psychiatry, 48*(4), 367–391. https://doi.org/10.1177/1363461511410240.

Bombay, A., Matheson, K., & Anisman, A. (2012). Personal Wellness and After-school Activities. In The First Nations Information Governance Centre (Ed.), *First Nations Regional Health Survey (RHS) phase 2 (2008/10): National Report on the Adult, Youth, and Children Living in First Nations Communities* (pp. 340–357). The First Nations Information Governance Centre.

Bombay, A., Matheson, K., & Anisman, H. (2014). Appraisals of discriminatory events among adult offspring of Indian Residential School survivors: the influences of identity centrality and past perceptions of discrimination. *Cultural Diversity and Ethnic Minority Psychology, 20*(1), 75–86. https://doi.org/10.1037/a0033352.

Bryman, A., & Bell, E. (2019). *Social Research Methods* (5th ed.). Oxford University Press.

Damasco, V. G., & Torres, R. A. (2021). Framework for Developing Resilience among Filipino-Canadian Youth during the COVID-19 Pandemic. In R. Torres, K. Leung, & V. Soepriatna (Eds.), *Outside and in-between: Theorizing Asian Canadian Exclusion and the Challenges of Identity Formation* (pp. 251–258). Brill. https://doi.org/10.1163/9789004466357_021.

George, P. (2017). Critical Arts-based Research: an Effective Strategy for Knowledge Mobilization and Community Activism. In H. Parada & S. Wehbi (Eds.), *Reimagining Anti-oppression Social Work Research* (pp. 29–38). Canadian Scholars.

Gupta, T. D., Man, G., Mirchandani, K., & Ng, R. (2014). Class borders: Chinese and South Asian Canadian professional women navigating the labor market. *Asian and Pacific Migration Journal, 23*(1), 55–83. https://doi.org/10.1177%2F011719681402300103.

Keightley, E. (2010). Remembering research: Memory and methodology in the social sciences. *International Journal of Social Research Methodology, 13*(1), 55–70. https://doi.org/10.1080/13645570802605440.

Kenten, C. (2010). Narrating oneself: Reflections on the use of solicited diaries with diary interviews. *Forum: Qualitative Social Research, 11*(2), Article 16. https://doi.org/10.17169/fqs-11.2.1314.

Kuhn, A. (2005). *An Everyday Magic: Cinema and Cultural Memory*. I.B. Tauris.

Lo, M. (2008, Spring). Model minorities, models of resistance: Native figures in Asian Canadian literature. *Canadian Literature*, 196, 96–112. https://canlit.ca/full-issue/?issue=196.

Nyaga, D., & Torres, R. A. (2017). Gendered citizenship: a case study of paid Filipino male live-in caregivers in Toronto. *International Journal of Asia Pacific Studies, 13*(1), 51–71. http://doi.org/10.21315/ijaps2017.13.1.3.

Padgett, D. K. (2017). Choosing the Right Qualitative Approach(es). In *Qualitative Methods in Social Work Research* (3rd ed., pp. 31–56). SAGE.

Pon, G. (2009). Cultural competency as new racism: an ontology of forgetting. *Journal of Progressive Human Services*, *20*(1), 59–71. https://doi.org/10.1080/10428230902871173.

Pon, G., Gosine, K., & Phillips, D. (2011). Immediate response: Addressing anti-Native and anti-black racism in child welfare. *International Journal of Child, Youth and Family Studies*, *2*(3–4), 385–409. https://doi.org/10.18357/ijcyfs23/420117763.

Razack, S. (2005). How is white supremacy embodied? Sexualized racial violence at Abu Ghraib. *Canadian Journal of Women and the Law*, *17*(2), 341–363.

Reay, D. (1998). Rethinking social class: Qualitative perspectives on class and gender. *Sociology*, *32*(2), 259–275. https://doi.org/10.1177%2F0038038598032002003.

Smith, L. T. (1999). *Decolonizing Methodologies: Research and Indigenous Peoples*. Zed Books.

Thobani, S. (2007). *Exalted Subjects: Studies in the Making of Race and Nation in Canada*. University of Toronto Press.

Torres, R. A. (2017). Transforming Indigenous Curriculum in the Philippines through Indigenous Women's Knowledge and Practices: a Case Study on Aeta Women Healers. In N. Phasha, D. Mahlo, & G. J. S. Dei (Eds.), *Inclusive Education in African Contexts: a Critical Reader* (pp. 173–189). Sense. https://doi.org/10.1007/978-94-6300-803-7_12.

Torres, R. A. (2021). Research Methodologies: History, Issues, Tensions. In R. A. Torres & D. Nyaga (Eds.), *Critical Research Methodologies: Ethics and Responsibilities* (pp. 24–32). Brill.

Torres, R. A., & Nyaga, D. (Eds.). (2021). *Critical Research Methodology: Ethics and Responsibilities*. Brill.

Yee, J. Y. (2015). Whiteness and White Supremacy. In J. D. Wright (Ed.), *International Encyclopedia of the Social and Behavioral Sciences* (2nd ed., pp. 569–574). Elsevier. https://doi.org/10.1016/B978-0-08-097086-8.28099-9.

CHAPTER 11

Application of Research to Africa's Peace and Security Conundrum

The Ethical and Moral Divide between the Ideal and Real

Michael Sitawa

1   Introduction

Research is considered a fundamental aspect in understanding the peace and security situation in Africa. The scientific research offers a number of advantages which include understanding the causes of conflict as well as the prerequisites for peace. Nutley, Percy-Smith & Solesbury (2003) posit that research offers a two-pronged analysis to peace-building in conceptual and instrumental use. Conceptually, through analysis, and instrumentally through informing policy formulation. In the case of the former, research is applicable in shaping understanding, attitudes and knowledge of conflict while in the former, it is meant to impact policy formulation to bring about more enhanced interventions. In either case, fundamental questions have been posed regarding who exactly crafts the policies on behalf of Africa.

In a bid to fully appreciate the scope of conflicts at whatever stage they lie in the conflict cycle, research methodology plays a prominent role. Keen to note is the level of adoption of scientific approach that various organs at global, continental and at national level (for some countries) have put in place in form of early warning, conflict monitoring as well as post-conflict reconstruction.

2   The United Nations Security Council (UNSC)

This is one of the six organs of the United Nations (with the others being the General Assembly, the Economic and Social Council, the Trusteeship Council, the International Court of Justice, and the UN Secretariat.) established under Chapters 5–7, Articles 23–54 of the UN Charter of 1945. The primary responsibility of the UNSC is maintenance of international peace and security. The Security Council, among other roles are calling for peaceful negotiation of disputes and the imposition of sanctions or authorizations of enforcement in order to maintain international peace and security. It takes the lead role in the identification and determination of potential threats to peace and stability as well as acts of aggression across the world (United Nations, 2021).

The Security Council activities are significantly informed by research findings from across the UN agencies, regional bodies and member states. Chapter 6 of the of the UN Charter also rationalizes the need to embrace early warning in a bid to avert conflicts. As Article 34 of the Chapter states,

> The Security Council may investigate any dispute, or any situation which might lead to international friction or give rise to a dispute, in order to determine whether the continuance of the dispute or situation is likely to endanger the maintenance of international peace and security.

The General Assembly and Security Council resolutions adopted in 2016 (A/70/262 and S/2282, respectively) on "sustaining peace", which include activities to that are aimed at prevention of the eruption, intensification, continuation and recurrence of conflict (United Nations Department of Political Affairs [UNDPA], n.d.). The Council points out a number of key elements which include the UN Resident Coordinators (RCs) and UN Country Teams. Through the support of UN, the RCs provide analysis and support conflict sensitive and preventive programming. This is made possible through the joint UNDP-DPA Programme on Building National Capacities for Conflict Prevention. Another element that is embracive of research is gender inclusion expertise which sees the UN engage in the deployment of experts on gender/women, peace and security who possess the ability to start and provide counsel on conflict analysis that is gender-sensitive in nature (UNDPA, n.d.). The aspects of gender-mainstreaming further draw their impetus from United Nations Security Council Resolutions 1325 and 2242 which lay emphasis on women's role in peace and security in their various capacities as military, police and civilian and a at various levels; strategic, tactical or operational.

3 Peace and Security Council (PSC) of the African Union

This is the African Union's (AU) principle decision-making organ on matters conflict prevention, management and resolution. Its configuration is meant to deliver on the continent's collective security and early warning response to conflict and crisis in a timely manner. As the key pillar of Africa's Peace and Security Architecture (APSA), among the various powers accorded to the Council as well as the Chairman of the African Union Commission is to anticipate and preclude conflicts, including policies and policy frameworks, which may result to massacres and other crimes against humanity. The anticipatory role of the PSC as stated above is indicative of the import that research offers to achieving collection and analysis of relevant data.

Africa Peace and Security Architecture is the main body that governs the African Union's key AU mechanisms on matters peace and security. It is composed of the African Standby Force, African Peace Fund, African Union Commission, Panel of the Wise and Continental Early Warning System. Figure 11.1 gives a diagrammatic presentation.

Of the five components, the Continental Early Warning Systems (CEWS) presents the strongest embeds of research as a critical aspect in solving Africa's peace and security conundrum. An establishment within article 12 of the PSC protocol, the Continental Early Warning System (CEWS) consists

FIGURE 11.1 Africa Peace and Security Architecture (APSA)
SOURCE: DESMIDT, S. (2016). PEACEBUILDING, CONFLICT PREVENTION AND CONFLICT MONITORING IN THE AFRICAN PEACE AND SECURITY ARCHITECTURE. EUROPEAN CENTRE FOR DEVELOPMENT AND POLICY MANAGEMENT. RETRIEVED ON 31-05-2023 FROM HTTPS://ECDPM.ORG/APPLICATION/FILES/8116/5546/8860/AFRICAN-PEACE-SECURITY-ARCHITECTURE-BACKGROUND-NOTE-ECDPM-2016.PDF

of an observation and monitoring centre referred to as the 'Situation Room' located in the Peace and Security Department. It also has satellite Observation and Monitoring Centres of the Regional Economic Communities (RECs) (AU, 2021). The Chairperson of the Commission uses the information gathered through the Early Warning System to provide necessary council to the PSC on impending conflicts and threats to peace and security in the continent as well as prescribe the most ideal course(s) of action (Desmidt, 2016).

In view of the sensitivity of its operations, it remains operational 24 hours a day (AU, 2021), receiving and analysing reports from potential 'hotspots', and dispatching them to the PSC Chairperson. In order to function at its optimum, CEWS has established collaboration with United Nations, its, agencies, research centres, international organisations, non-governmental organisations (NGOs) and academic institutions (Okumu, 2020).

4 Structuring Peace Support Operations in Africa

Africa has over the decades witnessed conflicts driven by various factors which revolve around resources, culture and power. In response, concerned actors such as the United Nations and African Union have structured responses in form of Peace Support Operations (PSOs). The United Nations under the United Nations Peace keeping. (PSOs) in their active sense can be defined as structured and deliberate intervention to prevent or de-escalate conflict, with the North Star being sustainable peace. From the above definition, PSO is applied in pre-conflict stage, active conflict and post-conflict. Within this framework, PSOs have been categorized into two: peacekeeping and peace enforcement. The latter aims to monitor and support the establishment of peace, usually in the context of a peace agreement and with the former focused on creating conditions for peace and are permitted to use force.

The Peace and Security Council (PSC) Protocol provides for Peace Support Operations (PSOs) to be a function and tool of the PSC and gives the Council powers to "authorize the mounting and deployment of peace support missions" and "lay down general guidelines for the conduct of such missions, including the mandate thereof, and undertaking of periodic reviews of these guidelines". PSC operations are also authorised by the UN Security Council in accordance with the UN Charter, Chapter 8, article 53(1).4

5 Conflict Triggers in Africa

Various models and theories have been fronted over time in a bid to shed light on reasons as to why groups in Africa (including others around the world) engage in violent conflict. An analysis of previous data sets and reports presented to and by the above-mentioned organizations all see them revolve around three issues: ideology, power struggle and resource control.

Within the ideological discourse, sociologists first conceptualize the term 'ideology' as the lens through which one observes and defines their surroundings and thus their 'world'. The concept of culture and socialization take a central role in shaping and calibrating this lens. Appreciative of the position taken by proponents of symbolic interactionism such as Herbert Blumer, George Herbert Mead, Peter Blau among others who opine that the family is the first agent of socialization, other agents over time interact with and shape the individual person. The result is a formed attitude. It is on the basis of varied attitudes and belief systems that persons may conflict. Individual persons will further, informed by socialization, respond to such conflicts differently which may sometimes culminate to conflict.

Africa has witnessed conflict that are triggered and fuelled by ethnic intolerance as witnessed in the Northern and the Middle Belt regions of Nigeria which according to Bolanle (2017), has manifested in form of Boko Haram insurgencies. These have left residents of cities like Gombe, Maiduguri, Damaturu and Bauchi living in constant fear. Boko Haram (Jamā'at Ahl al-Sunnah li-l-Da'awah wa al-Jihād), founded in 2002 by Muhammed Yusuf, often translated as "Association of the People of the Sunnah for Preaching and Jihad" or "People Committed to the Prophet's Teaching for Propagation and Jihad". In Somalia, the case is the same with respect to The Al Shabaab or youth who broke away from the Islamic Courts Union in 2006. According to Hansen (2013), in his research contextualizes the group as a hybrid Islamist organisation that is for Somali nationalism, bound by the dictates of international jihadism.

Power struggle is a dynamic that is well presented by the position taken by Ralf Dahrendorf (as cited in Weingart, 1969) who avers that conflict is an offshoot of power and authority tussles that exist between the rulers versus the ruled (super-ordinate and the subordinate). After giving a systematic account of the manner in which group formation is driven and dictated by social class, the *raison d'etre* is to emerge to have their way to or secure (a) seat(s) at the decision-making table. Dahrendorf lays out four potential outcomes: revolutions, coalition formation or democracies which, either way, grant the 'ruled' access to the corridors of power. The contrary is sometimes the case, when the ruled either scatter or completely annihilate the uprising mounted by the ruled. Throughout the entire process, there are situations that may be characterized by tension, such as in group formation, while others may degenerate into active conflicts such as revolutions. The above-stated situation of an overthrow in the African context can be illustrated in the case of President Yoweri Museveni's ascension to power in 1986 when he and former president Yusufu Kironde Lule formed the National Resistance Movement (NRM) deposing Milton Obote. The Arab Spring in the Sahel region is another pointer to deposition of leaders across various states in North Africa such as Zine El Abidine Ben Ali of Tunisia and Muhammad Hosni El Sayed Mubarak of Egypt in 2011.

Resource control and class consciousness are conflict triggers with their foundations/roots in Marxist philosophy by Karl Heinrich Marx (1818–1883). In his arguments, there are 'haves' and the 'have-nots' also referred to as the owners of the means of production and the wage workers/labourers. He is of the notion that owners of the means of production maintain resource control through ideological means such as religion or through the use of state machinery such as police or military. The use of the latter has often been characterized by tension with situations turning into violent conflict. Africa as a continent has witnessed a number of such cases; some of which have been presented by the ethnic banner. The divisions are therefore a direct assault on the unity that Africans once held, serving as key platforms for various social, economic and cultural engagements. The writings of Walter Rodney (1973) give a chronological analyses of how society's modes of production has transitioned over time across the following epochs: slavery, feudalism and capitalism. His predictions informed his position of society advancing to a socialist economy and finally to one of effective communism. A classic case within the African context is the overthrow in King Idriss 1 by Colonel Moumar Gadaffi whom in 1969 at the age of 27 took over a poverty-stricken desert country in a bloodless coup (Global Edge, 2021), and transforming it into one of the strongest social welfare states in Africa and the world.

6   Drivers of Conflict: Human Rights Watch on the Rwanda Genocide

Upon having identified the reasons behind conflict, also referred to as the conflict triggers, research and intelligence is also important in identifying the individuals, groups and organizations behind the in its nascent or active stages. Research (inquiry to inform truth) and intelligence (inquiry to inform specific parties) are also vital in tracking any forms of morphing or metamorphosis that these groups are undergoing in a view to fuel or engage in violence. As a result, necessary measures can be taken to mitigate or avert their activities. In the case of Rwanda, prior to the genocide of 1994 that claimed between 800, 000 to 1, 000, 000 lives over a three-month period, sources of information various quarters, Walter de Bock and Gert Van Langendonck (as cited in Human Rights Watch, 1999) point out that the UN had to situate its peacekeeping force in Kigali as per the Arusha Accords. The report by Human Rights Watch further points to intelligence reports being furnished to diplomatic representatives of Belgium, the U.S., France, and Germany from the Rwandan community. Notable in their reports was limited structured interchange among their military intelligence services over the situation in Rwanda.

The details of this intelligence reports were clear in terms of the volatility of the situation based on the 'palpable' tensions across the country and more-so in Kigali, the capital of Rwanda. There were concerns that the *Intarahamwe* were planning to attack peace-keepers of Belgian nationality. The former President Juvenal Habyerimana was also adversely mentioned as being responsible for the distribution of grenades, machetes and other weapons to the *Interahamwe* and to CDR young people. The looming threat of violence posed by these two groups had been confirmed with information from desperate Rwandans.

In as much as there was sufficient intelligence to inform action, it is said that this intelligence never got to the right actors which in this case were the United Nations Assistance Mission in Rwanda (UNAMIR). As Brigadier General Romeo Antonius Dallaire, the Canadian Force Commander put it,

> "A lot of the world powers were all there with their embassies and their military attachés," Dallaire said. "And you can't tell me those bastards didn't have a lot of information. They would never pass that information on to me, ever."

7   Wages of War: Winners vs. Victims

Just like peace requires initiative to arrive at and maintain, the same applies in conflicts as there are existent forces that invest in activating and sustaining them. This move is indicative of deliberate investment by persons in various quarters from both within and without Africa that have identified potential benefits to starting and fanning the flames of war. Africa as a continent had, has continued to register such cases with the rationale of such activities aiming to destabilize regimes with the aim of harnessing resources; a discussion that often takes place under the resource curse banner. Nigeria's oil-rich Niger delta has for a long time been in this category as according to International Crisis Group, based in Brussels, Belgium, government, military and foreign oil companies were indirectly behind the situation based on their lukewarm approach to ending the conflict (Harsch, 2007).

The Eastern part of the Democratic Republic of Congo (DRC) is well endowed in Coltan (Columbite-Tantalite): an essential component used in production of electronics and has for a long time played host to multinationals headquartered in the West either directly or indirectly through appendages (licensed or unlicensed companies). The resource-rich region has also seen continuous presence of rebel forces as well as Rwandan and Ugandan governments (and their armies) (Tololo, 2009).

Johnson (2002) opines that Sierra Leone is potentially one of Africa's most complicated cases, dating back to 1935 when mining of Diamonds was controlled by De Beers, a UK-based mining company which operated in conditions that saw change of hands over time to a point where the state of affairs regarding exploitation deteriorated to total anarchy. Armed groups, mercenaries, forces from neighbouring states got involved in direct and unregulated exploitation of the resource. The tag of war manifested in a nine-year civil war that was concentrated in and around the diamond districts of Kono, Koinadugu, Kenema and Kambia.

With the above-mentioned situation replicated in various parts of the continent where minerals are found (expect for few cases such as diamond-rich Botswana, gold-rich Ghana among others), lives of locals do get disrupted. According to the International Committee of the Red Cross and Red Crescent (1999).

Times of armed conflicts have seen increased numbers of civilians getting wounded or even losing their lives. For those who manage to survive, they end up getting undergoing treatment devoid of human dignity. They may be put in detention arbitrarily and sometimes end up getting separated from their families. In the process of the conflict, civilians find themselves on the receiving end as soft targets, forced to flee from their homes, and denied fundamental rights as human beings, such as the right to supplies essential to their survival. This is commonplace in "failed states" when the central government is no longer in a position to provide service delivery as it is effectively not in control over much (International Committee of the Red Cross, 1999). Over and above the aspect of mass displacement, conflict affects various age groups and genders in society in various ways. The ICRC identifies the most vulnerable categories as women, children, persons with disabilities and displaced persons. Manocha (2014) also adds the environment to the list of losers in conflict.

According to Save the Children (2020), it was noted that an approximated 415 million children across the world resided in conflict-affected areas in 2018. In as much as the figure was less than that reported in 2017, research findings still pointed to the most grievous violations on children in these zones. These were such as maiming resulting from hazards of conflict either directly targeting them in the case of genocides (Human Rights Watch, 1995) or as collateral in cases where explosive devices (Smith, 2011) are used. Children are also recruited into militia and rebel groups to take part in conflict as child soldiers. They also get abducted and subjected to various forms of slavery that sometimes involve sexual abuse (Save the Children, 2023. Within conflict areas, they do suffer malnutrition in view of the challenges of accessing and using routes to these areas (UNICEF, 2021).

In as much as the environment through uncontrolled exploitation has contributed to 40 per cent of internal conflicts around the world, it is considered as the silent casualty of war (Manocha, 2014), according to the United Nations Secretary-General Ban Ki-moon on marking the International Day for Preventing the Exploitation of the Environment in War and Armed Conflict.

8   The Ethical Dilemma in Research on Peace and Security in Africa

In as much as Africa has elaborate structures in place to shed light on the conflict stages, from early warning to phases of post-conflict reconstruction (and recurrence), it is worth noting that the continent remains riddled with conflicts. This then begs the questions? Is Africa blind to the causes of conflicts in the continent or is it a case of turning a blind eye to the underlying causes and triggers of violence?

Various scholars have fronted their views on what exactly drive certain types of conflict in Africa, with some of their indicators pointing to internal dynamics and others pointing to drivers outside the continent. Further, the commitment to responding to the signs of conflict based on underlying interests have also been mentioned from time to time. From the actual research perspective, questions have been asked about the influence of donors and agencies that support research on the packaging of research findings. This in specific looks at the truths against the convenient truths behind the real conflict triggers. An assessment of the disparities between early warning versus early response may not necessarily be accidental. As a result, many prescriptions/recommendations steer clear of the real issues thus protracting conflict.

9   Interests or Lack in Conflict Resolution

The case of Rwanda is one whereby rudimentary early warning signs were ignored. The first indicator was regards to the early warning response of the pre-conflict stage. In as much as Force Commander of UNAMIR Brigadier General Romeo Dallaire argues that he was not informed of the potential magnitude of the killings, literature sources point to there being an uncoordinated but robust intelligence collecting apparatus, which had sufficient knowledge on the same. The United Nations had two and a half thousand personnel in the country observing the situation. Even with the mass killings and displacements ongoing, the International Community did little to stem the violence. The country was left to its own devices with the Rwanda Patriotic Front (RPF) bringing the fighting to an end after taking over the capital of Kigali. Calls for UN peace keeping troops by Dallaire were not forthcoming (Power, 2001). UN Security Council voted to cut down the UN peacekeeping force in the Rwanda to 270 from 2,500 soldiers (United States Holocaust Museum, 2021). In justifiable scepticism of engagement in a conflict that they did not understand, the U.S. did not send troops to Rwanda after the failed peacekeeping mission in Somalia (Baldauf, 2009). The lack of interest by the International Community in the small Eastern African country did not warrant further intervention after the safe extraction of foreigners working in the country in the early days of the killings.

The ethical dilemma therefore dogs the lack of response to this conflict situations that displayed all signs of turning deadly at a massive scale. With all the relevant information, it raises fundamental questions on the genuine spirit of the international community in upholding the Preamble of the UN Charter which states:

> **we the peoples of the united nations determined**
> to save succeeding generations from the scourge of war, which twice in our lifetime has brought untold sorrow to mankind.

10 Ideological Differences

Matters of peace and security have from time to time been acted upon on the basis of 'empirical' evidence presented by the powers of the day. The powers of the day are once again the bourgie from the strictest sense of Marxist philosophy. In this regard, it is worth noting that some conflicts in Africa have been driven by interests either to destabilize governments or depose leaders who may not be willing to align their ideological dispositions and convictions to those of the core states. In Africa, the assassination of Patrice Lumumba of the Democratic Republic of Congo (then Zaire) was motivated by his desire to engage the world through strategies and approaches that would protect the interests of the citizens. This was a matter of significant concern to the international community, because of the wealth of natural resources that had been freely exploited for nearly a century by the time of Lumumba's declaration (Williams, 2017). This followed his portrayal by the international media as evil (France 24, 2021) justifying his elimination. Since then, the story of the Congo has been one of conflict in the Eastern side of the resource-rich nation.

A similar narrative revolves around the toppling of the Libyan leader, Colonel Maumar Qadaffi as earlier stated in this chapter. The position of the former President of the United States of America Barack Hussein Obama regarding his authorization of the NATO-backed invasion of Libya points to regret on his end (British Broadcasting Corporation [BBC], 2016); an outcome he argues was based on the inadequate planning of the post-conflict reconstruction (*The Guardian*, 2016) after the deposition of the leaders of one of Africa's success stories. Gwaambuka (2016) points out that in as much as some of Qadaffi's value systems and philosophical convictions ended up infringing on the rights and freedoms of the Libyan people, the social welfare system he put in place was responsive to education, healthcare, women empowerment, food security and many more placing it higher than some first world countries.

Qadaffi, before his deposition and death, made mention of interests by Western powers in his country's oil reserves, which are the largest in terms of deposits in Africa (*The Guardian*, 2020). Further, indications of the talk surrounding the United States of Africa and the adoption of gold as the currency of choice for the African continent did not go down well with the Western powers (Chothia, 2011). From the above, the ethical dilemma in research as a vital organ to peace and security in Africa falls short in forestalling some of these conflicts both at the UN as well as the pre and AU formation. Who did the bidding for the invasion of Libya? How is it that the post-conflict reconstruction phase was left out in the planning of the invasion? Could it be that the phase was deliberately 'left out' in order to give room for 'reconstruction' in a manner that would suit certain interests? How could a country, ranked by the United Nations Development Programme (2010 as cited in Baspineiro, 2020) as a high-development country in the Middle East and North Africa within a year merit deposition of the same ruler who worked to get it there?

11 Commitment of Resources to Early Warning and Early Response: Where Real Priorities Lie

The desire to influence positive change for peace comes with significant financial investment at any stage of the conflict cycle. This therefore means that nobility and commitment to peace and stability in Africa should be reflective of financial support channelled to governments and bodies mandated to deliver on these aspects. Further, withdrawal of development assistance to countries that do not meet certain rights and freedoms, democratic governance and transparency among others should apply such that these governments are forced to uphold these important values and by extension, the rights of the people. This plays especially into the conflict prevention part of the conflict cycle where governments would be open to coalition arrangements of democracies that embrace views of the majority. However, in the case of the United States of America for example, according to the Congressional Research Service (2020), top proposed recipients in FY2021 include a number of countries which according to them have questionable governance records (e.g., Rwanda, Uganda, Tanzania and Nigeria). Figure 11.2 shows the U.S. aid to Africa in FY2021.

From the above, analysts have raised questions regarding the possibilities of these resources being channelled to such governments being used to buttress oppressive activities of abusive security forces or prevent U.S. influence on matters of democracy and governance. Further, questions have been raised on the balance between programmes geared towards good governance and those of health and development.

The ethical question of the above among other arrangements then raises concerns of genuine commitment towards emancipating the citizenry from

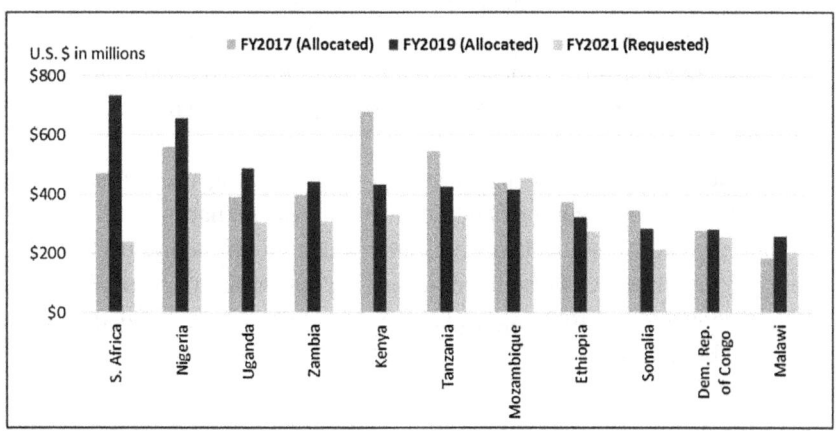

FIGURE 11.2 U.S. aid to Africa, top recipients, recent allocations vs. FY2021 request
SOURCE: STATE DEPARTMENT, CBJS FOR FY2019-FY2021. CONGRESSIONAL RESEARCH SERVICE. (MAY, 2020). U.S. ASSISTANCE TO SUB-SAHARAN AFRICA: AN OVERVIEW. RETRIEVED FROM ON 31-05-2023 FROM HTTPS://WWW.EVERYCRSREPORT.COM/FILES/20200520_R46368_9E9ECBF330872 5CCF131115CBC658FEF70796D00.HTML#_TOC40863960

allegedly oppressive regimes that have been accused of corruption and underdevelopment or continuous dependence on the West for basic needs. Another ethical concern raises questions on what potential benefits such arrangements could be forthcoming to such African governments and supporters of such regimes. Could it be a case of propping up the comprador bourgeoisie?

Lack of data on budget documents i.e., bilateral budgetary allocations on matters of peace and security channelled to African countries have raised concern with regard to policy dilemmas further posing a challenge in impact evaluation of these funds. An example of such is country- and program-level breakouts of some security assistance such as for the Global Peace Operations Initiative (GPOI).

In Mocimboa da Praia in the Cabo Delgado region of Mozambique, the gas-rich region which had been taken over by Islamic State insurgents forced Total, firm to pull out of its $20 billion liquified natural gas project. A total of 1, 000 Rwandan troops supported the Mozambican government to repel the groups from the region. Financing for the Rwandan troops' mission in Mozambique is said to be coming from France (Meldrum & Bowker, 2021). This joint military response has so far been quiet on sustainable peace initiatives; an issue which merits priority status based on triggers of this violent movement relating their activity to poverty, weak public services, corruption, unemployment and youth radicalization by national and foreign preachers (Faria, 2021). Research findings point to the need for a civilian military cooperation (CIMIC) arrangement, modelling those sanctioned by the UN and AU under peacekeeping missions/operations. Further, Faria among his recommendations highlights the need to protect the interests of the local communities in the region as resources are being extracted by foreign companies as well as provision on basic services for the locals.

In the above cases, ethical issues emerge questioning the genuine spirit behind maintaining certain ties with some regimes and nations and not others that may need support. Questions are also raised on the interests behind financing stabilization efforts in some sub-regions within regions of conflict without confronting providing a plan for sustainable peace reflective of all aspects of human security.

12   Addressing Climate Change

Research studies have pointed to there being a correlation between climate change and conflict. Of the 20 nations states most susceptible to climate change, 12 of them are experiencing conflict. Research on 'heat-aggression relationship' avers that, there, armed conflict has increased by 10–20%; an association made with each 0.5°C increase in local temperatures (Hussona, 2021). The above situation points to water, or the lack of it in sufficient quantity being a trigger for conflict. Boutros Boutros-Ghali, while foreign minister of Egypt, and who later on became the UN Secretary General in 1988, opined that the next wars his country and the Middle East experienced would be based on the waters of the Nile (Kameri-Mbote, 2007). Fast forward to 2021, Fitzpatrick (2021) reports that Egypt and Sudan called for the intervention of the UN Security Council after Ethiopia began filling the reservoir behind the Great Ethiopian Renaissance Dam (GERD) on the Nile that would significantly reduce volumes of water into Egypt.

The situation in the Horn and Eastern parts of Africa due to drought and locust invasions as well as in the Northern part of the Central African Republic, scarcity of and thus competition for pasture are cases that buttress the above-stated position (Mulhern, 2020). Hussona also adds that the conflict situation in the Darfur, Lake Chad basin and the Boko Haram situation in North Eastern Nigeria have triggers pointing to climate change; which result to a multiplier effect that exacerbate the conflict situation on the continent.

With these conflict trends affecting Africa in such a magnitude, it is important to note that Africa contributes to a paltry 2% of global emissions. It therefore begs the question; who are the leading polluters and what are they doing to address the worsening situation? China (30%), United States (15%), India (7%), Russia (5%) and Japan (4%) according to UNHCR, World Bank and The Times of India had been identified as the leading polluters in 2021 (Occonia, 2019).

With various initiatives in place to reduce climate change such as the Kyoto protocol of 1997 and the Paris Climate Agreement (COP 21) of 2015 (United Nations Framework Convention on Climate Change, 2021) that given accurate and alarming projections of the effects of climate change, it would be expected that the global super-powers would commit to their achievement. However, little has been done in this regard as temperatures continue to increase. With three of the top five polluters holding permanent membership on the United Nations Security Council, should optimum commitment to curbing climate change for the sake of peace and security in Africa and the rest—informed by continental statistics and trends on conflict—be a far-gone conclusion?

Africa is also without blemish as on the Kenyan scene, issues of protracted conflict in the Arid and Semi-Arid Lands (ASALs) majorly the Northern Frontier Counties have witnessed climate trends that have exacerbated the cultural practises such as cattle rustling leading to inter-communal conflicts. Undercurrents based on research findings and media reports have also shown that this trend is beneficial to some influential elements who engage in cattle rustling for no other reason but for trade of meat. Further, political scores are settled within the melee; dynamics that drive the proliferation of small arms and light weapons. This then begs the ethical questions; why would the pursuit of the trappings of power by the local leadership take precedence over the wellbeing of the local communities?

13 Health, Pandemics and Epidemics

The health security situation in Africa has for a long time lagged behind. As a result, the continent has continued to experience low rates of life expectancy partly occasioned by diseases such as HIV, malaria, TB, cholera among others. Infant mortality rates are also relatively high especially in areas experiencing war. Pandemics such as the Ebola virus has from time-to-time ravaged the Western parts of Africa claiming lives across the region. The COVID-19 pandemic which has seen the global economy contract, creating massive job losses and by extension, an immense multiplier effect across the various factors of human security. Reports from leading pharmaceutical companies observe that rich nations representing 14% of the global population procured up 53% of the most effective vaccines as at December 2020 (BBC, 2020). The position was corroborated by Kelly, Kirk and Ahmed (2020), who provided statistics that pointed to three in every four persons in the developed countries having received the COVID-19 vaccine. This was in contrast to the situation in the developing nations where 1 in every 500 had received the jab. Udayakumar (2021) puts this situation in real figures where he observes that the countries of the global North had in their possession 4.6 billion doses of the vaccine, while those in the South 670 million in their possession. Jefferson Sachs (2021) during the United Nations Food Systems Pre-Summit in 2021 where mentioned the need for powerful nations to release hoarded vaccines to the rest of the world, especially to developing nations.

Ethical questions are therefore raised based on the disparities pointed out, as well as the need for affirmative action pointed out in order to tip the scale in the fight against COVID-19 for the whole of humanity. Appreciative of the COVAX initiative, the divide is still significant. Why would the global powers hoard the doses of the vaccines? Why would it require such intervention for the north to support the global fight against COVID-19?

The above health security situation is also reflective of investment in research and development as well as investment in health infrastructure in Africa. Many African countries have not dedicated required resources to this very important sector. Further, resources channeled from development partners to assist in improvement of healthcare infrastructure have on many occasions been unaccounted for. According to Omondi (2021), the International Monetary Fund has asked the government of Kenya to disclose the names of the persons who were behind the controversial Kenya Medical Supplies Authority (KEMSA) irregular procurement processes that cost the USD 78 million.

Some ethical questions arise from such kind of alleged financial improprieties. Why would there be such pilferage of resources that should be channeled to such a noble cause? Is it that the Government of Kenya (GoK) was/is not alive to the devastating impact of the pandemic to the economy? Why would the GoK not see the need to channel such resources to prudent use in order to boost its struggling healthcare system?

14   UNSC Composition/Representation and Camaraderie

The current composition of the UNSC has five permanent members (United States of America, The United Kingdom, China, Russia and France) and ten non-permanent members that hold the seats on rotational basis. It is without doubt that the need for the Council as stated earlier in the chapter is important. However, some fundamental questions are raised with regard to the utility of the membership composition formed in 1945. Further questions are raised on how responsive it is to contemporary global threats as well as demographic representation. At the global level, how effective is the SC without representation of Latin America and India? At the continental level, how does the Security Council appreciate challenges facing Africa's peace and security without a permanent voice in form of a member/representative from the continent? It is in this regard that the former Secretary General of the United Nations, the late Kofi Annan (n.d.) observes that the SC should be reformed with the aim of allowing additional seats that will include India and an African country to represent a close to three billion of the seven billion people plus. He proposes as well, the inclusion of Japan on the SC as it is a significant financial contributor to the UN.

A candid analysis of the nature of the relationship of some of the permanent security council members raises concern on their ability to put global interests before national, regional and allies' interests. In a meeting of the U.S. and EU, officials branded China as 'aggressive and coercive' with regard to its economic policies and honouring of global treaties (Cook, 2021). In response, China responded with the President Xi Jinping warning, as reported in *The Standard* (2021),

Anyone who dares try to do that will have their heads bashed bloody against the Great Wall of steel forged by over 1.4 billion Chinese people.

From the above scenario, the world finds itself in a 'Catch 22' situation as core members of the UNSC who are supposed to protect the UN Charter and avert another World War go at each other with open declarations of aggression. The fundamental question from a scientific perspective is the ability of the members to deliver on the spirit on the UN Charter for the sake of the greater good of humanity. Is it possible to uphold the 'peer' aspect that should guide debate in terms of tone and difference with such kind of a tensive relationship existent? For the greater good, will the world be treated to objective 'review' of issues brought before them?

15 Conclusion

From the above, it is evident that Africa has sufficient data regarding conflict across the conflict cycle. This is in as much as African Peace and Security Architecture Report of 2010 among many more point to frailties in the present working especially of APSA. From the above analysis, it is evident that doubt can be justifiably cast on the true spirit of the global organizations and powers in responding to the underlying causes of conflict in view of the overwhelming evidence of available data. Committing resources to organizations mandated to secure Africa has proven to be a challenge with the African Peace Fund operating on a constrained budget. Vested interests at country level have been observed from the past as significantly influencing Africa's governance, peace and security trajectory. This then raises more questions than answers as the effects of instability begin to affect the world as well. The current refugee/migrant crisis with the collapse of the 'Libyan wall' between Sub-Saharan Africa and Europe, extreme weather patterns affecting various parts of the world occasioned by the greenhouse effect and the COVID-19 pandemic that has indiscriminately shaken the global economy claiming the lives of millions are some of the main challenges that Africa and by extension, the world is currently grappling with. The world will sooner or later, address Africa's conflict situation either as a primary or secondary concern to the challenges they face today or in future. With most of these challenges point to one trigger which is unethical practice by private sector both in the North and South, the conclusion therefore is that not if, but when the world is ready to relook at research findings on conflict drivers in Africa with the required ethical and moral lens, then the continent will begin to make substantive strides towards stability.

For Africa and for Africans, the reawakening of the true spirit of Ubuntu is the 'silver bullet' to getting Africa on the path to peace, stability and prosperity. As previously observed, the issues affecting Africa have, are and never will be genuinely discussed by governments outside of her borders. Africans must therefore take it upon themselves as an obligation to today's and to the future generations to kickstart and spearhead the agenda. The term Ubuntu, a Nguni Bantu word that can be loosely translated as "humanity" is pedestalled upon the phrase "I am because we are" and by extension, calling for Africa to be seized of the philosophy of "humanity towards others". It is only when the children of Africa take this trajectory of thought will the continent identify and deal with the contemporary enemies of progress, with their immediate ones being poverty, hunger and illiteracy. Ethical research will therefore focus on the broad-spectrum of causes and effects of these three factors and remain guided on crafting solutions to address them. Community-based approaches to solving local problems will also gain more traction with conflict resolution mechanisms embracing home-grown approaches to sustainable peace. At this point in time, human security will take centre-stage thus solving the peace and security dilemma and plugging the ethical and moral divide between the ideal and the real.

References

AU, (2021). The Continental Early Warning System (CEWS). Link: https://www.peaceau.org/en/article/the-continental-early-warning-system#:~:text=As%20stipulated%20in%20article%2012,data%20collection%20and%20analysis%3B%20and. Date retrieved: 13/08/2021.

Baldauf, S. (2009). Why the U.S. didn't intervene in the Rwandan genocide. *The Christian Science Monitor*. Retrieved on 12/08/2021 from https://www.csmonitor.com/World/Africa/2009/0407/p06s14-woaf.html.

Baspineiro, R. (2020). Libya: Before and after Muammar Gaddafi. *teleSURHD*. Retrieved on 13/08/2021 from https://www.telesurenglish.net/analysis/Libya-Before-and-After-Muammar-Gaddafi-20200115-0011.html.

British Broadcasting Corporation. (2016). President Obama: Libya aftermath 'worst mistake' of presidency. Retrieved on 12/08/2021 from https://www.bbc.com/news/world-us-canada-36013703.

British Broadcasting Corporation. (2020). Rich countries hoarding Covid vaccines, says People's Vaccine Alliance. Retrieved on 13/ 08/ 2021 from https://www.bbc.com/news/health-55229894.

Chothia, F. (2011). What does Gaddafi's death mean for Africa? *BBC News*. Retrieved on 12/08/2021 from https://www.bbc.com/news/world-africa-15392189.

Congressional Research Service. (May 2020). U.S. assistance to Sub-Saharan Africa: an overview. Retrieved from on 13/08/2021 from https://fas.org/sgp/crs/row/R46368.pdf.

Cook, L. (2021). U.S., Europe, NATO close ranks to counter 'aggressive' China. *AP News*. Retrieved on 15/08/2021 from https://apnews.com/article/europe-antony-blinken-china-ursula-von-der-leyen-europe-6c7c4a0da00ed5a8f529efa3392975cd.

Desmidt, S. (2016). Peacebuilding, conflict prevention and conflict monitoring in the African Peace and Security Architecture. *European Centre for Development and Policy Management*. Retrieved on 12/08/2021 from https://ecdpm.org/wp-content/uploads/African-Peace-Security-Architecture-Background-Note-ECDPM-2016.pdf.

Faria, C.J. (2021). The rise and root causes of Islamic insurgency in Mozambique and its security implication to the region. Policy Brief. *Institute of Peace and Security Studies*. Addis Ababa University. Retrieved on 13/08/2021 from https://reliefweb.int/sites/reliefweb.int/files/resources/Policy-Brief-The-rise-and-root-causes-of-Islamic-insurgency-in-Mozambique-1.pdf.

France 24. (2021). Family seeks justice for Lumumba, DR Congo's murdered hero. Retrieved on 13/08/2021 from https://www.france24.com/en/live-news/20210115-family-seeks-justice-for-lumumba-dr-congo-s-murdered-hero.

Global Edge. (2021). Libya: History. *GlobalEDGE (via Michigan State University)*. Retrieved on 13/08/2021 from https://globaledge.msu.edu/countries/libya/history/.

Gwaambuka, T. (2016). Ten reasons Libya under Gaddafi was a great place to live. *The African Exponent*. Retrieved on 13/08/2021 from https://www.africanexponent.com/post/ten-reasons-libya-under-gaddafi-was-a-great-place-to-live-2746.

Hansen, S. J. (2013). *Al-Shabaab in Somalia: the History and Ideology of a Militant Islamist Group*. Oxford University Press.

Harsch, E. (2007). Conflict resources: From 'curse' to blessing: Transforming an African war risk into a peace asset. *Africa Renewal*. Link: https://www.un.org/africarenewal/magazine/january-2007/conflict-resources-%E2%80%98curse%E2%80%99-blessing. Date retrieved: 22/03/2021.

Human Rights Watch field notes, Nyakizu, Butare, July 20, 1995.

Human Rights Watch, (1999). The Warning. Link: https://www.hrw.org/reports/1999/rwanda/Geno4-7-01.htm. Date retrieved: 22/03/2021.

Hussona, J. (2021). How is climate change driving conflict in Africa? Action on armed violence. Retrieved on 13/08/2021 from https://aoav.org.uk/2021/how-is-climate-change-driving-conflict-in-africa/.

ICRC, (1999). Protection of victims of armed conflict through respect of International Humanitarian Law. Retrieved on 03-05-2021 from https://www.icrc.org/en/doc/resources/documents/misc/57jpzn.htm.

Johnson, E., (2002). Blood diamonds: the conflict in Sierra Leone. Link: https://web.stanford.edu/class/e297a/Conflict%20in%20Sierra%20Leone.htm. Date retrieved: 22/03/2021.

Kameri-Mbote, P. (2007). Water, conflict, and cooperation: Lessons from the Nile River Basin. *The Wilson Center*. Retrieved on 15/08/2021 from https://www.wilsoncenter.org/publication/water-conflict-and-cooperation-lessons-the-nile-river-basin-no-4.

Kelly, P., Kirk A., & Ahmed, K., (2020). Covid vaccine figures lay bare global inequality as global target missed. *The Guardian Newspaper*. Link: https://www.theguardian.com/global-development/2022/jul/21/covid-vaccine-figures-lay-bare-global-inequality-as-global-target-missed. Date retrieved: 15/08/2021.

Manocha, V. (2014). Environment is one of wars' greatest victims. *Down to Earth*. Retrieved on 04/05/2021 from https://www.downtoearth.org.in/news/environment-is-one-of-wars-greatest-victims-47280.

Meldrum, A and Bowker, T. (2021). Rwandan, Mozambican forces retake port from insurgents. *AP News*. Retrieved on 13/08/2021 from https://apnews.com/article/europe-africa-rwanda-595f475f3cb737974f96dd8990f7cb18.

Mulhern, O. (2020). Climate change and conflict in Africa. *Earth.Org*. Retrieved on 13/08/2021 from https://earth.org/data_visualization/climate-change-and-conflict-in-africa/.

Nutley, S., Percy-Smith, J., & Solesbury, W. (2003). *Models of Research Impact: a Cross-Sector Review ofLliterature and Practice*. London: Learning and Skills Research Centre.

Occoina, (2019). Top 5 most polluting countries. Sustainability for All. Link: https://www.activesustainability.com/environment/top-5-most-polluting-countries/?_adin=02021864894. Date retrieved: 21/08/2021.

Okumu, W. (2020). Conflict prevention from the ground opportunities and challenges for closer cooperation between AU, RECS and civil society: On conflict prevention in Eastern Africa. *Friedrich-Ebert-Stiftung*. Retrieved on 12/08/2021 from http://library.fes.de/pdf-files/bueros/fes-ua/17398.pdf.

Power, S. (2001). Bystanders to genocide. *The Atlantic*. Retrieved on 12/08/2021 from https://www.theatlantic.com/magazine/archive/2001/09/bystanders-to-genocide/304571/.

Sachs, J. (2021). Jeffrey Sachs' speech at the UN Food Systems Pre-Summit (full speech). *YouTube*. Retrieved on 17/08/2021 from https://www.youtube.com/watch?v=WZ1xc491mnU.

Save the Children, (2023). Child Soldiers: The Tragic End of Childhood for Boys and Girls in Conflict. Link: https://www.savethechildren.org/us/charity-stories/child-soldiers. Date retrieved: 05/09/2023.

Smith, K. (2011). Devastating impact: Devastating impact explosive weapons and children. Retrieved on 03-05-2021 from https://www.refworld.org/pdfid/4f2678082.pdf.

The Guardian. (2016). Barack Obama says Libya was 'worst mistake' of his presidency. Retrieved on 13/08/2021 from https://www.theguardian.com/us-news/2016/apr/12/barack-obama-says-libya-was-worst-mistake-of-his-presidency.

The Guardian. (2020). Gaddafi's prophecy comes true as foreign powers battle for Libya's oil. Retrieved on 12/08/2021 from https://www.theguardian.com/world/2020/aug/02/gaddafis-prophecy-comes-true-as-foreign-powers-battle-for-libyas-oil.

The Standard, (2021). 'We'll bash your heads bloody against the Great Wall'. https://www.thestandard.com.hk/section-news/section/11/231750/'We'll-bash-your-heads-bloody-against-the-Great-Wall'.

Tigray's children in crisis and beyond reach, after months of conflict: UNICEF. Retrieved on 04/05/2021 from https://news.un.org/en/story/2021/01/1083102.

Tololo, E., (2009). Coltan and conflict in the DRC. ReliefWeb. Link: https://reliefweb.int/report/democratic-republic-congo/coltan-and-conflict-drc. Date retrieved: 12/08/2021.

Totolo, E., (2009). Coltan and conflict in the DRC. International relations and security network. Retrieved 22/03/2021 from https://reliefweb.int/report/democratic-republic-congo/coltan-and-conflict-drc.

United Nations, (2021). Main bodies. Retrieved on 11/08/2021 from https://www.un.org/en/about-us/main-bodies.

United Nations (2021). The United Nations Security Council. Retrieved on 11/08/2021 from https://www.un.org/securitycouncil/.

United Nations Framework Convention on Climate Change, (2021) The Paris agreement. Retrieved on 13/08/2021 from https://unfccc.int/process-and-meetings/the-paris-agreement/the-paris-agreement.

United States Holocaust Museum, (2021). Pleading for help. Retrieved on 12/08/2021 from https://www.ushmm.org/genocide-prevention/countries/rwanda/case-study/response/pleading-for-help.

Weingart, P. (1969). Beyond Parsons? acritique of Ralf Dahrendorf's conflict theory. *Social Forces*, 48(2), 151–165.

Williams, S. (2017). Congolese uranium and the cold war. *New African, 568*, 24–7.

PART 4

Reflexivity and Ethics

∴

CHAPTER 12

Ethics of Doing Research in the Indigenous Community

Rose Ann Torres

1   Introduction

Research as a political process looks at how local contexts matter in the process of producing knowledge. This means that people's ways of life—including their values and belief systems—should take a central role in knowledge production. Knowledge production, in turn, should be not only a process of rationalism but also one that is ethical and geared towards humanizing those so defined as emotional and instinctual beings. As an ethical process, research calls for reimagining the immeasurability of the other, in ways that esteem participants beyond the quantification metrics of science. In other words, research seeks to visualize instead of merely understanding the other, in ways that acknowledge human beings' complexity beyond the simplification that is science. The act of researching the other thus becomes a process beyond commodification and production of the other in ways that make researchers disidentify with what they have been told is the only process of producing truth. Research as an ethical process therefore should (re)imagine knowledge production beyond the industrial processing and rationalizing of the other and instead think of ways in which we can de-industrialize the process to accommodate (and validate) other ways of truths. In so doing, the histories of communities should help researchers validate the ways in which those communities come to know what they know, as well as the values corresponding to their social being.

These major conceptual frames of the *how* of research are fundamental aspects that I want to share with you in this chapter. The next section describes my study's participants, followed by a discussion of recruitment and data collection. The chapter's analysis section focuses on implicating the self and my relationship with the Aeta women healers.

2   The Participants

My participants were the Aeta women healers in the Philippines. They have been situated in the northern part of Luzon, located in the foothills of Steep Mountain on the western side of the Sierra Madre, the Philippines' longest mountain range. They believe that Cagayan is where their ancestral terrain is located—where their ancestors were buried and where they practiced their culture and tradition. This is also the place where they continue their healing practices, following in the footsteps of their ancestors.

When 19th-century Spaniards colonized the Philippines, they brought with them physicians from Spain. Indeed, the creation of public health and Western medicine were integral parts of the ideology of empire (King, 2002, p. 765). This ideology of colonial "curing" is one of the justifications given by colonizers, on the pretext that they were bringing the best quality of life for Indigenous people. The idea that the Spaniards were out to save the newly found heathens from their uncivilized way of living was planted in the minds of the Indigenous people (Torres, 2017); it did not matter if the colonizers ravaged, demonized, or dehumanized the lives of the Indigenous people whom they ostensibly sought to "save."

The so-called colonial way of curing has been used to cover up of the ongoing process of colonization. In fact, history bears witness to several diseases in different countries where colonies were established. In other words, colonial medicine was a means of achieving the goal of colonization, insofar that Indigenous healers' traditional roles were completely disregarded. Alfred Crosby (1972/2003), in *The Columbian Exchange: Biological and Cultural Consequences of 1492*, forcefully argues that the main destructive effects of the conquistadors and other settlers was the introduction of alien animals, plants, and diseases and that much of the project of genocide was operationally realized by these forces. In the case of North America, colonization ultimately led to more than five million deaths and a radical alteration of population demographics, and it subsequently paved the way for the land expropriation, such as the Manifest Destiny in the United States. Similar analyses have been done and should be expanded upon to include the Philippines. In some ways, the Aeta were protected from earlier ravages by their comparatively remote location.

Expansionism works on logic, not unlike cancer: it is sustained by uncontrollable and unsustainable growth. In this respect, it is hardly surprising that all people, including the Aeta, are exposed to expansionism's nefarious forces. The Aeta women's work therefore is linked in the deepest ways to the connections between Nature, health, and society and is a counterpoint to what may be seen as the crisis medicine approach introduced (or more exactly, imposed).

by the West. The Aeta women healers explain the differences between their healing practices and the Western way of healing; Singli, for example, states that in her healing she uses herbal medicine and prayers. She also mentioned that without the help of the Creator, the herbal medicine that she uses for her patient's body will be useless (Torres, 2021). Holmes (2002) states that ways of knowing are not based on the limits of one's own physical sense and may include prayer, prescience, dreams, and messages from the dead (p. 37). This has been affirmed by the Aeta women healers who state that their healing practice focuses not only on the use of herbal plants but also on other ways of healing.

Aeta women healers' extensive healing knowledge is well-known both in their community and in other communities in the province of Cagayan Valley. The Aeta are well-respected by their own people and their community has been recognized for the work they have been doing. They are consulted in times of tribulation and have been called upon to make major decisions for their community. Their healing practices continue to exist, despite the presence of Western style health centers and public health practitioners in their community. They choose to use their own healing practices to cure their people; they share their knowledge of healing with others; and they continue to apply their healing practices, despite the dehumanization they have been subjected to by the public health community at a national level. The Aeta women healers believe in themselves, and their belief is a strong force in maintaining their identity. They believe in the efficacy of their healing knowledge, despite the continuing disruption by the non-Aeta people. It is important to recognize their ways of disrupting coloniality in their community through their ways of healing.

The main purpose of this research was to explore the healing practices of Aeta women. It also sought to document the resiliency and elements of agency that have contributed to the continuity of this knowledge (Torres, 2017). The Aeta women healers' agency is related to economic, spiritual, social, political, and cultural factors. The research examined the different forms of resistance against the imposition of colonized knowledge, and how Aeta women healers negotiated their positions in a society that valued the knowledge of men over women. However, in this chapter, I will not delve into the research project; instead, I will discuss the ethical process of doing research with the Aeta women healers. I have published numerous articles about my research, but I have not discussed the ethics of doing research. This is what I want to accomplish in this chapter.

3 Recruitment

As a researcher, I had to appreciate that participants' claim that they are "story lines" was a fundamental form of imagining their lives and how we were to produce knowledge. It was also clear that such narrative was dialogical, and community based. The act of cooking sweet potatoes became the central methodology of my study, because while they were cooking, they would tell stories that were underpinned by Indigenous epistemologies. The Aeta women healers welcomed us and offered us some rice cakes to eat. The act of offering the rice cakes reminded me of the vulnerability and humanism that should guide the *how* of doing research in the community. To that end, one can see how an exercise that was supposed to recruit members into the research process became an orientation into Aeta Indigenous ways of life, which I affirm should guide my methodology.

4 Data Collection

Aeta women healers asked me about my study. It was then that I informed them about my study. They were very excited and agreed to share with me their healing practices. I presented them with consent form to sign. But before that, they questioned what it entailed. This aspect of asking for information reminds me that while I may be re-presenting their stories in my research, it nonetheless remains a political process, and such a request for information confirms that this group is not docile and that they have ways of resisting colonial encroachment. The provision of food before such an engagement presents an art of resistance that humanizes ways of producing knowledge in ways that are dialogical and non-violent.

As much as they experience challenges in their daily life because of the scarcity of resources and the continued oppression of imperialism, the Aeta remain strong as a community in facing the adversities of in their daily lives. The study allowed me to hear about their perspectives on healing and its implications in relation to the academic discourse. I also realized that researchers (such as myself) can never impose the preeminent methodology in conducting research among this community. Allowing participants to co-determine which methodology to employ led to a much more meaningful dialogue between me and the Aeta healers. As Graveline (1998) reminds us, "to speak is a privilege" and "spoken thoughts-words-are sacred" (p. 139). My engagement with the Aeta women healers helped me reflect on my position as a researcher who had been immersed in a Eurocentric discourse, because there was a possibility that I could unknowingly use my position to oppress them.

My engagement with the Aeta women healers helped me to critically reflect on my privileges, prestige, and power and how these could be used as oppressive tools in representing the participants' agency and identity. The research offered a lens through which to see how the external world demonizes the Aeta women healers. It enabled me to represent them from their perspectives, because they allowed me to hear and to write about their knowledge on healing and its implications for the academy after internalizing the discussions. This helped me understand the importance of honoring their knowledge and being consistent with their worldview (Sevilla et al., 1992). This is particularly important in this study as it was the Aeta women healers who had helped me select the methodology for gathering information.

In this study, the research embarked on a new production of knowledge (Spivak, 1996) that highlights the healing practices of the Aeta women. This study reveals that Indigenous knowledge is an important part in both political and academic discourses. The study also provides new material for "the grasping of the production and determination of literature ... and a research about the conditions of women" (Spivak, 1996, p. 59).

The Aeta women healers also told me that others who would subsequently listen to me would listen as if it was their voices that they were hearing. Furthermore, the women healers were emphatic that trying to write down notes while they were speaking was ineffectual because, at times, whatever they would be telling me would not be able to be translated into words but rather communicated through their actions.

I listened attentively and asked about their healing practices. We also talked about identity, agency, and representation. They told me that if I had any questions, I could ask them. I felt the support of the Aeta women healers. Their smiles always reassured me that I would be fine in this journey. I went home and transcribed all that I had heard. I also wrote my own reflections and observations on the things that they had said.

I situated myself in the Aeta community as a student who was ready to learn and to be taught. I took this experience to unlearn the things that I had heard about the Aeta and replaced such prejudices with the knowledge that I had received from the Aeta women healers. Indeed, this experience has shaped my way of theorizing, writing, and researching about Indigenous peoples. I hope that this study will not only challenge our way of thinking about the Aeta women but also re-orient our Eurocentric gaze with respect to Indigenous contributions to the academy, the political arena, and public health.

5 Data Analysis and Coding

Data analysis was also guided by the data collection procedure; rather than merely asking participants closed ended questions, I also allowed them the opportunity to reflect on what they had said. The process of differentiation of data collection and analysis smacks of colonialism and demarcates those who do analysis as experts and those whose data is collected as consumers and emotional beings. This dualism in terms of research process serves the capital in ways that analysis comes to be given more prominence and data collection becomes a process that is touristic and dehumanizing. To decolonize such a process is to call for ways in which participants can take a central role in both the collection and analysis of data in ways that decolonize this dualism.

6 Implicating the Self: Who Am I in Relation to the Aeta Women

I grew up in Cagayan in the Philippines near the Aeta community. I still have not forgotten of the times when my mother would take me for a visit to the Aeta community to play, enjoy meals, share stories, and exchange gifts with their children. I learned from then on, that life was a gift shared with each other in ways that remind us of our interconnected vulnerabilities, relationality, and humaneness. To seemingly look vulnerable in the eyes of the other was a way of reminding us of our human self that cannot stand without the other. This aspect of integrating me with the community provided me with the requisite route toward defining my axiological, ontological, methodological, and epistemological perspective towards this study. To speak of research that is based on values, realities, and ways of being is to claim that research is political. This political claim is to affirm that research should be grounded within communities' ways of social life.

In this chapter, I present to you the lived experiences of Aeta women healers in the Philippines. While doing so, I must also ask: Who am I to represent this Indigenous community? This aspect of representation is political and needs deeper critical reflexivity for me to identify my ethical duties and responsibility. Even though I grew up with the community, it is my prerogative to identify how insider/outsider politics play a complicated part in the representation of the people we claim to represent. I therefore ask: Why I should be the one to do this representational dance—and moreover, do I even need to do so? Allyship should remain a kind of a complicated dance for somebody like me who lies within the borderline of insider and outsider. This border point is violent and only they who are ready to sit in its discomfort can work within the complexities of this representational politics. First, being with the community does not give me a figurative passport to such cultural representation. Pon (2009) reminds us that cultural identity is "highly discursive and linked to how subjectivities are formed through desire, language, and representation" (p. 64).

This could be such an easy route to remove my self from such complexities that are cultural and ethical. While as a human being I may choose to remain in my comfort zone, I ask myself how such comfort will continue to denigrate this community that I grew up with. My comfort and appearance are political because they efface such communities. If I fail to represent such stories to you, I am implicated in the disappearance of the community. If I present their stories without critically nuancing their stories and who I am, I remain implicated. That said, I will reiterate that a presentation of the lived experiences of Aeta people does not mean that they cannot represent themselves. In fact, they have known how to represent themselves even beyond the rational Western representation of the self. This aspect points to the fact that while they may seemingly be presented as docile and emotional, they use multiple ways of representation that transcend dominant (and again Western) styles of presentation.

I conducted this research 10 years ago, and I am still agonizing and reflecting on how I can best represent this work ethically without denigrating and terrorizing the community of Aeta women. I was a doctoral student, and the goal was to undertake research that would empower and help the community realize self-determination. Such a determination of empowerment and self-determination is not without nuances and raises some important questions: Who am I to empower them? What would that empowerment look like? If empowerment is bringing them to the centre, how would that centre look like? If that centre is a White centre, we could be now engaging with an ethical prerogative and asking questions regarding how such a single form of centre may marginalize the margin-margins in which these communities have called home. So, to speak of ethics and self-representation, we need to ask how the self that is to be represented has been created over time, such that what may be representation of the self becomes representation of the other. That would mean that even stories given by those whom we perceive as being oppressed could be a presentation of an account that is colonial and, as such, we need to critically reflect and engage with the participants. Self-determination therefore becomes a process of re-imagining research in ways that constitute not only a provision of data to policy makers but also a process of mirroring communities in ways that raise awareness of the colonial atrocities meted on them. This would ethically and politically change the ways in which we think of research, such that communities come to be brought together by the mirror image reflected on them by the research. This places onus on the research to unite and form coalitions in ways that are non-violent and meant to bring change in the community through social capital. The system knows exactly how to do this through laws, legislations, protocols, and other mechanisms of controls, especially for Indigenous and marginalized groups, and we have seen this happen in our society today. It is within this framework that I argue that while research has been a violent process of misrepresenting Indigenous communities, Indigenous communities continue to subvert such representation in ways that are non-violent and meant to disorganize the metrics of knowledge production through contextual arts such as healing practices.

According to Torres and Nyaga (2021),

> researchers aim is to understand and imagine themselves and others differently. There are different ways through which we come to understand (read quantitative research) and imagine who we are and our becoming (read qualitative). In a nutshell, research is about engagement with us and others to imagine who we are and who we could become. This imagination in research is a back-and-forth movement from familiar to unfamiliar spaces of our being.
>
> p. 120

In addition, Torres and Nyaga (2021) argue that

> to reimagine the research process from critical, performative, transformative, and reflexive ways help center communities' needs and aspirations as fundamental in meaning making and knowledge production. For a while, research has been and continues to be an ivory tower beyond community's reach. Production of knowledge has become a neoliberal process that alienates community members from the very knowledge that is supposed to emancipate them. Knowledge production is an industrial process that squeezes blood from communities without giving back.
>
> p. x

7 Conclusion

I will end this chapter with a call for an engaged process of engaging participants in research in ways that humanize them and make them take control of their life through research (Wilson, 2008). This helps mark research as critically reflexive and ready to mix the blood and the mincemeat in ways that go beyond the normalized process of making knowledge.

The methodologies of research and practice help imagine communities beyond their everyday experiences and start acknowledging how such experiences both resist and uncouple colonial boundaries of knowledge production. Through a critically reflexive research process, research takes an ethical tangent in ways that identify everybody as having the power to produce knowledge. Ethical obligation is a fundamental necessity of any critically reflexive research. As Levinas would say, we come to engage with the face of the other in ways that mark us as late (Llewelyn, 1995; Perpich, 2008). This means that the role of the researcher as the knower of the other is flawed and contradictory and steals the life out of communities. For researchers to be ethically responsible, they will have to come to terms with the fact that they cannot understand the face of the other. Rather, they can only imagine and acknowledge the pain of the other. To do this, every researcher will have to "kill" (read necropolitics) the urge to be the expert of the other. This means the death of self for the resurrection of another self that imagines others and their point of need.

References

Graveline, F. (1998). *Circle Works: Transforming Eurocentric Consciousness*. Fernwood.

Holmes, L. (2002). Heart Knowledge, Blood Memory, and the voice of the Land: Implications of Research among Hawaiian Elders. In G. Dei, B. Hall, & D. Rosenberg (Eds.), *Indigenous Knowledges in the Global Contexts: Multiple Readings of Our World* (pp. 37–53). University of Toronto Press.

King, N. B. (2002). Security, disease, commerce: Ideologies of postcolonial global health. *Social Studies of Science*, 32(5–6), 763–789. http://doi.org/10.1177/0306312 70203200507.

Llewelyn, J. (1995). *Emmanuel Levinas: the Genealogy of Ethics*. Routledge.

Perpich, D. (2008). *The Ethics of Emmanuel Levinas*. Stanford University Press.

Pon, G. (2009). Cultural competency as new racism: an ontology of forgetting. *Journal of Progressive Human Services*, 20(1), 59–71. https://doi.org/10.1080/1042823090 2871173.

Sevilla, C. G., Ochave, J. A., Punzalan, T. G., Regalla, B. P., & Uriarte, G. G. (1992). *Research Methods* (Rev. ed.). Rex Printing Co.

Spivak, G. C. (1996). *The Spivak Reader: Selected Works of Gayatri Chakravorty Spivak* (D. Landry & G. MacLean, Eds.). Routledge.

Torres, R. A. (2017). Transforming Indigenous Curriculum in the Philippines through Indigenous Women's Knowledge and Practices: a Case Study on Aeta Women

Healers. In N. Phasha, D. Mahlo, & G. J. S. Dei (Eds.), *Inclusive Education in African Contexts: a Critical Reader* (pp. 173–189). Sense. https://doi.org/10.1007/978-94-6300-803-7_12.

Torres, R. A. (2021). Feminization of Pandemics: Experiences of Filipino Women in the Health Care System. In R. A. Torres, K. Leung, & V. Soepriatna (Eds.), *Outside and In-between: Theorizing Asian-Canadian Exclusion and the Challenges of Identity Formation* (pp. 189–204). Brill. https://doi.org/10.1163/9789004466357_017.

Torres, R. A., & Nyaga, D. (Eds.) (2021). *Critical Research Methodologies: Ethics and Responsibilities*. Leiden: Brill.

Wilson, S. (2008). *Research is Ceremony: Indigenous Research Methods*. Fernwood.

CHAPTER 13

A Reflexive Gaze on Qualitative Policy Research
Deconstructing Traditional Policy Research with the Interface of Youth-Voice and Arts-Based Focus Groups

Dawn Onishenko and Julie Erbland

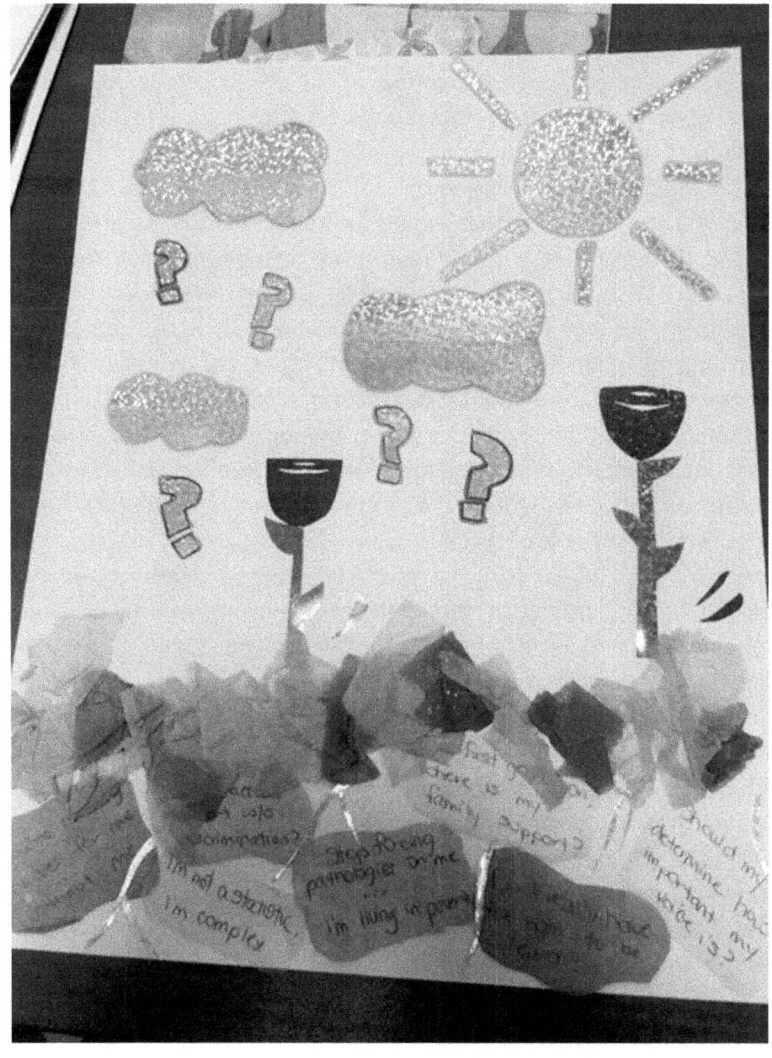

FIGURE 13.1a   Policy research as a tool for youth resistance

Policy development, and ways of understanding policy through its various forms of analysis, are situated in models and approaches that tend to be removed from those most impacted by the policies in question (McKenzie & Wharf, 2010); policy *research* is no different – with its preponderance of policy models, wicked events, policy windows, evidence, experts, and actors. When it comes to systems and structural policy issues that impact young people, children and youth are rarely invited to the conversation in a fulsome manner (Grover, 2004). Failing to *meaningfully* include those with lived experience, we argue, exacerbates the fissures between neoliberal policy evaluation, that serves to further marginalize already excluded groups, and critical policy development that seeks effective (transformative) operational change. This chapter represents the reflexive ponderings of two researchers as we consider the choices taken as we engage in a qualitative research process to learn about how youth from the Central American and the Caribbean diaspora *experience* rights-based policies (Figure 13.1a).

This chapter speaks to the structure and the nuances of the research methodology and the ways in which peer researchers, facilitating focus groups in 'messy spaces' – with food, circuitous discussion, construction paper, glitter, and magazines – contribute to deep understandings of the realities of the migration of youth in relation to youth rights and how those rights are situated within a Canadian social policy context. What surfaced from the research process that upended traditional policy research and its linear approach to question formation, data collection and analysis, was a deep and critical analysis of policy as stories of lived experience. In an environment of making art, where focus groups followed less of a rigid, linear, 'data collection' structure and embraced the texture of youth engagement – listening and learning from one another, making art, engaging in spirited debates, laughing, expressing a multitude of emotions, and forming relationships – emerged stories of the divide between what youth understand as their rights and entitlements (purported to be entrenched in social policies and programs), and what they *experience* in this country, in the very institutions meant to uphold those rights. From stories of an education setting instructing a youth to cover their dreadlocks or leave, with no understanding of their spiritual significance; to a shared acknowledgement of the precarious employment that youth engage in to make up the gap in household income, and the risks that come with working in those locales of exploitation; to the knowing exchange of what it means when trying to educate their parent on the policies related to child protection when, in a different cultural context, the issue would have been dealt with in a manner that would not involve the gaze of protection agencies, are just a few of the experiential examples of the way in which youth rights fail to be reflected in the policies that impact them. However, analysis did not end there; youth were astute in identifying and deconstructing the policies that perpetuate exclusion and had critical ideas for redressing the divide. This chapter affords us an occasion to engage in much-needed critical reflexivity pertaining to policy, and policy related research models, so that the research can better inform decisions and become pathways to transformative change.

1 Research Methodology

This chapter draws on a qualitative policy research study exploring the perspectives of immigrant youth and the impact of systems and institutions, and their corresponding layers of legislative, government and organizational policies, on understandings of individual and collective experiences of social rights. The research hears from youth who migrated to Canada from Latin America and the Caribbean and explores how they experience rights, and how those rights are shaped by systems of the state and realized through policy.

More and more, Canada is adopting the discourse of youth inclusion through the promotion of youth rights, youth engagement and the participation of youth as a form of social inclusion. For example, Canadian provincial governments reference the United Nations Convention on the Rights of the Child as a part of provincial legislation (i.e., Ontario's amendments to the Child and Family Services Act) and youth advisory committees are cropping-up as a means of gathering youth input into the policy making process at the most senior levels of government (i.e., Prime Minister's Youth Council). However, child and youth rights are increasingly situated within a neoliberal discourse of individualism wherein young people and their families are expected to take responsibility for their own wellbeing while social welfare supports are increasingly eroded (Goddard, 2012; Houdt & Schinkel, 2014; Rice & Prince, 2013). Acknowledgement of the systemic and structural factors that discriminate against youth that migrate to Canada are positioned against a responsibility discourse that expects youth to take personal responsibility for their own wellbeing and largely ignores the impacts of colonization and racism (de Finney, Loiselle & Saraceno, 2011). Thus, this research uses a rights framework to explore how and where those rights are situated in sectors impacting youth (youth justice, education, health care, child welfare, immigration) and how those policies are experienced by youth.

The exploration of intersections between youth as policy users and their rights as defined in those policies enables new understandings of how youth define individual, social, and collective rights and opportunities to exercise those rights. The research aims to build understanding in regard to Canadian social policy in three key areas: 1) whether opportunities to actualize rights support social citizenship or perpetuate the colonization of the Global South through neoliberal policies; 2) consider factors which support and/or hinder the translation of children and youth rights from the diaspora populations in Canada; 3) map how and where rights are expressed and document the connections/disjunctures between policies that speak to and provide opportunities for access to youth rights and the youth lived experience of those rights.

Qualitative methods and data resulting from lived experience is devalued as a form of evidence (Denzin & Giardina, 2008) compared to policy research that rely on methods considered to have more grounding in evidence, such as discourse analysis and quantitative methods. This research prioritizes arts-based qualitative focus groups with youth ages 16 to 29 from El Salvador, Honduras, Nicaragua, Dominican Republic, Trinidad and Jamaica. Four focus groups, facilitated by two Spanish speaking peer researchers and one principal investigator, with 23 youth, sought to understand how youth understand rights within key domains of the research project (youth justice, child welfare, education, immigration) and how they conceptualize their own rights. Focus groups were 3 hours long, beginning with a brief presentation about youth rights, followed by a broad rights question on each of the domains, and then looking at each of the areas from a human rights framework and from youths' perspectives. (Note: it was intended originally, that each domain would be discussed in the focus group before moving on to the next domain). The focus groups included an arts-based activity, the development of posters, to provide an alternate form of communication beyond the traditional research milieu. Artworks were vetted to eliminate identifying information. Focus groups were analyzed for themes and youth voice compared with Canadian policies that claim a youth rights framework to understand the disjuncture/connection between youth experience and policies that provide opportunities for access to youth rights. Through an iterative process, over thirty policies were collected, from formal to informal, and including legislative, administrative and policy frameworks. Focus group themes were used to identify, select, and guide a content analysis of the policies.

The research path did not follow a traditional policy research process but was, rather, emergent, iterative, discursive, and at times circuitous, following the lived experience of the youth which then generated possibilities for new questions and new meaning. As Strega and Brown (2015) remind us, as principal investigators we must to stop and reflect and ask ourselves "[w]hose story will our research tell, why, to whom, and with what interpretations?" (p.4). Data was not simply themes, nodes, and codes, but included posters with drawings, words, poems, collage, and pictures to represent and express considerations, experiences, ideas, and solutions. Latitude was given to two peer researchers, with their own lived experience, to drive the data collection process and to unsettle the insider-outsider dynamics between researcher and participant.

1.1 Not All of the Set-Out Approaches to the Research Were So Clear in Practice!

Peer researchers, with an abundance of art supplies and food and a tolerance (enthusiasm!!) for creative chaos, established a welcoming setting in which to talk, engage, debate, and express themselves in ways that the youth who participated indicated they had not previously experienced in terms of an opportunity to talk about the intersection of their experiences of immigration and rights/policy/social institutions (indeed, at the end of each group, youth expressed a desire to attend another group in the future, with the same participants, to continue the discussions). Co-constructed grounded theory, as a methodological approach, enabled the peer researchers and, in some ways, the youth themselves, to be a part of defining the research areas, including the identification of which polices needed to be included in the content analysis, which institutions needed be discussed, and what questions needed to be asked.

The research proposes to critically interrupt notions of policy development that exclude youth as policy actors and desires to challenge traditional strategies of policy analysis and development by engaging peer researchers (young people) with lived experience in all aspects of research design, from participant recruitment to data collection. The peer researchers attended multiple planning, training, and debriefing sessions with the principal investigators on the research design, the literature that informed the study, the intended approach to focus groups, and recruitment. The desire to include youth voice in as many of the research aspects as possible required us to set aside preconceived notions of how the focus groups would be constructed. Even though the principal investigators had experience with focus groups and working with young people, as white adult researchers we were challenged by the peer researchers – from the amount of information that would need to be provided to the youth prior to the group discussion (our oversimplification of the context), to the way in which the information would be delivered (discussion of each domain individually), to our assumptions of what the type of art supplies youth would want (we did not include magazines with diverse ethnocultural representation that could be used in collage making), to how the art should be integrated into the focus group (concurrent with the 'talk focus group' rather than at the end as a reflection on the discussion), to the very complicated and intersectional nature of policy exclusion (i.e., health policy and education) – our training with the peer researchers proved to be as much of a learning for us as it was for the peer researchers – and required a leap of trust on our part to shift our 'carefully planned approach' to one which was far more 'boisterous', 'disorganized', and evolving.

To understand the challenge to established approaches it is necessary to first consider traditional focus groups and the exclusion of youth from policy research. The following sections outline approaches to focus group research and the role of youth in relation to policy development and considers the ways in we, as researchers, re-visioned these approaches (or, more accurately, witnessed them *being* re-visioned). We then present the words of the youth themselves to illustrate how the creation of research environments that make room for exploration and critical conversations, where youth voices are the main holders of space, through personal sharing and listening to one another, and the chance to create narratives in multiple ways, including on large pieces of blank paper, led to new understandings of the ways in which policies can fail the various rights they are intended to uphold.

2 Focus Groups

On the surface focus group research seems straightforward – who has not seen the show *Madmen* and the use of the focus groups as marketing research to decide the best approach to advertising the product of the day. Focus groups are frequently regarded as an expedient way to collect a significant amount of data, and ascertain the opinions of multiple people, in a short time (Redmond & Curtis, 2009). Research literature includes varying approaches and definitions of focus groups. Barbour (2007) notes that most definitions use terminology that refer to "group interviewing," "focus group interview" "focus group discussions" (p.3). Perhaps what is most straightforward is understanding focus groups as a group discussion, with ideas that surface as a result of the guidance of the researcher. "Any group discussion may be called a focus group as long as the researcher is actively encouraging of, and attentive to, the group interaction" (Kitzinger and Barbour as cited in Barbour, p. 3). Focus groups provide the opportunity to explore ideas and gain a broader and richer understanding of a topic based on the perspectives of a number of individuals (Redmond & Curtis, 2009). Our research embraced this value of using focus groups for data collection. We thought about ways that could disrupt the notion of *extracting data* from youth, individually, in isolation, for our own purposes, to one which includes fostering opportunities to learn and share experiences as part of a collective consciousness raising possibility, as well as creating the opening to think about strategies of resistance. We anticipated that focus groups may help breakdown neoliberal notions of responsibilization and individual failings and encourage a collective acknowledgement of structural exclusion grounded in social conditions. Further, we anticipated that the focus group would act as both data collection in and of itself as well as provide the framework for carrying out an analysis of policies identified by the youth.

It must be noted that there are limitations of focus groups, a key one being that the researcher and their style can impact the flow between the group and the discussion between the participants (Morgan, 1997). For this research, peer researchers were critical contributors to the research as their lived experience both influenced our approach to the research as well as allowed for discursive interaction between interviewer and participant.

Focus group research speaks to the importance of considering group dynamics that take place and how in-group interaction shapes the outcome of the research. Redmond and Curtis (2009) refer to the focus group in relation to a "form of group interview where the aim is to understand the social dynamic and interaction between the participants through the collection of verbal and observational data" (p.57). Focus groups are not discussions simply for the sake of conversation, but to generate data and information. Morgan (1997) considers focus group research in terms of "a research technique that collects data through group interaction on a topic that is determined by the researcher" (p.130), describing the core elements of the focus group as data collection, data collected from interaction through group discussion, and the role of the researcher. Although our intent was certainly aligned with initiating an opportunity for group discussion, we also wanted to initiate possibilities of shared learning in the act of bringing youth together. Focus groups support interaction between individuals and their ideas with a primary benefit coming from the ideas generated from group discussion (Gibbs, 1997; Redmond & Curtis, 2009). To give voice to counterhegemonic collective narratives, to listen and learn from those with lived experience, to include an insider political and personal perspective, helps us to explore whether the policies intended to actualize youth rights function to support and uphold social citizenship or, in fact, serve to perpetuate the domination and subordination of diaspora youth from the Global South.

3 Youth as Policy Actors

Finding multiple ways to let youth co-construct the research at all stages is situated in the awareness that youth are not considered policy actors. There is minimal research that portrays youth as true policy actors, with youth informing the policies within which their rights intend to be embedded. Youth are not characteristically regarded as the ones to define the solution to the problem, but rather in need of being managed via policies and programs. Youth are positioned within deficit-based constructs such as "citizens in the making" (Marshall, 1998, p.100), a "social problem" (Beauvais, McKay & Seddon, 2001, p. 5), risky, dangerous, difficult – in need of containment and being managed … (Besley, 2009; Creaney, 2013); youth are seen as an adjunct to policy rather than a legitimate policy actors. Our research strives to challenge notions of policy that relies almost exclusively on 'expert knowledge' produced by sanctioned epistemic communities and presents policy from the perception of young people to reveal how youth are policy experts in their deep critical awareness, from an experiential perspective, on policy impact.

Within the literature on diaspora youth and social policy, there is a lack of research that includes the youth voice perspectives on the intersections of youth migration in Canada and child and youth rights. Human rights frameworks are increasingly popular within western policy-making approaches; therefore, hearing from those most impacted, specifically youth, on how rights are implemented within the policies that are applied to the systems with which they intersect, is critical. While there are criticisms of rights-based approaches, such as their inability to effectively address issues of a systemic nature (Hertzman, 2002) and their focus on the individual as opposed to collective rights, rights-based discourses exist as the "only benchmark for a common global language" within youth-serving sectors (Goldson & Munice, 2012, p.61). Therefore, while child and youth rights approaches are limited, they offer a policy framework for less punitive approaches within state systems that have been criticized for a lack of youth inclusion (i.e., education, child welfare, and youth justice) and can evaluate their policy approaches. Rights-based discourses and related policies may foster the participation of children and youth as decision makers as a mechanism to counter neoliberal impacts on social programs such as education, youth justice and child welfare. In fact, Oyeleye (2014) points out, youth face significant challenges because of the global and economic impacts of neoliberalism, including unemployment, contract work, low paid jobs, and lack of opportunities for career advancement. These impacts of neoliberalism have been met with resistance driven by young people in the form of:

uprisings, protests and resistance movements that have been championed by youth across the world, with a growing consciousness of the universality of each national episode in terms of the systemic origin of the oppressive experiences and the conditions that are being felt across national, race, gender and, increasingly, class boundaries, represent a collective global demand for social justice, and a refusal to be written out of history.

p.67

On the other hand, literature points to the limitations of the participation models and questions whether they are effective. For example: "a frequent criticism is tokenistic consultation, where children and young people are asked for their views but never receive feedback and never know if their views have produced any change in policy or practice" (Tisdall & Davis, 2004, p. 132). Consequently, any consultation with youth as policy stakeholders must be approached with the dual recognition of their deep understanding of social inequity as well as the unique agency and capacity to effect change youth command and must be situated in a commitment to ensuring that the insights advanced are included as legitimate and valuable policy drivers.

3.1 *Youth Speak to Their Exclusion from the Policy Process*

What better way than listening to the voice of the youth themselves to illustrate the ways in which they are excluded from policy development. Youth participants shared they are invisible in the polices made for and about them. They challenged that adults need to stop making policies without them and that their experiences should not be reduced to policy themes, statistics and outcomes. The text in Figure 13.1b reads: "You're making policies for me ... without me". "Could we access support w/o discrimination?" "I'm not a statistic, I'm complex". "Stop forcing pathologies on me ... I'm living in poverty". "I'm first generation where is my family support?" "Do I really have the right to be heard?" "Should my age determine how important my voice is?" The concerns articulated in this poster are deep, complex, and passionate. They demonstrate a desire to be included in the discussion and the capacity to identify a social problem; indeed, it firmly positions youth as policy actors.

Our process endeavored to be driven by youth in as many ways as possible. From leveraging critical anti-oppressive youth organizations for recruitment, to the inclusion of peer researchers in most aspects of the research, it was an intentional approach to politicize the research process itself in order to disrupt adult centric notions of policy development, analysis and research and the very institutional systems which hold those policies tight as foundations

FIGURE 13.1b   Deconstructing traditional focus group research and the use of youth voice

of their operating frameworks. We started with acknowledgement that the traditional relationship between the researcher and researched contributes to how knowledge is constructed. As an intentional process of disruption, our data collection centered on the inclusion of peer researchers who brought lived knowledge of child welfare, youth justice, education, and social media. The peer researchers met with the principal investigators in advance to put together the focus group questions, plan the structure of the focus groups, and contribute to strategies of recruitment.

Focus groups began with a presentation of the key areas of education, child welfare, immigration, youth justice and social media and the types of systems and policies that impacted those areas. The peer researcher explained that we were not looking for institutional critiques but rather were seeking to understand more broadly each of the areas from a human rights framework and from the youths' perspectives. The peer researcher framing of the research allowed new interpretations of the areas to emerge that may not have been explored. Examples explored by participants, such as – just because they had the *right* to access education, it did not mean that they experienced inclusion within school settings; experiences of violence attached to unregulated labour and precarious employment that youth engage in so that they can support families, resulting in criminalization, have repercussions for accessing services; the ways in which immigration status builds barriers in accessing health care, potentially impacting youth in care, led to a more complex discussion and understanding of the impacts of policy on youth from the diaspora. The youth, via the peer researchers, became co-constructors of the knowledge as they defined how they experienced each of the policy areas and how they defined their experience of rights within those contexts.

4   Art as Critical Policy Research Methodology

In reflection, while we may have recognized the power of creating opportunities to hear from youth with lived knowledge, we may have underestimated their power and capacity to educate us both through their narratives and through the art that they created. We set the conditions to bring youth together and a research approach that was flexible in its ability to adapt to the moment, but it was the youth themselves that took hold of what was available, and it was their decision to trust the process enough to share their multiple truths; unanticipated was use of art to critically interrupt traditional research paradigms that would have simply seen us collecting and coding the narratives from the youth. In the making of art as a means of storytelling, the focus groups in and of themselves became a process of learning for the researchers and for the participants. Before going further into the power of the art it is important to speak to the original intent. In our planning we regarded the art as a culminating activity that would take place at the end of the focus group. After listening and engaging in the focus group, participants would reflect and pull together the threads of the discussion into posters. Our thinking was that this approach would provide us a window into how the youth synthesized the emerging themes and would provide an alternate form of expression and communication in recognition that youth need opportunities to express themselves beyond the traditional research interview and focus group setting.

It was the peer researchers that asserted that art supplies should be made available at the outset of the focus group so that youth could engage with the materials as they preferred. If we had any hesitation that the art may distract from the discussion, we were wrong; rather, it allowed for a way for youth to remain engaged as they listened and to create and communicate simultaneously. We started the focus group with nice, neat, organized piles of bristol board, markers, glue, glitter, scissors, and magazines and, within minutes of starting the group, the table was a heap of mixed method chaos – laughter, quiet reflection, discussion, and attentive listening dominated the room. We had mistakenly assumed that youth may co-create an art piece – but instead each hand went into the pile, with each youth wanting their own poster board for their creation. What resulted was an opportunity for youth to express their multiple truths while engaging in deep, personal, and at times painful, discussion and the posters were a vehicle for expressing their expert knowledge.

To illustrate we will share two key findings from the research and the ways in which the use of art was able to support youth participants to exercise their personal agency as a part of making meaning of the subject matter.

4.1   Lived Experience as Policy Expert

The ways in which youth live policy is different than how they see it defined in legislation, standards, frameworks, and the various tools of state and organizational bureaucracy. Lived experience goes beyond the current state definition of categories of rights and what the youth taught us was that they live rights as a part of their experience. Youth described living policies in ways that were disconnected from the ways in which policies are defined. They shared that their experiences should be a part of how policy is interpreted and operationalized, otherwise policy merely reflects the neoliberal status quo. Figure 13.2 highlights the incoherence between formal rights and lived experience in relation to health care, education, employment, and culture. Had we simply utilized a traditional focus group methodology we may not have accessed the opportunity to build collective and individual knowledge.

4.2   Policy Is Intersectional and Layered

Through their stories, youth emphasized that policy cannot be reduced to an institutional category. For example, the experiences youth have in the school system crosses into other sectors and, as a result, those policies come into play (Figure 13.3). Therefore, policy cannot be understood simply as a set of institutional constructs if one wants to understand how policy is actually lived and experienced. Instead, the experience of policy is layered and messy – rather than a set of discrete categories, policies are experienced as crossing from one policy sector into another. We were also challenged to look past adult centric views of what policies most impact youth and hear from them in terms of their experiences. For example, the lack of access to health care and the ways in which precarious labour led to dangerous situations for young people were unanticipated themes. Such emergent themes were in part possible because of a critical research methodology that infused flexibility and valued the importance of forming relationships with the youth then provided opportunity and space to generate and articulate knowledge.

5   Conclusion

We cannot end this discussion without centering and decentering ourselves as researchers in this process. To those reading in the hopes of an 'ah ha moment' to inspire their own research, this is not a research process that can be simply replicated without first interrogating oneself as researcher. To understand the power of the methodological journey that we took alongside the youth it is vital to reflect on our whiteness, adult centric viewpoints, and the Eurocentric

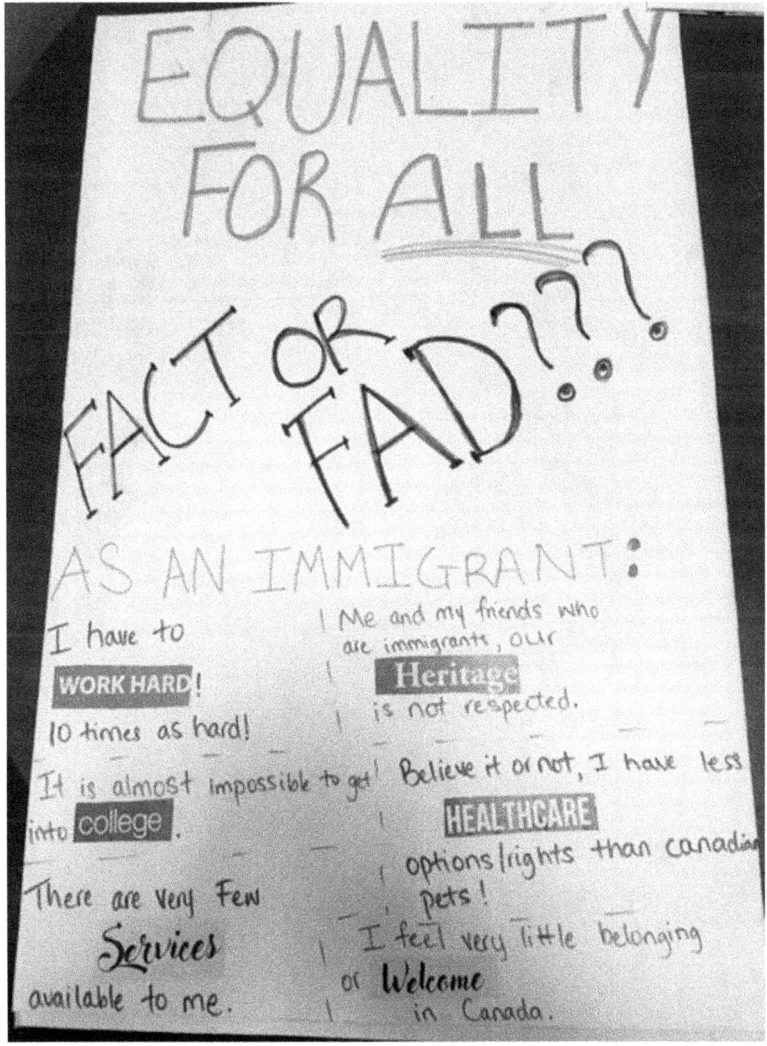

FIGURE 13.2 Youth as policy experts

and western models of evidence and linear approaches to research methodology and policy development in which are steeped. Despite our intention at the outset to outline a methodological approach that would upset traditional research processes, it is only now in this process of critically standing back and engaging in reflexive self-critique, that we are able to fully begin to see the importance of challenging what we, as researchers, impose on the process in ways known and unknown. It was not *us* that allowed for this journey to

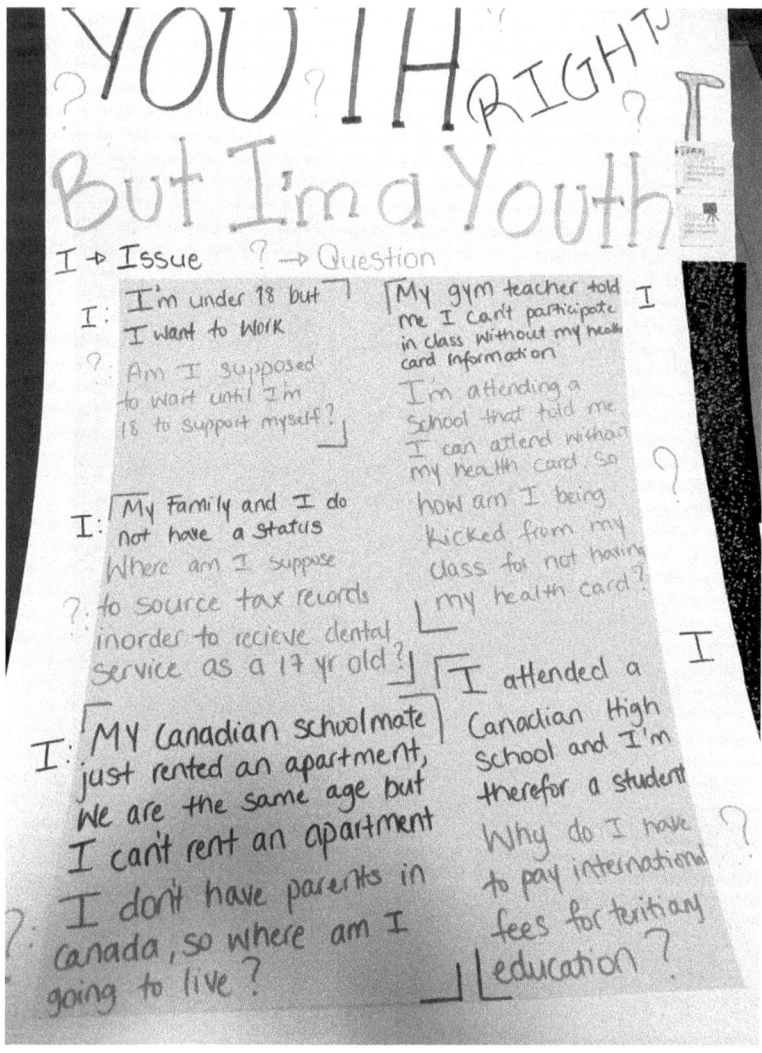

FIGURE 13.3 Policy is intersectional and layered

occur – it was the youth that got us there, insisted their knowledge be shared, and it is their power must be centered.

In reflection, the youth taught us that as researchers and critical thinkers we must find ways to lean into the dual purpose of research: research as a means of creating and contributing to new knowledge but also centering the role of research as a means of social change and activism. It was the youth that showed us how the researched and researcher can come together to disrupt spaces held as expert. The youth challenged traditional notions of engagement, where they have been invited in with strict parameters only to be shown the door once we have taken what we need. We entered into a space to learn about the translation of youth rights into lived experience, and in this we already saw ourselves as cutting-edge. In coming together and exerting self-determination, the youth and peer researchers made us take a step back from a predetermined process to allow for a methodology that was emergent— a shared space of critical deconstruction. We mused that the youth came as their own ethics committee, wielding their shared power instead of edits on a page, to influence the process in a way that worked for them. If, as researchers, we had remained cemented to our planned approach— reading policy definitions tied to traditional notions of systems and structures – we would have been stuck. If we had not been open to the talking over one another, the laughter, the agreements and disagreements – we would not have heard the complex shared stories. Had we pushed the silent ones to speak in order to draw out a verbal contribution, we may not have witnessed the flowers emerging from the earth, and with those petals, the themes of pain, exclusion, and opportunities for change. What we learned is that deconstructing traditional policy research with the interface of youth-voice and arts-based focus groups was the power of youth as researchers. Our own privilege and expertise were confronted by the power that came with allowing youth to interrogate a process that centered listening to their lived realities in whatever way that wanted that to emerge. As a result, we gathered rich, personal, and deeply meaningful knowledge about the lived realities of youth rights in relation to journeys of immigration – a set of lived experiences that critically challenges how we must think about and develop policy not for, but with, youth.

Our goal was to hear from youth and to gather their experiences of youth rights so that we could compare what we heard to the policies we collected. Our intent was to explore the disjuncture/connections between youth experience and policies that speak to and provide opportunities for access to youth rights. What we did *not* anticipate was the way in which the methodology would in and of itself provide an opportunity for change – that, bringing youth together in spaces of non-traditional research, with multiple opportunities to be included, whether through art or the peer researchers, itself facilitated agency and empowerment through shared learning and knowledge. One of the goals was to find ways to understand the spaces of exclusion of youth in policy in terms of their experience of systems, but what we heard is that youth need to be a part of policy development and research to influence how policy is defined, interpreted and applied. Do not be fooled: in the image of pink tissue paper and glitter sunshine, a youth states that they "are not a statistic" but rather "complex"; under the earth and the bright red roses in the earth, and under the tissue paper grass, the youth yells at us to ensure they are included – to not erase them based on their age (see Figure 13.1a).

This chapter has encouraged us to reflect on the power of young people, their agency, and their right to be a part of those conversations that most deeply impact them. We will continue to reflect and find ways to not just bring youth to the conversation, but to help construct how the conversation takes place, as it will be in this confluence of relationship building and critical reflexivity that youth and adults can come together. Where adults and their power can be challenged, and where youth can control the space – this is where new and valuable meaning will emerge.

References

Barbour, R. (Ed.). (2007). *Doing Focus Groups*. London, United Kingdom: SAGE Publications Ltd.

Beauvais, C., McKay, L., & Seddon, A. (2001). A literature review on youth and citizenship. *Canadian Policy Research Networks Inc.* Retrieved on April 1, 2014 from: www.cprn.org/documents/29502_en.pdf.

Besley, T. (2009). Governmentality of youth: Beyond cultural studies. *Contemporary Readings in Law and Social Justice*, 1(2), 36–83.

Creaney, S. (2013). Beyond pre-emptive criminalisation: Towards a child-friendly youth justice. *Safer Communities, 12*(3), 101–110.

Denzin, N. K., & Giardina, M. D. (2008). Introduction: the Elephant in the Living Room, or Advancing the Conversation about the Politics of Evidence. (pp. 9–51). In N. K., Denzin & M.D. Giardina (Eds), *Qualitative Inquiry and the Politics of Evidence*. California: Left Coast Press.

de Finney, S., Dean, M., Loiselle, E., & Saraceno, J. (2011). All children are equal, but some are more equal than others: Minoritization, structural inequities, and social justice praxis in residential care. *International Journal of Child, Youth and Family Studies*, 2(3/4), 361–384.

Gibbs, A. (1997). Focus groups. *Social Research Update*, (19), Department of Sociology, University of Surrey, 1–7.

Goddard, T. (2012). Post-welfarist risk managers? Risk, crime prevention and the responsibilization of community-based organizations. *Theoretical Criminology. 16*(3) 347–363.

Goldson, B. & Muncie, J. (2012). Towards a global 'child friendly' juvenile justice? *International Journal of Law and Crime and Justice*. 40(1), 48–64.

Grover, S. (2004). Why won't they listen to us?: On giving power and voice to children participating in social research. *Childhood (Copenhagen, Denmark)*, 11(1), 81–93.

Hertzman, C. (2002) Leave No Child Behind! Social exclusion and child development. The Laidlaw Foundation Working Paper Series.

Houdt, F. V., & Schinkel, W. (2014). Crime, citizenship and community: Neoliberal communitarian images of governmentality. *The Sociological Review*, 62(1), 47–67.

Marshall, T.H. (1998). Citizenship and Social Class. In Shafir, C. (ed.) *The Citizenship Debates* (pp. 93–111). Minneapolis: University of Minnesota Press.

McKenzie. B. & Wharf, B. (2010). *Connecting Policy to Practice in the Human Services* (3rd ed.). ON: Oxford University Press.

Morgan, D. L. (1997). Focus Groups as Qualitative Research (2nd Ed.). *Qualitative Research Methods Series. Sage Publication.*

Oyeleye, A. (2014). Lost and found? Globalised neoliberalism and global youth resistance. *Critical Arts.* 28(1), 57–68.

Redmond, R. & Curtis, E. (2009). Focus groups: principles and process. *Nurse Researcher,* 16(3), 57–69.

Rice, J.J. & Prince, M.J. (2013). *Changing Politics of Canadian Social Policy* (2nd Ed). University of Toronto Press.

Strega, S. & Brown, L. (2015). *Research as Resistance: Revisiting Critical, Indigenous, and Anti-oppressive Approaches.* Toronto: Canadian Scholar's Press.

Tisdall, K. & Davis, J. (2004). Making a difference? Bringing children and young people's views into policymaking. *Children and Society.* 18(2), 131–142.

CHAPTER 14

A Co-constructed Critical Autoethnographical Conversation with Social Work Students regarding Reflexive Research Engagement

Marco Giuliani, Michelle Brochu, Albina Magomedova, Michelle Boehm and Dawn Onishenko

This co-constructed autoethnography seeks to bring to the foreground the lived experiences of four undergraduate social work students engaged in grounded theory research on marginalized youth homelessness in a time of COVID-19 as part of our fourth-year placements. This chapter explores the tensions and congruences between our theoretical understandings as social work students at a critical anti-oppressive institution and the concrete realities of conducting qualitative research. Through critical reflexivity, we, the authors, explore qualitative research practices that were employed as research assistants, to compare and contrast the ethical and political congruences as student researchers. This chapter engages with key concepts of anti-oppression, the research processes, ethical considerations, the student experience, and challenges that arose from the pandemic.

1   Methodology: Why a Critical Co-constructed Autoethnography?

Our critical reflexivity on our experiences as social work placement students working on an anti-oppressive research project is situated in critical co-constructed autoethnography.

> Critical co-constructed autoethnography as a methodology [is] steeped in critical theory, critical pedagogy and critical race theory. It provides a way for collaborating activist researchers to reflect on the tempo, uncertainty, and complexity of research relationships that cross boundaries into more personal spaces such as friendships. Further, critical co-constructed autoethnography creates spaces for collaborating researchers to work across differences.
> CANN & DEMEULENAERE, 2012

As a methodology, critical autoethnography allows us to take on the roles as both researchers and participants, and utilize this opportunity to situate our identities, values, and beliefs within our research. Critical autoethnography highlights the importance of "turning our gaze inwards" (Freeman & VanKatwyk, 2019, p. 152), whereby the researcher observes their own experiences, including the social and political context which informs personal conduct (Chew et al., 2015, as cited in Freeman & VanKatwyk, 2019). Through this inward gaze, the researcher is no longer a passive player in colonial theoretical frameworks, but rather, acknowledges their subject position to identify challenges and contradictions in the operationalization of power, with possibilities of resisting colonial and positivist notions of objectivity (Freeman & VanKatwyk, 2019; Heron, 2005).

While this critical autoethnography was a reflexive practice that began in the final stages of our placement as student researchers on a grounded theory project on marginalized youth homelessness, we came together as a research team for weekly meetings and continued to meet after our placement had ended, staying on as research assistants on a voluntary basis. During these meetings, we asked each other questions on our experiences as social work students conducting research on youth homelessness and how our academic teachings of critical AOP aligned, or did not align, with conducting research. In these rich discussions we came to appreciate the value of developing reflexive skills. We critically reflected on grounded theory as a methodology, the ethical considerations of researching marginalized populations, and the challenges of conducting anti-oppressive research as 'academics' in mitigating top-down research on vulnerable persons. We began by writing individual critical reflections, then merged them into a combined critical autoethnographic analysis. However, the critical autoethnography became too watered down and so we individually revisited the merged document to thicken our analysis. Rather than breaking down into themes, we collectively decided to present our analysis in the same chronology as the research process. As a group, we believe this best reflects our growth as student researchers, but also recognize how this structuring may be helpful for future social work students hoping to engage as student researchers as part of their placement.

2   Beginning the Story by Situating Ourselves

At first glance, it might have been difficult to spot our shared connection as student researchers. We represent four different decades in our ages and four significantly different stages in our careers. We are a diverse quartet with various social work practice interests. As social work students, situating ourselves is critical to challenging positivist and colonial understandings that researchers are objective and neutral (Heron, 2005), but to maintain some degree of anonymity, we chose not to disclose our names when providing each student's subject position and unique reason for being drawn to the research project. Our personal agendas varied from preparation for first-time entrance into full-time work, to shifting careers, to updating credentials, and to augmenting skills for the sake of increasing one's scope of knowledge and practice. Despite these differences, we all share a passion for people who are vulnerable to homelessness and a keen interest in developing our skills to be the best critical anti-oppressive social workers that we are capable of becoming. The magic element that facilitated blending our collaborative energies was the environment imposed on us by the pandemic and the structure of the research project.

When receiving the opportunity to participate in a research placement related to youth homelessness, each of us consciously went through a personal reflection period where we took time to consider what this research meant to us. We note that the placement was not open to any student, but rather clearly available only to those students who brought a passion for and an understanding of housing precarity, homelessness, youth and social exclusion. It was important for each of us to seek out the connection we had with youth homelessness, in order to confirm our offer and move forward with the interview process and hopefully secure the position. Three of us identify as white. As it turns out, each of us holds experiences and identities that intersect with youth homelessness, each bringing a unique lens and spirit to the interview that ultimately resulted in each of us being invited to the project.

To better illuminate the relational dynamics that we brought to the research, we will discuss some of the connections we observed from one another. Two students had direct experience with homelessness as service users. One now works as a service provider in the field. Those of us that had previous experience with homelessness described feeling a sense of duality throughout the research process when walking the line of privilege that separated service users and service providers. We were able to understand stigma, marginalization, and the feeling of being disenfranchised in a deeply personal manner and found it difficult and almost ironic to sit in a place of privilege and power, when we could recall and reflect so easily what it was like to be on the other end, years ago. This also accentuated the importance of self-reflexivity and "turning our gaze inwards" (Freeman & VanKatwyk, 2019, p. 152), to recognize that our personal narratives cannot be stripped from our role as a researcher, but rather hold that awareness in our decision making and when reflecting on our interactions. Having both navigated the social work system before, we approached the study and the research participants with a high level of compassion and 'survivorship' that grounded us and propelled us forward from a particular lens. One student, in particular, had lived experience of hidden-homeless, while also experiencing cultural erasure and abuse of power by persons of authority. This student had a preconceived notion of the stresses and struggles that contributed to homeless youth becoming disenfranchised. However, as student researchers, we collectively came to recognize how self-reflexivity is fundamental to avoiding the danger of making unconscious expectations about participant perspectives and experiences. This will be explored further when discussing interviewing.

2.1 *Social Location*

As a group, in the process of our critical reflexivity, we came to unpack the lens we held collectively and individually. We came to recognize that the complex intersectionality which we brought to the research team was silently influencing us. Three of us identify as white, two of us have lived experience connected to the 2SLGBTQ+ community and all of us have witnessed and/or experienced gender-based stigma and violence. One student identifies under the 2SLGBTQ+ umbrella and lived in Toronto's gay village, which led to personal encounters with homelessness, including couch surfing, sex work, and survival sex. Another has family members who have experienced gender-based violence. Two of us identify as profoundly compassionate and connected to the disability community – one as a professional and one as a family member – and have deep concerns for what homelessness looks like when living with a disability. Two are single parents; one supporting their child alone and having experience of gender-based stigma and trauma and one having experienced damage that can occur in a social services system that is wrought with gaps. Two of us have lived experience of homelessness and have experienced stigma, marginalization and understand being disenfranchised in a deeply personal manner.

One of the students has been working in the non-profit sector supporting disabled young adults with their transition into adulthood and the workforce, some of whom are precariously housed. With this experience, this student felt a responsibility to advocate for the active inclusion of individuals who identified as having a disability and how their experience with homelessness may look different compared to others. This disability-based lens and perspective helped challenge the research study in terms of how we conceptualized homelessness. In team meetings we discussed that, "just because you have a roof over your head, this does not mean an individual has been provided with a quality standard of living" – that they have a *home*. This was evidenced by the number of disabled individuals that lived in group homes throughout the pandemic and were relegated to living in solitude throughout the lockdown. In addition, we saw from our interviews the high number of homeless individuals who self-identified with some form of being differently abled and/or forewent being placed in a shelter during the pandemic due to not wanting to live in isolation for the two-week quarantine period.

Another student has been working in the homeless sector for a decade and has deeply personal interest and volunteered or was employed in community services for decades. As a person who initially viewed social work through the lens of a front-line worker, it seemed that there was a disconnect between the lens of theoretical academia, including research, and the lived experience of doing direct service with clients. The experience of this placement quashed that personal view and enabled the rethinking of social work practice to include research which raises the participant voice beyond the individual service provider and bridged voices to the community and to policy makers. For this student, the placement became an opportunity to consolidate knowledge and reimagine social work practice to be inclusive of academia, within the context of the political environment. The student had intersectional factors of lived experience, including being a first generation Canadian whose life was impacted by the influence of colonialism, of being a support person to LGBTQ family members, of being a parent of children with disabilities and mental health system involvement, and who had lived experience of gender-based disenfranchisement and marginalization. The student, who had great appreciation of the connection between the personal and the political, came to have great respect for the role of social work research in raising participant voices to facilitate bridging gaps in policy.

The research team member who identified under the 2SLGBTQ+ umbrella was drawn to the project from their experiences living in the Church and Wellesley area, a predominantly Rainbow community in Toronto, which led to personal encounters of persons who were living rough, couch surfing, and engaged in survival sex.

> These were not just people I would pass by on the street. They were my neighbours, my friends, and people I came to know and care about while living in this dynamic community. And because people come to this neighbourhood in hopes of finding acceptance, and in some cases fleeing discrimination from their hometowns, or even violence in their families, there is also a lot of vulnerability, trauma, and housing precarity there, visible and invisible.

We each brought lived experience and preconceived concepts of homelessness to the placement. We also had awareness of the privilege that comes as a researcher, a role which inherently has power (Heron, 2005). Consequently, we all needed to address the ways in which our lived experiences influenced our worldviews. It is only in naming this that we could ensure that we had the capacity to be self-reflexive and do social work research that truly raised the voices of our research participants using anti-oppressive anti-racism transformative practice.

3 Reflexive Engagement with the Research Process

3.1 *Grounded Theory*

As we began our placement and learn more about the research, part of what made this research project so exciting to all of us was its methodology. Grounded theory was first developed in the 1960's by Glasser and Strauss and is currently the most widely used methodology in qualitative research (Padgett, 2017). Eventually Glasser and Strauss had differing perspectives on how grounded theory should be conducted (Padgett, 2017). Our research project took on a less rigid and more feminist approach to grounded theory in which it was not the quantity of participants that was viewed as significant, but rather the thick, rich quality of data that emerged from participants. Grounded theory begins with questions that are informed by the existing research on a topic and our current understandings of the phenomenon. Padgett (2017) describes grounded theory as an "inductive–deductive feedback loop in which hypotheses or hunches are tested as the conceptual model is built" (p. 62). In other words, it is an iterative process in which our research questions, data collection, and data analysis continuously inform one another as part of an ongoing process.

As student researchers, the iterative process of grounded theory became evident when the interview questions that we created, which were based on relevant themes we derived from our preliminary literature review on youth homelessness during COVID-19, were continuously revisited and checked against the new themes that emerged by participants. One student remarked:

> This really made the importance of qualitative research come alive for me. Suddenly, we are not just a research team asking important questions that we derived from our initial understandings of the subject area, but rather, the voices of participants themselves brought forth data to inform future questioning, the important questions for us to be asking moving

forward. The participant's voice, their experience, their knowledge, it informs the research process.

As social work students at a critically anti-oppressive school, we agreed that this iterative process is aligned to the work that we want to be doing as social workers and as student researchers. It also makes sense when researching a phenomenon such as COVID, in which things change quickly, such as availability of vaccines, agency policies, and the changing provincially mandated restrictions.

4 Learning from the Research Team Engagement Process

4.1 *Team Meetings*

While reflecting on our experience of participating in the research process, it seems imperative to draw attention to our team meetings because they acted as the foundation of support for our critical reflexivity. As part of our placement requirements, each week or so, for a few hours, the whole team would come together via Zoom. The group consisted of the principal researcher, two co-investigators, as well as us four placement students and, at times, community members. It was within the collaborative dynamic of our research team meetings that we were given the opportunity to reflect on methodological and logistical issues, as well as all ethical situations that arose. In other words, this is where the magic happened in relation to our personal transformative social work practice. From the very first meeting, our participation involved seeking, contributing, and learning about how to do research. With an open floor policy for discussion, we were able to address situations as a group, where multiple and often contradicting opinions would come up that ultimately challenged our thought processes over and over again. Some of the topics we discussed revolved around previous decisions such as risks, honorariums, and participant inclusion/exclusion criteria. More specifically, questions such as the following were freely discussed:

> What kind of risks were involved when it came to interviewing frontline workers, and how do we ensure that we do everything we can to maintain their well-being and job security? Would frontline workers and managers be eligible to receive an honorarium? How do we justify in the REB that only homeless youth would be receiving an honorarium? How strict do we choose to be in our inclusion/exclusion criteria for the homeless youth and how will allowing them to self-identify benefit our study?

From a pedagogical perspective, this comprehensive and inclusive learning environment modeled anti-oppressive social work in that our perspectives as social work students, combined with our own unique connections to homelessness, were welcomed as valuable contributions to the conceptualization of the project. This was an especially unique situation because we were having these kinds of discussions with academic professors that had been working and teaching these concepts for years. Never did we feel downplayed or self-conscious about coming forward with thoughts or ideas because the culture of respect that was cultivated during these meetings was so strong. This was in no way tokenistic, but instead shifted our roles as student researchers to co-creators of the project. And while you might assume that having such a large research team with student researchers may have impeded the expediency of the overall project, we found that this actually led to a profoundly more meaningful learning experience as both placement students and future social workers (and, our principal investigator maintains that student contribution and challenges made the research stronger and more comprehensive).

Moreover, with neoliberal structures creeping further into academia and field education, these kinds of relational meetings seem to resist neoliberal trends. According to George et al., (2013), it is becoming increasingly common for field placement environments to house neoliberal ideals through concepts of competition, efficiency and individualism. This illusion draws a stark contradiction to our experiences, which was especially felt during our meetings. At no point in the project was the focus centred on concrete tasks and deadlines, although those also had to be met.

Likewise, though our tasks as placement students were often assumed to be able to complete alone, our team meetings acted as an opportunity for learning and support as we embraced each challenge. As one student reflected as we discussed the team opportunities:

> Of course, there was tension as we were working hard to evolve our social work practice, but we always knew that if needed, we had a team behind us. This sense of comradery thus replaced any desire or need for competition between one another ... Consequently, even when in the crucible of working in a small team, our natural inclination was to work together. The principal researchers also modeled this collegiality and extended it to us as part of the team. This created a safe space where we could contribute ideas and seek responses and feedback without fear or judgement.
>
> One such example was when a student expressed upset at having learned of how people experiencing homelessness were being given tickets by public transit constables when they entered transit without paying

a fare. The discussion that followed evolved into a discussion with the theme of the ways in which people experiencing homelessness are sometimes easily identified and then targeted, creating a systemic structure which profiled and criminalized specific people. Initially the student was feeling upset about having spoken to someone who experienced this and shared the incident with the team as a means of self-care in a safe place. This evolved into shared compassion and a fulsome discussion of the harmful ways that the homeless are disenfranchised. If there were any air of competition between the students, they would have not shared isolated personal experiences and would have focused on coming to meetings with only research specific academic material to share in the discussions.

4.2 *Conceptualization*

Part of the important learning came from the high levels of autonomy given to us throughout the research study. This learning is akin to that described by Preston et al. (2019): We were given significant freedom and responsibility in the research process: creating interview questions, filling out the REB protocol, and developing recruitment material and consent forms. As a team we would spend hours discussing and working on these research components and then come to our principal investigator for feedback and approval. In this way, our placement experience aligned with the transformative social work values of our school. This was reflected in the leadership of our research supervisor and principal investigator who encouraged meaningful critical discussions and created a platform that allowed us to re-conceptualize elements of marginalization and homelessness. This platform also critiques the rigid colonial conceptualizations of what it means to exist in the margins and how individuals experience homelessness. It was important for us to broaden the context of what it means to be marginalized in order to better understand the participants we were interacting with and the challenges they experienced throughout the pandemic.

In order to maximize our learning as social work students, we were not simply assigned tasks, but rather included by the principal investigator and co-investigators when finalizing details of the project for the ethics proposal. To our surprise, we students became contributors to the design and process of creating the research. This included our direct input into the design, REB, execution and coding the research. This was a profound learning opportunity including adapting to challenging pandemic-related tensions while prioritizing critical anti-oppressive practices. Navigating the system of doing research that was approved by REB while employing AOP practices required that all REB concerns be addressed fully and that the research participants had a positive experience of participating in the interview.

The placement was an opportunity to form our own views of the political nature of social welfare which has contributed to our own transformative social work practice development. By witnessing the gaps and associated consequences that the participants experienced we saw the connection between social welfare policy and social welfare programs. This placement experience gave us the opportunity to politicise our practice, rather than a more common experience in which the ways that social welfare is depoliticized in community settings (Preston et al., 2019). As discussed with each other, our previous agency placements in other academic programs involved attending community services settings. Typically, these placements involved being mentored in the inner workings of the agency and mechanically learning how to replicate the work that was being done rather than examining the mechanism of systemic barriers and changes that would create a more transformative AOP environment in the placement's setting.

5   Application of Learning

In this broad context, we wanted to intentionally shift power dynamics by providing participants with the agency to self-identify and lead the discussion of how they conceptualize marginalization (Fook, 2002). As AOP student researchers we felt a personal responsibility to honour the research participants by making the initial contact with participants one where the student researchers consciously attempted to set aside any preconceived notions and bias in order to create a safe space for participant disclosure. Student researchers focused on ensuring that participants had the agency to self-identify and to not be labeled by the researchers. This was a means for students to cope with the sense of dissonance and personal ethical conflict which the students recognized as part of the social work practice development that they felt in relation to how we used these labels of marginality, either assigned or self-proclaimed, and if we were perpetuating further marginalization towards these participants.

5.1   *Research World Weaving with AOP Front Line Work*
While, as students, we admit that we had not previously seen the link between research and front-line social work practice, as the placement progressed and particularly as we reflected on the experience, the connections became very apparent.

As an experienced front-line worker, I had perceived that there was a disconnect between the theoretical academia of research and lived experience of being on the front line doing direct service with clients. However, this project demonstrated how research can be a platform to facilitate clients' willingness to share thoughts and to have voices be heard. The act of doing research also contributed to my refining and developing my own social work professional practice skills. Ultimately, I came to view research as a crucible in which one has the opportunity to rethink social work practice through the development of a research project and the action through completion of the research project. The experience of being a facilitator to elevate the client voice is evidence reaffirming anti-oppressive social work professional practice.

Though our project was research, the placement taught us the underlying implication of our approach to research and social work practice. Not only did the research give us the opportunity to self-reflect on what we believe our social work practice ought to look like and our personal core beliefs about social work practice, it also gave us the opportunity to grow in our practice.

At the time of the placement, we were not cognizant of the ways in which the COVID-19 pandemic would become the backdrop for reimagining our field education experience. In hindsight, the pandemic acted as a catalyst for influencing changes to the landscape of social work placements and social work practice as the pandemic-related restrictions evolved. As students we were not permitted to meet with participants in person; virtual phone or video appointments were set. Honorariums were paid by e-transfer or snail mail. Recruiting participants was by agency contact and email. The environment in which homeless youth received support was up-ended and changed without warning: Supports made a pivot from working directly with clients to using phone and video contact. In the process, as the homeless sector workers informed us in interviews, they were forced to hone their skills of assessing voices, sound of respiration, and skills of conversation in the absence of access to the body language which informed practice. Homeless sector workers connected with the homeless youth and completed network coordination while concurrently surveying services that had the capacity to support the homeless. Protocols and available supports shifted seemingly daily at times and staff learned to be flexible and work within a changing landscape of potential supports. The youth were seeking support from a system that was inundated with clients who had critical needs to access food and shelter when capacity of available services was frequently exhausted. As such, as students, we had an awareness that we were preparing to engage with participants who were facing deep life crisis.

5.2 Research-Social Work Crossover

In our team meetings and with our placement supervisor, we had the opportunity to engage in complex discussions such as exploring the concept of what 'duty to report' means. "The textbook definitions of duty to report seemed very clear to me when reading them in class. However, it became more complex in the context of speaking with people who relay their lived experience in a web of disclosing both past and present events". The issue was quite important to us since homeless youth are at such high risk of having had traumatic childhood experiences (Kidd et al., 2021). The textbook lessons did not represent intersectionality in the lives of participants. The complex discussions of what our obligation and our duty look like in the research setting helped us to understand the complexities involved in our duty as social work practitioners when working with vulnerable youth. It also reminded us of the power dynamics inherent in every social work interaction.

The substantial discussions of what our obligation and our duty look like in the research setting helped us to understand the complexities involved in our duty as social workers. So, the research project taught us a great deal about the reality of being face-to-face with vulnerable people. Though our discussions were focused on the research participants, the context of our discussions most certainly helped us to form a better concept of what transformative social work practice in the field looks like through applying academic and legalistic language into real world situations where decision making, situational insight and discretionary skills would be exercised.

Such discussions are examples of how we received a meaningful opportunity to experience what being mentored looked like. The principal investigator/placement supervisor supported us as we processed such circumstances and what they mean to subject participants and to us as social work practitioners. One student shared, "At that moment I didn't realize what a significant example of mentoring that was taking place in our team meetings. In hindsight, now that I can step back from the mitigating details of the discussion, I now see it is this mentoring that taught lessons that will be carried forward into the future". The skill of noting mitigating circumstances as history, historical events, timing, intent, level of collaboration of parties involved and appropriate documentation of all observations were reviewed in the context of vignettes from research participants, yet such skills would be relevant in our future practices in the field.

5.3 Trauma-Informed Lens

An integral part of being critical anti-oppressive researchers is having an awareness of the interrelatedness between youth homelessness and trauma

(Morton et al., 2012o. More specifically, traumatic life events often precipitate experiences of youth homelessness, while experiencing homelessness itself also leads to further traumatization (Kidd et al., 2021; Morton et al., 2020). While the research project was not specifically identified as trauma-focused, a trauma-informed lens was integral to every step of the research project. This entails taking pauses, picking up on physical and verbal queues of participants, and ensuring the safety of the participant to the best of your ability (Hallett & Crutchfield, 2018; James & Gilliland, 2017; O'Hara & Levine, 2016). As researchers were careful to not ask leading questions so that participants could have the freedom to speak. Researchers asked if there is anything else that they would like to share. Researchers were cognizant of hierarchical nature of interviews and therefore created a safe environment by having a conversation with participants rather than a question/answer session. One student remarked,

> Youth participants were often seemingly comfortable when speaking about their experiences. They were forthright and shared so much. I believe part of this is because having an opportunity to speak about your lived experience is so meaningful to people, but I also think that as a researcher, as a social work researcher in particular, making a connection with the participant from the start is part of trauma-informed care.

As a team of student researchers, we grew to strengthen our interviewing skills. We wanted our participants to get a sense of how we would be conducting the interview prior to commencing, not just in words, but through actions when providing informed consent. This is where we believe transparency is part of being trauma-informed researchers – and, indeed, was part of our placement training about informed consent and power. By letting youth participants know what the project is about, what the interview will be like, and what the possible risks to participating would be, it gives them power to decide whether they want to participate. Part of trauma-informed lens is also recognizing how persons of authority, such as a researcher, might be intimidating, so not only are participants informed that they could skip questions they do not feel comfortable asking, but they can also terminate the interview at any time without jeopardizing their relationship to the interviewer, the school, or the project.

As student interviewers, creating a space in which participants genuinely felt comfortable, the option to withdraw from the research was important to us as a tool of self-determination. This is also important to relationality and anti-colonial research (Strega & Brown, 2015). In the end, not a single participant withdrew from the interview process, with many participants having shared during the post-interview debrief that the interview was the first time they had felt heard. One student reinforced how important relationality and taking the time to be present with participants is, particularly for socially excluded participants.

> I think for vulnerable populations such as youth experiencing homelessness, informed consent is an opportunity for participants to get a sense of what you stand for, of what kind of space you will be creating during your time together so they can get a sense of whether they feel safe and at ease.

During the setup of interviews and when the interviews took place, researchers focused on creating a safe environment. Though contacts were virtual, either via video conversations or telephone, interviewers focused on creating a safe environment and building rapport with the participants. Any concerns or issues were addressed with immediacy such that the participants could feel comfortable. Researchers were careful to not ask leading questions that could influence responses. This also encouraged participants to voice their experiences and what life looked like to them. Giving participants the freedom to share any issues which they wished to share also contributed to the development of understanding the complexity of the lived experience of being homeless.

5.4   *Allowing Participants to Define Marginalization, and Homelessness*
We were not looking at marginalization as a one-dimensional domain by allowing participants to define and self-identify as being marginalized. This same conceptualization applied to intersectionality, the lens that looks at how minority status and marginalization combine to shape the experiences and identities of people based on the intersecting domains (Cho et al., 2013). As we know from our own lived experiences, our culture, age, gender, and socioeconomic status can sculpt the way we experience various forms of contextual and ever-changing privilege and oppression. Consequently, it is no surprise that, as a team, we had a number of discussions regarding marginalization. In effect, these discussions led us to us feeling confident in being student researchers in which participants had the power to self-identify in these domains rather than being placed into a limited and oppressive box by outsiders, and as researchers.

Such discussions became quite significant as we were not accepting the textbook definitions which we had learned; rather, we were taking the terminology and exploring it in relation to what it is like when one is face-to-face with the homeless youth who have no relationship to textbook definitions, but rather only their own lived experience as a young, at risk and/or homeless person. We began to talk about notions such as honouring the personhood of each individual study participant.

5.5 Research Ethics Board Protocol and Processes

The history of research within marginalized communities, particularly Indigenous communities, is steeped in unethical social work and research practices, including knowledge that has been extracted with significant oppression and exploitation at the expense of marginalized individuals (Nygård & Saus, 2016). As student researchers from a critical AOP school, we were very cognizant of the research implications and, given the nature of our research study, we felt during the self-implication process it was important to situate our identities in relation to the history of colonization and the perpetuation of stealing and re-purposing narratives for the benefit of the researcher and knowledge production (Nygård & Saus, 2016). This type of reflective thinking is what propelled our research as well as our intermediary discussions within every step of the research and gaining ethics approval from the REB.

As social work students, we encountered many unexpected situations in gaining the approval from the Research Ethics Board (REB). We were bound by the details of our study and over the course of many months continued to complete our application, submit for approval, receive REB feedback, adjust our application, re-submit and await further approval. Between periods of re-submission our team would reassess important points such as risk management and how that would look for marginalized individuals, as well as our responsibility to report prior abuse. We quickly realized there were many considerations in terms of what we thought was right as social workers and what was expected from the point of view of an ethics panel. As one student reflected:

> It was a discussion such as these that I came to respect the REB process. If it were not for the REB process, we would've not had such discussions. It became clear to me that part of the value of the REB was not merely the ethical behaviour when acting out the study, but also reviewing the core beliefs of our own ethics and values regarding the research itself and the participants with whom we would interact. The process of working through the REB necessitated that we process our thoughts and discourse to ensure that we were aligning with our goal of being unbiased and reflective such that the research would focus on the voice of the participant.

6   Recruitment

Recruitment of participants is one of the most important elements of any research project – with knowledge and diversity of participants being critical to strong research findings. As one of the students, who had a primary responsibility for recruitment reflected:

> Since I came into the research as a placement student later in the year, I was tasked to begin the first phase of recruitment. At this point in my placement, I had a very limited understanding of my role and even what recruitment really entailed. Although apprehensive, I figured the best approach for me to wrap my mind around the process would be to revisit some of the skills and knowledge I gained through academia. As I considered the research and recruitment, I thought about issues of positionality and power dynamics, and how I was personally implicated in them, as well as the group as a whole. I thought about the critical, anti-oppressive lens that this project held, and what that meant for me. I knew that I needed to situate myself within the research as an able-bodied, white, heterosexual, cis-gendered woman researcher, who was not homeless, nor was I considered a youth. With these multiple identities illuminated, it was, and still is, obvious to me that I hold privilege in our society, which translates to power within relational interactions. As these clear power relations revealed themselves, my intuition informed me of the profound responsibility I held in relation to how I chose to move forward, especially when considering how I would work with youth with these marginal experiences and identities. As I held space for these bodies of thought, it became clear that what I was actually doing in this moment was critical reflexivity.

Critical reflexivity requires social workers to remain present and reflective during practice, as a way to hone in on the underlying assumptions that they may be reflected through their choice of language and the approaches they use during direct practice with clients (Napier & Levine, 2016). We know that language employs authority, "and so by taking the time to hash out these issues with my own social location and the ways that my privilege and oppression potentially interact with others, I was able to prepare myself mentally, so that I could be as intentional of an anti-oppressive researcher as possible".

With this kind of reflection occurring in relation to the recruitment process, conceptual ideas were revisited during larger team meetings in order to predict some of the spaces we assumed homeless youth existed in our society.

Hidden homelessness became an important concept in our conversations. We started thinking about sex workers and survival sex; newcomers and the issues of undocumented and isolation; and members of the LGBTQ community and the issue of safety in relation to the shelter system (Côté & Blais, 2019). Above all, it was concluded that we, as student researchers and professional researchers, were in no position to make assumptions of where homeless youth exist, especially during a pandemic that has altered the social landscape beyond anything we could have imagined. Recruitment, thus, needed to be strategic in order to ensure that the project was being promoted to diverse populations of youth, but also to frontline workers and those holding managerial positions in areas of the community that connect to our research population. Logistically, Excel became a huge support during this journey, as it allowed for a place to create and build a document that outlined all of the agencies that needed to be contacted. This included executive, managerial and frontline workers at youth-specific agencies and non-youth specific agencies, as well as reaching out to drop-in centers and known hangout areas, and contacting respites, encampments, supervised consumption sites, Ontario Works and ODSP, newcomer specific agencies, and sex work committees and outreach programs. Once the main template was created, the next step was to start calling each agency on the phone and talking to whoever was available to take down the information and get the word out to the youth and staff at the agency.

While talking to front desk workers, or frontline workers, I always tried to get other more specific contacts within the agency, or even confirmations with whoever I was speaking with to either participate personally or agree to put up flyers or send them out electronically. Interestingly, the more connection I was able to make early on, helped dramatically with how much engagement and follow through I received in return from them. This was only one example of the many times I realized, in life and research, how vital communication can be in producing positive action. The first few phone calls I made, I remember feeling tense and unsure about what was going to be asked and whether I would know the answers, but as time went on, call after call, it became easier to answer questions and speak clearly and fluently about the research project. With that being said, it needs to be acknowledged that as a social work placement student reaching out to social work agencies, and having affiliation with an affluent University, the power dynamic between myself and the other person would likely not be a barrier for me to make progress in my recruitment. This is simply because as I called and introduced myself, the recipient would recognize these identity buzzwords, and since they were likely to also be social workers, or some other kind of helping professional, that person would naturally be more receptive to the information I brought to the phone call and also likely be more apt to engage and help out. If the power dynamics were less aligned, and I was, in fact, a complete outsider, the connection and engagement I reflected on would likely not have happened so easily and it would be important to find other, more dramatic ways to break down barriers and forge an authentic connection.

While relying on frontline workers to get the word out for us, and hang up flyers, the youth ultimately had to make the autonomous decision to call or email to set up an interview. When a youth called or emailed, it was expected that we would filter the candidates by finding out what kinds of marginality they identified with. Although in theory this step made sense, because we needed to ensure that the recruits were, in fact, suited for the study; it felt unethical, in practice, to demand that they give up this kind of vulnerable information before establishing a more developed rapport. Likewise, from an anti-oppressive lens, it seemed counterintuitive to me to deny any of these willing youth the opportunity to tell their story and receive the honorarium because they obviously needed the support and in my mind, I thought, "who am I to deny them a chance to gain a bit more financial security and safety?". I knew that both of these instances would be beneficial to them, and their well-being and I didn't want to be a gate-keeper between deserving and undeserving, even if it meant risking the integrity of the study. For this reason, I often skipped this step, or at least modified it. When asking for the youth to disclose their perceived marginality in relation to their homeless status, I was often met with resistance and confusion from the youth, where they either were offended or just didn't understand what I was asking. I was often met with the rebuttal that they were marginalized just for being homeless, and I agreed. I can remember receiving a number of calls from youth who resided at an agency in a small town. It was clear that diversity was less established where they were, and so when I inquired about their relationship to marginality and homelessness, I was given answers that I wouldn't consider to be traditional domains of marginalization. One of the youth even struggled to come up with something, and so together, through conversation, we were able to materialize a new concept that had not yet been explored – criminality. As each youth came up with a unique perception of their own marginality, I let them know that the next step would be to have a conversation with my supervisor and then after getting the 'go ahead,' I would call them back to set up an interview time. When speaking with my supervisor about these different and new categories of marginality, there was some hesitation about whether to accept them. This hesitation illuminated for me the ways in which research can be exclusive and I would imagine that if this isn't recognized the kinds of data produced would be limited as well. Luckily, my supervisor also realized the value these youth brought to the study, and we were able to accept them for interviews. Interestingly enough, upon interviewing and allowing these youth to open up about their lives, many other hidden marginal identities and experiences came to light that were invaluable to the study. This instance reminds us that connections in research exist in hidden and unusual places and can only be found and explored if the research allows for it.

6.1   Interviewing

With all of our hard work during the first round of recruitment, we found that our schedules filled up with interviews quickly. Youth interviews were especially complex since each youth embodied their own set of unique and intersectional identities, each identity informing their homelessness in some way or another. At times, it was tricky to navigate these complexities for us because as interviewers, it required that we pay close attention to the often changing power dynamics throughout the interview. What I mean by this is that as interviewers, we really had no idea who these youth were or what they had been through, and with each of these unique positionalities, we could only control how they perceived us throughout the interview to a certain degree. Therefore, power relations were consistently changing and evolving between the youth and the interviewer as they took their time to present us with new information surrounding each of their identities that they used to describe how it related, good or bad, to their homelessness. The nuances that existed between and in relation to all of the different identities and experiences that they held, which were so vastly different from one youth to another, required fervent listening and comprehension skills to keep the interview moving forward, while also maintaining the youth's trust and respect that really acted as the vehicle for the interview's progress. Interviewing was important to all of us, and students reflected:

> Interviewing for me was quite intense, because I wanted to show up for the youth as an intentional anti-oppressive researcher; however, due to the nature of research, I found that an inherent tension existed between my training as an AOP social worker and now as a student researcher. Finding a way to mediate this tension was a task that I think we all struggled with individually and on the collective level.
>
> I found that sitting in a place of power provoked personal anxieties in me, because I knew that with power came responsibility. I felt unsettled because I was unsure whether I would ask the right questions to honour the stories of the youth and uphold the integrity of the research. One way that helped me overcome this overwhelm was to find a sense of

grounding by reminding myself that the interview was not about me, and so I should stop making it about me and prioritize the wellbeing of the youth. By doing that, I was able to reorient my emotions, so that all of my energy and focus was being projected on the project and the outcome, which ultimately seemed to work out.

It was exciting to witness the transformation that took place as the others completed the interviews. Following interviews, we processed the dissonance between being passive students studying textbooks and who prepared scripts for the researcher interview guide to the reality of being confronted with the intersecting roles of interviewer, responsibility to anti-oppressive practice and finding peace with the experience of a new subject position as researcher/practitioners. As a worker in the homeless sector returning to the university setting, participating in this process prompted me to reflect on my practice in the context of competing domains of daily engagement with the community. These discussions enriched all of our self-reflection and skills.

One strategy we found useful that helped to mitigate the power dynamic that exists within the interviews was asking for the youth's preferred pronouns, and then using them throughout. Our intention for using this strategy was to establish an interview environment that centred the client early on by letting the youth know that we interviewers understand and respect gender nonconformity, and we are open and willing to embrace them in whatever form they chose at that moment and however they self-define. We hoped that this helped the youth to see that we valued their dignity as participants and people and were interested in more than just their homeless status. Although some youth were not familiar with the concept of pronouns, the majority were prepared to give them and even expected to be asked. It seemed to be a useful tactic because it seemed to help the youth relax and open up more and engage with the questions with more enthusiasm.

Similarly, we let the youth lead the interviews through a conversation-like format, where we did our best to employ our best active listening and empathy as they spoke. This was a strategy we used to convey the message that we are holding safety and space for them to open up in whatever way feels comfortable and right for them. This was important because we really wanted the conversation to be authentic and aligned with the youth's experiences. For this reason, we each used the interview guides loosely, and worked to maintain fluidity between the conversation and new topics of discussion. Moreover, we intentionally used open-ended questions and avoided leading questions to reduce any interruption to the flow that the youth created. Consequently, the interviews developed in unique ways, and it seemed that each youth spoke to what they knew and valued, giving each interview its own form based on the things they highlighted or understated.

6.2   Transcribing Interviews

Transcribing turned out to be surprisingly transformative for our social work practice; however, it was a long, tedious process for all of us. As I am sure most of you can imagine and probably even relate, the process of watching and hearing yourself doing something that you have not yet quite mastered, is horrifying. It is unpleasant because as social work placement students, we wanted to perform at our best, but of course, we can only do our best in that moment and try to do better the next time. Transcribing turned out to be a great resource for facilitating this kind of learning, because transcribing, quite literally, has you watching the interview as a spectator. This process requires that while you follow every word, sentence structure and theme during the interview, you also pay attention to the more subtle verbal and non-verbal cues that shadow the whole performance. It is unbelievable how much deeper we were able to dive into each interview, observing emotions and tones that did not seem so obvious during the actual interview.

> During interviewing, I realized that I often had an anxious emotional response when acting as the primary interviewer. Transcription gave me the opportunity to observe my anxiety, while interviewing, from the outside. This was invaluable to me because before seeing these videos, I only understood my anxiety through whatever experience I was having at the time it occurred. For this reason, I always understood it internally and could only imagine, dreadfully, what it was like for others to see. By observing myself in these moments, I realized that the intensity that was felt in my body was not always as obvious to others as I thought. This perspective helped me to find courage to push through in those moments, and stay focused on the interviewee, which was really my main goal all along.

Additionally, our placement supervisor and principal investigator reviewed each audio/video interview and discussed it with us in our one-to-one supervision meetings. There we could process what occurred and get feedback on how to improve and what was working well for us; she even commented that after a while we identified all of the areas for improvement and had strategized how to address these concerns before we met with her! Since we each did transcribing individually, in our own spaces, we were able to take a step back whenever we felt we needed to pause the video, and really deconstruct the ways that we approached subjects with the clients. We would decide if the original method we chose was, in fact, the best way. If we decided that it was not, then within our own individual reflection we had a chance to think of a more pronounced and intentional way we could approach it next time if something similar came up. Ultimately, with so many unique interviews going on, many instances that we reflected on did not come back up, but others most certainly did, and so, although painstaking at times, transcribing helped us a lot to fine tune our skills in interviewing and anti-oppressive practice.

7 Research during a Time of COVID-19

Conducting research with youth experiencing homelessness presented multiple challenges to recruitment due to the transient nature of youth who are precariously housed. These challenges were further heightened by the COVID-19 pandemic since the University, following Public Health guidelines had placed strict protocols for researchers in order to prioritize both researcher and participant safety and wellbeing. Consequently, we were unable to go to agencies or canvas the streets to inform workers and youth about the project in hopes of obtaining willing participants. This not only created a heavy reliance on agencies to recruit youth on our behalf, but also an additional barrier to accessing youth participants who were not in the care of agencies or connected to a worker in some capacity. While snowball sampling is generally an effective method of recruitment when it comes youth, this approach was inaccessible due to lockdown and strict isolation mandates.

Another barrier created by COVID-19 was the shift to virtual interviews. This made it a necessity for participants to have access to a phone or an internet device in order to participate. While in some cases, this may have in fact made participation more accessible to participants since geography was no longer a barrier, it also meant that anyone without access to technology would not be able to participate.

Finally, a lack of private space is not uncommon for youth experiencing housing precarity, since living environments often include staying in dormitory style shelters, couch surfing at a friend's, or residing in places where it could be dangerous to speak openly during an interview. Thus, some participants had difficulty finding private spaces from which to do the interview.

7.1   Honorariums and Vulnerable Populations

While managers and frontline workers were not compensated monetarily for their contributions to the research, youth participants were provided with a $40 honorarium to cover any phone or data changes they may have incurred in addition to their time and contributions. Both COVID-19 and the precariousness of experiencing homelessness made it difficult for all youth interested in participating to access the honorarium. Without the ability to meet in person due to COVID-19 restrictions, this meant funds had to be e-transferred to youth. As a team, we brainstormed alternatives that would still adhere to our university's research protocols. In the end, alternative solutions included mailing a gift card of the participant's choosing to an agency, worker, or an address of their choosing, as well as e-transferring the funds to a designated worker or person of their choosing. As one student researcher remarked,

> Excluding participants that don't have bank accounts, email addresses, or phones would further marginalize some of the most vulnerable youth out there. Those are probably the most critical voices to include, since this places them at risk of being invisibilized. From a critical AOP lens, we wanted to ensure that we did everything possible to ensure any youth wanting to share their perspectives could do so.

From an anti-oppressive perspective, there is contention around providing honorariums to research participants from vulnerable communities, such as youth experiencing homelessness. On the one hand, it is ethical to provide compensation to someone for their time and contributions, yet it can also be viewed as coercion to someone where income is scarce, particularly for youth who are more likely to be swayed by monetary incentives (Ensign & Ammerman, 2008). That being said, the research team discussed why providing honorariums is an ethically appropriate decision, why $40 is an appropriate amount based on the cost of a monthly phone and data plan. It is also important to note that youth participants could withdraw their participation at any time during the interview and they would still receive their honorarium without jeopardizing their relationship to us or to the university. This helped ensure that the narratives youth shared were not influenced by the honorarium.

As critical anti-oppressive researchers, it is important to note that in spite of this being clearly stated in the consent forms and explicitly reviewed by interviewers prior to the interview, a power dynamic will always exist in which youth participants might feel unable to express their desire to terminate the interview. This is where important social work skills come into play, into being able to sense the comfort level of participants either through what they are saying, or by what they are not saying (pauses, hesitations, short responses). Additionally, many youth participants did not appear on video, either by choice or because they were calling into the meeting through a phone. The lack of visual cues did not appear to impede the ability to engage in a dialogue with youth or to sense their comfort (or discomfort), as evidenced by the detailed narratives they shared. In fact, as research students, we were all quite amazed by how highly engaged youth participants were, with many expressing gratitude for having an opportunity to share their experiences. Perhaps, as students we had lower expectations of our ability to elicit comfort in participants which would facilitate willingness to share their story. Ultimately, we were thrilled to have supported the youth to be heard.

8   Ethical Dilemma

An ethical dilemma that we as researchers were faced with is that how do you research marginalized populations without further marginalizing them. Although well-intentioned anti-oppressive practitioners that were equipped with an integral social justice university education, it became apparent that in order to work ethically with vulnerable persons, we would need to situate ourselves in the research. When it comes to AOP, Yee (2013) reminds us that "it is not about intent, but rather about the invisible, if not insidious ways, in which power and domination can cloak themselves amongst those who are privileged, including those who are subject to oppression" (p. 345). As white researchers, working to illuminate the experiences of marginalized youth homelessness, we held a deep responsibility to hold our privileges accountable.

Self-reflection and reflexivity skill development allow practitioners to write themselves into their practice, so that their personal narratives of domination and marginalization are visible and anchored in such a way that they can practice consciously by reducing and limiting harm, as much as possible (Heron, 2005). This process became pivotal in our ability to drive the project forward both individually within our sections, but also as a team. By bringing critical reflexivity to our positionality, privileges and bias that could influence our research we were able to offer a comfortable space which ultimately led to participant engagement.

8.1   *Finding Peace with the Dissonance*
One theme that led to a lot of discussion in our reflexive journey is the dissonance that we felt due to the hierarchical nature of research and the privilege and power we held as student researchers. As a first experience of being in the

researcher/ interviewer role, we felt responsible to ensure that AOP practices were actioned respectfully. We recognized the need to be self-reflective in order to find a sense of balance that would feel comfortable when in the process of interviewing participants. It was important for us, as student researchers, to align with participants in the creation of a safe environment for the research interview to take place. One of the students, who was employed, working with street-involved homeless during the pandemic, evolved through various stages of insight into the value of research to lift the voices of participants as they represented so many homeless who were not heard. The students also spent a lot of time processing self-care strategies as they were immersed in witnessing the gaps in the system and consequences suffered by the homeless most of their waking hours.

9 Final Thoughts/Conclusion

Our experiences as researchers have changed us personally and in our understandings of what anti-oppressive research can look like. While we are not youths experiencing homelessness/housing precarity, nor frontline workers dedicated to serving youth, we view our roles as researchers as both an honour and a responsibility because we have been entrusted with the knowledges and experiences of participants, and with that comes a responsibility to share their perspectives. According to Strega and Brown (2015), "every decision a researcher makes, from choices about topic and research site to the ... relationships with participants to the means by which findings are disseminated, has political significance and therefore affects the social justice potential of our work" (p. 7). This was certainly the case with our team, in which painstaking care was placed into every decision from, as Potts and Brown (2015) state, "a commitment to anti-oppressive research means committing to social justice and taking an active role in that change" (p. 17). Thus, qualitative research is well positioned to be a pathway to anti-oppressive practice but must be carefully and consciously re-visioned to take into account every decision and must be grounded in researcher critical reflexive self-examination of self and research choices.

9.1 *Advice for Future Student Researchers from These Student Researchers*

> As I take a moment to visualize all that this experience has embodied in me, as an upcoming social worker, my advice for future student

researchers is to take a chance on the unknown. It seems you really do need to find that bit of courage inside you that is hiding and take a leap of faith. You have everything you need to succeed and cope with the task ahead, and the research community needs your unique skills, and perspectives. Even if they aren't developed completely yet, this might be the opportunity that will spark the transformation you need. I wish you nothing but success and happiness, and I'm so proud of all of you.

References

Cann, C. N., & DeMeulenaere, E. J. (2012). Critical co-constructed autoethnography. *Cultural Studies, Critical Methodologies,* 12(2), 146–158. https://Doi.Org/10.1177/15327 08611435214.

Chew, K. A. B., Greendeer, N. H., & Keliiaa, C. (2015). Claiming space: An Autoethnographic study of Indigenous graduate students engaged in language reclamation. *International Journal of Multicultural Education,* 17(2), 73.

Cho, S., Crenshaw. K., & McCall, L. (2013). Toward a field of intersectionality studies: Theory, applications, and praxis. *Signs: Journal of Women in Culture and Society, 38*(4), 785–810.

Côté, P., & Blais, M. (2019). Between resignation, resistance and recognition: a qualitative analysis of LGBTQ + youth profiles of homelessness agencies utilization. *Children and Youth Services Review, 100,* 437–443. https://doi.org/10.1016/j.childyo uth.2019.03.024.

Ensign, J., & Ammerman, S. (2008). Ethical issues in research with homeless youths. *Journal of Advanced Nursing, 62*(3), 365–372. https://doi.org/10.1111/j.1365-2648.2008 .04599.x.

Fook, J. (2002). Theorizing from practice: Towards an inclusive approach for social work research. *Qualitative Social Work: QSW: Research and Practice,* 1(1), 79–95.

Freeman, B. & VanKatwyk, T. (2019). Testing the waters: Engaging the Tekéni Teyohà:ke Kahswénhtake /Two row wampum into a research paradigm. *Canadian Journal of Native Education, 41*(1) 146–167.

George, P., Siver, S., & Preston, S. (2013). Reimagining field education in social work: The Promise unveiled. *Advances in Social Work,* 14(2), 642–657.

Hallett, R. E., & Crutchfield, R. (2017). Homelessness and housing insecurity in higher education: A Trauma-Informed approach to research, policy, and practice. *ASHE Higher Education Report,* 43(6), 7–118.

Heron, B. (2005). Self-reflection in critical social work practice: Subjectivity and the possibilities of resistance. *Reflective Practices, 6*(3), 341–351. https://doi.org/10.1080 /14623940500220095.

James, R. K., & Gilliland, B. E. (2017). Approaching crisis intervention (pp. 3–25). In James, R. K., & Gilliland, B. E. (Eds.), *Crisis intervention strategies* (8th ed.). Cengage Learning.

Kidd, S. A., Thistle, J., Beaulieu, T., O'Grady, B., & Gaetz, S. (2019). A National study of Indigenous youth homelessness in Canada. *Public Health* (London), 176, 163–171. https://doi.org/10.1016/j.puhe.2018.06.012.

Morton, M. H. (2020). The complex predictors of youth homelessness. *Journal of Adolescent Health,* 66(4), 381–382. https://doi.org/10.1016/j.jadohealth.2020.01.003.

Napier, L., & Levine, K. (2016). Practicing critical reflection (pp. 2–14). In O'Hara, A., Weber, Z., & Levine, K. (Eds.), *Skills for human service practice* (2nd Canadian ed.). Oxford: Oxford University Press.

Nygård, R. H., & Saus, M. (2016). Emphasizing Indigenous communities in social work research ethics. *International Social Work,* 59(5), 666–678. https://doi.org/10.1177/0020872816646815.

O'Hara, A., & Levine, K. (2016). The Microskills of interviewing (pp. 107–127). In O'Hara, A., Weber, Z., & Levine, K. (Eds.), *Skills for human service practice* (2nd Canadian ed). Oxford: Oxford University Press.

Padgett, D. (2017). *Qualitative methods in social work research* (3rd ed.). Thousand Oaks: Sage.

Potts, K. L. & Brown, L. A. (2015). Becoming an anti-oppressive researcher (pp. 17–42). In Brown, L. A., & Strega, S. (Eds.), *Research as resistance: Revisiting critical, Indigenous, and anti-oppressive approaches* (2nd ed.). Canadian Scholars' Press.

Preston, S., George, P., & Silver, S. (2019). Field education in social work. *Critical Social Work,* 15(1). https://doi.org/10.22329/csw.v15i1.5908.

Strega, S., & Brown, L. (2015). From resistance to resurgence (pp. 1–16). In Brown, L. A., & Strega, S. (Eds.), *Research as resistance: Revisiting critical, Indigenous, and anti-oppressive approaches* (2nd ed.). Canadian Scholars' Press.

Yee, J. Y., & Wagner, A. E. (2013). Is anti-oppression teaching in Canadian social work classrooms a form of neoliberalism. *Social Work Education, 32*(3), 331–348. https://doi.org/10.1080/02615479.2012.672557.

CHAPTER 15

Arendtian Phenomenology of Politics

Lawrence Ofunja Kangei

1 Introduction

The elucidation sets out to tackle the Arendtian phenomenology of politics by delving into the dissimilar constituents of this philosophical approach and why it is relevant in the jurisdiction of research. The preceding outlook will be facilitated by making an allowance for hermeneutics to the degree that it nourishes phenomenology in respect of operation to acquire a consolidated logic. The issues appertaining to public and private, unitive sense and judgement besides the rationale for Arendt's change of approach form the corpus of this clarification as in the subsequent segments.

2 Hermeneutic-Phenomenological

By developing and explicating her use of hermeneutic-phenomenological materials and methodologies on the one hand, and shared historical-political experiences on the other, she is able to show how she combines the two, on the other, the exposition defends an interpretation of Hannah Arendt's work that integrates its various dimensions, such as political theory, philosophy, historiography, literary theory, and her journalistic contributions (Arendt, 2003, p. 34). The key notions of 'world' and 'worldliness' are the subject of this explanation in terms of relating the theory or *ought* and practice or *is* of research. The thesis here is that Arendt's work offers a primarily implicit but strong and convincing description of an as yet undefined perspective that we call a hermeneutic phenomenology of politics. This perspective can be loosely defined as concrete studies of political-historical experiences with the objective of comprehending the connotation of those experiences. This necessitates the politicization of hermeneutic phenomenology over and above the conception of a hermeneutic-phenomenological perspective within political philosophy and research (Arendt, 1968, p. 20).

There are various reasons for the current scarcity of integrated and truly interdisciplinary viewpoints on Arendt's work identifies research as part of the lacuna that calls for urgent and requisite focus for the society to delve into holistic meaningful headway. It has been interpreted overwhelmingly within established independent disciplinary frameworks, such as political theory, historiography, or philosophy, each time at the handicap of other viewpoints. Most philosophers, including those who are skeptical of any claims to universality, avoid contextualizing philosophers' research work for fear of jeopardizing its general validity. Scholars of political science and historiography who are more empirically oriented, on the other hand, usually reject to draw general conclusions from specific historical and political conditions so that to maintain the sanctity of the province of research (Arendt, 2003, p. 33). Another significant reason is ideological in nature. Arendt's work has been arrogated in highly polarized debates that transcend its context, most notably in the United States of America, by exponents of both sides of these deliberations and advocates of a middle ground or reconciliation of the two sides, owing to the often-polemical nature of her own writings. The immensely prominent dispute between so-called modernist and postmodernist scholars of her work is one such example. The dispute between liberals and communitarians, as well as the one against her political thinking's purported aestheticism, are two previous examples (Arendt, 1970, p. 47).

The chapter suggests a hermeneutic-phenomenological reading of Arendt's historical and political accounts, as well as a more contextual reading of her philosophical research-oriented discoveries. The forgoing is precisely what a political hermeneutic phenomenology aspires to. Arendt's work is distinguished by the relationship she establishes between a historical-political and a philosophical sensibility, which she does through a continuous hermeneutic-phenomenological research political approach. The study argues that Arendt's work is best understood as a collection of phenomenologically informed reflections on politics and politically informed phenomenological research exercises (Arendt, 1972, p. 50). The totalitarian loss of the world taught her to value what is at stake in the world, both experientially and politically, and to regard humans as worldly beings in the first place who form comprehensions for science and technological advancements guided by their contextual needs. Arendt's analysis of totalitarianism provides clues to a diagnosis of the political human condition that centers around plurality and freedom by examining the aspects of human existence that totalitarianism disables, such as belonging to a lawful, political community, spontaneity, indeterminacy, plurality, and common sense. Her goal is to preserve the appearances of events, particularly political ones.

The goal is to look at Arendt's hermeneutic phenomenology via the prism of a concept that sits right at the crossroads of political theory and hermeneutic phenomenology: the concept of "world." Any interpretation that reduces Arendt's conception of the universe to either a phenomenological or a political figure ignores Arendt's thought's complexity and uniqueness which are key rudiments in the sphere of research (Arendt, 2003, p. 34).

Furthermore, Arendt's hermeneutic-phenomenological assessments of political phenomena and events are improved by method and its implications for her phenomenological anthropology, which are classified under the two fundamental dimensions of her phenomenological notion of the intersubjective world, namely, its commonness and publicity or visibility (Stangneth, 2014, p. 18). Each nomenclature demonstrates how these analyses emerge from thoughts on the totalitarian experience and highlights the new insights enabled by a hermeneutic phenomenological interpretation of Arendt's political analyses. Arendt's phenomenological impulse is obvious in her treatment of political events as lived, intersubjective, perspectivist, and worldly experiences. Arendt's work is characterized by the pervasiveness of distinctions and paradoxes as a result of her focus on experiences (Arendt, 1977, p. 49).

Arendt's method is called hermeneutic phenomenology for the reason that she focuses on comprehending the connotation of experiences and events in their uniqueness and contingency, thus, serving as a bases for specificity which is core in the realm of research for knowledge production. In her opinion, the exercises in understanding, as she termed them, are dual-sided. They are, first and foremost, crucial. Arendt's goal is to give justice to political life's original, non-derived character, the *vita activa* (Arendt, 1960, p. 30) and to save it from philosophical preconceptions and fallacies, as well as the imposition of the *vita contemplativa's* laws (Arendt, 1998, p. 55). Arendt's method for dismantling preconceptions is not denial. Instead, she insists on exploring how the history of political experiences and phenomena is condensed and sedimented in our language, that is, disclosed or hidden in traditional political notions, in a genealogical manner for the rationale of pursuing the backdrop of historicism. Second, Arendt's hermeneutic exercises comprise of understanding and narration, and they are experimental. Stories have the potential to stay true to the political's phenomenal nature, notably its character of appearance. We can begin to understand phenomena and events by narrating them, thereby initiating processes of reconciliation with past events and reorientation toward the future (Arendt, 1996, p. 34). Arendt promotes a hermeneutic phenomenology of politics, as she is primarily interested in comprehending political occurrences, events, and experiences, or, to put it another way, in what occurs in public space and in facts.

3 Arendt's Approach Shift

Arendt's method differs from traditional methodologies and paradigms in the humanities and social sciences that aim at explanation, that is, establishing causes, reasons, and regularities, because of her emphasis on understanding and interpretation. Explanatory approaches to history and politics, she believes, avoid the painstaking and detailed task of understanding, and risk devolving into scientistic and metaphysical constructs (Arendt, 1973, p. 12). As a result, they are ideological constructs that cause political issues. They tend to be deterministic by establishing laws that determine the course of human history and from which predictions about the future can be obtained. The promotion of determinism is often accompanied by a lack of sensitivity to the novel, which can lead to normalization and the loss of agency and resistance capacity.

The historical and political context of her method is just as important as its phenomenological inspiration. Arendt's rejection of philosophical and scientific approaches reflects a deep and vividly felt feeling that "the thread of tradition is torn," as she puts it. Totalitarianism's ascent had resulted in a fundamental break with tradition. Arendt adds that, in addition to grieving this truth, the loss of tradition presents us with the opportunity to reclaim a sense of reality by shedding the burden of metaphysical and scientific traditions, which nourish and cultivate a disengaged attitude (Arendt, 1994, p. 46).

Arendt's method is, thus, not exterior to the themes she analyzes, unlike more traditional research paradigms. The methodic ideal of objectivity as defined by scientists or empiricists requires the scholar to act as a fair-minded onlooker of the matter under inquiry while employing a method that is equally detached from the subject. This abstract or quasi-universalistic viewpoint, known as the Archimedean perspective, is presupposed to transcend all individual points of view (Arendt, 1992, p. 28). The Arendtian phenomenological scholar, contrariwise, is an involved looker-on or addressee, that is, someone who allows herself to be addressed by the subject she is studying, because the observer's third-person position prevents access to meaning, which is what hermeneutic phenomenology is all about. The scholar-as-engaged-spectator rejects the scholar-as-disengaged-subject-object observer's duality (Arendt, 2006, p. 41). The inherent significance of human conduct replaces the objectification of human action. The spectator's judgment is not universal or detached, as the disengaged observer's perspective is, but rather appeals to imagination, that is, taste, and representative thinking, that is, imagining others' possible perspectives on a given scenario for oneself. This creative process bestows a specific validity on judgment, which could be christened situated impartiality (Arendt, 2010, p. 23).

Arendt's method has raised a number of highly persistent and continually repeating concerns and caused significant misunderstanding (Arendt, 1970, p. 45). Her appeal to experience and her awareness of facts, others claim, are simply empiricist or even scientistic blunders. Likewise, the rifeness of her many distinctions is frequently interpreted as a sign of essentialism. These arguments, it is suggested, are misunderstandings that may be cleared up by explaining the widely misunderstood hermeneutic-phenomenological context of these notions and distinctions in Arendt's work. Furthermore, the chapter argues that Arendt's commitment to experience, facts, and clear distinctions is informed by sound political considerations. An attempt is made to rescue the appreciation of experience, factuality, and making distinctions for a critical and responsible study of politics by correcting these common misunderstandings.

Since Arendt's hermeneutic-phenomenological approach of the political is first and foremost focused at comprehending the worldliness of human experience, we portray it as a phenomenological anthropology of the political. Issuing from her reflections on the totalitarian experience, we argue, Arendt's phenomenological anthropology is an exemplary example of situated, contextual and experience-based political inquiry. Her phenomenology of the worldly human condition was shaped by her dictatorial experience of world loss. In *The Human Condition* (1998) and *The Life of the Mind* (1982), we analyze the evolution of her phenomenological anthropological view. Arendt's analysis of the worldly human condition focuses on how a range of human factors, such as life itself, worldliness, plurality, and natality, shape human experience and existence. Human circumstances are characteristics of the common human situation that both determine and are determined by it. Human beings and their natural and physical surroundings are inextricably linked. Conditionality's phenomenological foundation ensures that conditions are both constants of human experience and existence, as well as historically changing in their unique constellation and meaning. Arendt's analysis of human situations, particularly the human condition of multiplicity, challenges metaphysical and scientific views of what makes a human being a human being, as articulated in universal and eternal human nature definitions.

4   Phenomenological Existence

A phenomenological topology of reality develops from this anthropology, describing the many experienced views on the environment we inhabit: nature and the material, or intersubjective, components of the world. Together, the material and intersubjective aspects establish the world as a living space. The world's material dimension provides stability and a constructed environment, which shelters humans from nature in some ways. Meaningfulness, on the other hand, is enabled by the intersubjective dimension. Arendt often argues as a phenomenologist that plurality is a paradoxical situation that deals with disparate and even contradictory experiences that are yet related and even mutually interdependent or conditional. The study goes on to address four extraordinarily diverse facets of the plurality paradox: difference and equality, difference and commonality, isolation and fusion, communication, connection or intersubjectivity, conflict, agonism, and uniqueness. The two aspects actually assume each other, contrary to the consensus in Arendt study that these pairs constitute dualisms. These paradoxes also imply that plurality and worldliness are conditional on each other and co-original. As a result, a loss of plurality entails a loss of worldliness. A loss of world results in a loss of individual uniqueness, equality, commonality, meaning, and a feeling of reality.

With respect to metaphysics, strong empiricism and scientism, and poststructuralism, this hermeneutic and anthropological phenomenology of the political is crucial. Arendt's phenomenology of human conditions calls into question metaphysical assumptions about human nature. For it assumes a subject-object dichotomy, metaphysical thought is dualistic. Man is viewed as a rational sovereign subject who is opposed to the world, much like the scholar-as-disengaged-observer according to the Archimedean ideal of objectivity. Since defining and determining the constants of human nature results in a generalization and objectification that is blind to distinctions between people and historical fluctuations, the philosophical tradition is also essentialist or naturalist. It is deterministic in the sense that it tends to ignore the contingency of factual truths in favor of forceful logical truths. Arendt, like the poststructuralists, believes in the historical diversity of specific human contexts. These conditions, on the other hand, yield constants. Poststructuralists' epistemological pessimism leads them to reject the meaning of experience, facts, and the ideal of impartiality outright. Any criterion for discerning normative differences is lost if experiences, facts, and impartiality are considered as nothing more than ideological, scientific constructs.

It is indispensable to elucidate the various intersubjective world's dimensions, which include: the immaterial; relational; dynamic and fragile space of meanings and stories in need of constant maintenance that arises whenever people relate to one another through words and deeds; and which vanishes when people no longer relate to one another. It is about the *res publica*, or what is of public concern to everyone, as opposed to one's private business. In

Arendt's words, the main aspects of the intersubjective world are the inter-esse or in-between, the space of appearances, and the web of relationships (Arendt, 2003, p. 14). The most general features of the intersubjective world that connect these dimensions are the phenomenal or public quality on the one hand, and the community quality on the other. The world of intersubjectivity is both a common and a public environment. In reality, the public sphere is a common world. The world is public because it comprises everything that is visible in public and is shared by all of its inhabitants. The world is a common world because it is visible to everyone. For the reason that everyone has a distinct viewpoint on the same reality we share, this commonality is pluralistic.

In conjunction with the above, an examination of a facet of the world's commonness, namely the interaction between citizens, community, and globe, is appropriate. Arendt sees community as a question rather than a solution. Her starting point differs significantly from that of many other political philosophers who are concerned about society's disintegration or fragmentation and are examining the topic of community. On the other hand, Arendt is concerned about the social trend toward, and coercion into, homogenization. The fact that her insights on political community are anchored on her analysis of the authoritarian experience has largely been overlooked by her philosophical readers. First, Blut und Boden's national-socialist ideology instilled in her a great suspicion of ethnic or other naturalist grounds and explanations for community, leading her to choose artificial citizenship (Arendt, 1993, p. 34).

5 Totalitarian Appraisal

Arendt's analysis of totalitarianism led her to identify two totalitarians' anti-political predicaments, the first of which is all-encompassing isolation, and the second of which is the merger of numerous individuals into a single Man (Arendt, 1979, p. 68). Arendt learned from her authoritarian experience that individuals require both temporary isolation and shared global space or being-together. When people become distinct without being together, solitude becomes the pathological condition of isolation; when people are together without being distinct, fusion occurs. As a result, Arendt rejects both classic communitarian and radical individualist approaches to the subject of community. Individuality and the common world are not mutually exclusive due to the paradoxical character of plurality (Arendt, 2003, p. 29).

True political community is artificial, heterogeneous, and non-given. It is a state of being together that does not emerge until citizens publicly exhibit their diversity of viewpoints and ideas. Its goal is not to establish agreement, consensus, or harmony by homogenizing or equalizing differences, as is the case in traditional communitarian communities (Arendt, 2000, p. 17). Rather, it is to give due consideration to the diversity and divergence of different viewpoints in order to create a shared universe. Community is never guaranteed since it lacks a solid foundation. What, then, do citizens as citizens have in common, as positively defined? If there is no foundation, how can humans create such a common world? Exchanging ideas and making commitments, common sense, and civic friendship are among the actions, practices, and situations that shape our relationship with the mutual world, according to Arendt.

This necessitates a comparison of Arendt's perspective on community with two classical political-philosophical positions within social contract theory: the quasi-liberal model of the social contract, based on enlightened self-interest and associated with Hobbes; and organic models of community, based on a sovereign people's general will and appealing to generalized complicity (Arendt, 1960, 29). According to Arendt, the political appeals to interest and will have fatal political repercussions because they have four properties: subjectivism or solipsism; unity, homogeneity, and immediacy; sovereignty; and naturalism. Arendt's main criticisms of both Thomas Hobbes and Jean-Jacques Rousseau's political thinking center on their antagonism to pluralism and their theories' blindness to worldliness. Their shared aversion to plurality stems from their obliviousness to plurality's paradoxes. As a result, they represent two influential approaches to do away with plurality, in Hobbes' case through one-man rule and in Rousseau's case through the fiction of the people as many-in-one. Both see plurality as a problem, an unfortunate reality that must be addressed if the polity is to survive.

In the civil war-like state of nature, plurality is related with selfish individual wills for Rousseau, and uncontrolled and still-irrational aggressive self-interests for Hobbes; to be precise, with a mere conflictual multitude of isolated persons for Hobbes. Similarly, they symbolize two ways to get around the planet and, as a result, undermine it. Rousseau's proposal to reduce distinct individuals' multifarious viewpoints to a general will, as well as his introduction of compassion as a public policy ideal, overlook political institutions that exist outside of, i.e., between, people and function as media in their connections. Compassion bridges the gap between people and, in particular, the common planet. In Hobbes' justification of enlightened self-interest, the individual comes to the conclusion that her long-term interests are best served when everyone transfers their freedom to the sovereign.

In contrast to interest or will, the study maintains that Arendt's paradigm is based on opinion, promise, and action-in-concert. She uses a civic community idea, which presupposes a mostly horizontal link between citizens. In this view, community refers to a shared reality rather than a shared human character, such as reason as defined by Hobbes (Sommerville, 1992) or compassion as defined by Rousseau (Rousseau, 1923). This shared reality is not a given, nor is it natural; rather, it is the result of citizens' concerted action, expressed through opinion and the formation of contracts based on promises. Opinions, by definition, necessitate the presence of others; moreover, they are often formed between citizens over the course of their exchange, rather than within people's heads.

Arendt places her outlooks on the commons in a separate lineage contained by social contract theory, which is loosely related with Locke; the horizontal contract between independent individuals who mutually bind themselves (Locke, 1690, p. 36). In contrast to the vertical relationship between individuals or ruled and the government or ruler, the horizontal contract assumes equality among its constituent components. Covenants, treaties, constitutions, the law, and so on all serve to institutionalize the promise-based social compact. These institutions exist in the shared common world, in the space between men. In the Rousseauan and Hobbesian social contracts, these intermediary institutions are conspicuously absent. These institutions, unlike basically short-sighted self-interest and the public will, create sophisticated frameworks with future linkages and ties without eroding the fundamental contingency of action. Unlike compassion and the sum of, even enlightened, self-interests, the law, in addition to its longer-term focus, is impartial. Arendt's very different model of foundation of power is the promise and the horizontal contract, which she perceives as action-in-concert rather than sovereignty.

6   Reflections on Common Sense and Judgment by Arendt

Many of Arendt's assertions regarding the common world are made in the milieu of taking into consideration reasonableness or *sensus communis*, a shared understanding of the world. She originally presented the topic as a preliminary solution to the question of which loss pulls people away from the conjoint world and how this process works, which has been largely disregarded in scholarship on Arendt's explanation of judgment. Arendt discovered that good judgment is linked to our perception of the real, and that its action is in opposition to authoritarian ideological thought. Common sense is inductive and intersubjective in operation (Arendt, 2010, p. 44). In contrast to philosophical thought, common sense discoveries are deduced from sensory experience inductively.

The bedrock of political understanding is common sense, which is intimately linked to feeling and is always in touch with the real world. Intersubjectivity is another crucial aspect of common sense, because it cannot function without the presence of others. Private senses are coordinated by common sense to create a single reality and to change the utter subjectivity and partiality of these sensations into intersubjectivity, but without establishing objective knowledge by Archimedean standards. It is stated at this point that horse sense has both a world-building and a world-disclosing impact, allowing us to make sense of reality. It also has an integrative effect, fitting us into a common reality by merging our five senses. The significance of the notion of common sense in Arendt's views on judgment is one of the most contentious questions in Arendt studies. Is it an a priori or empirical notion? When one considers Arendt's hermeneutic-phenomenological foundation, as the disquisition claims, it becomes clear that realism is not an a priori faculty nor does it refer to a specific society, but rather is co-original with the common world. Common sense assumes that there is a common reality and that humans fit into it.

7 Civic Friendship and Politics of Friendship via Political-Philosophical Debate

The point of departure is that, while Arendt and Derrida are critical of the prevalent conception of community, they do not reject community in its entirety (Habermas, 1984). Similarly, Arendt and Derrida resist communitarian concepts of community, which they associate with the classical figure of brotherhood. Both, on the other hand, are opposed to extreme individualism. For both, the issue of community boils down to how to construct a civic tie or political being together that isn't reducible to the communitarian conception of community, or, to be more specific, brotherhood. Both point to a specific vision of friendship as a viable alternative. Aside from critiquing classical philosophical assumptions about politics, particular political developments, particularly the rising influence of nationalistic and other quasi-naturalist beliefs on the general definition of political community, have prompted them to reconsider political community.

Following a thorough examination of their respective viewpoints on civic friendship, we arrive to the inference that for Derrida, the political community, the non-communitarian friendship, is always 'yet to come.' As a result, the community is elevated to a higher plane since it will emerge from outside our shared human and civic existence. As a result, it is "worldless" in the Arendtian sense. Arendt is unconvinced by such messianism. Friendship in the

Arendtian sense is focused toward the preservation of the common reality that exists between us and is the result of our shared action and speech in regard to that world. Only when citizens exhibit their multiplicity of viewpoints and opinions in public space does a political, non-natural, non-homogenous, but pluralistic society arise. Its goal is to bring to life the multitude and diversity of different views in order to create a common universe. This is exactly what happens in a friendly conversation. The prevalent conception of community, as well as the 'coming community,' do not reflect this common world.

In Arendt's terminology, the visible or civic quality of the intersubjective universe is the space of appearances. Arendt's anthropological concern on appearance and visibility stems from a deconstruction of metaphysical two-world conceptions that prioritize Being above appearance. Arendt's political prioritization of appearance and visibility suggests a political strategy that prioritizes action and speech in public space, to be precise, civic involvement. It is based on a phenomenological examination of the pre-totalitarian experience of expulsion from the public realm and annihilation of private spaces.

Arendt's phenomenological and moral distinction between the private and public spheres, on the one hand, and the social and political spheres, on the other, as distinct but connected dimensions, is characteristic of her theory of the space of appearances. These distinctions give a framework for distinguishing between good and bad kinds of visibility and invisibility, namely, politically sound or suitable forms of in/visibility that are conducive to human dignity from those that are politically destructive and anti-human dignity (Bradshaw, 1989, p. 13).

In terms of participation and citizenship, Arendt sees public visibility and private or natural invisibility as two sides of the same coin of good political action. Citizens require more than just natural quality protection through the private personality that the private sphere allows. Even in the public domain, citizens require additional concealing of their natural features through legal personhood, which Arendt compares to a mask that hides an actor's face on stage while revealing and amplifying his or her unique voice. This cliché is invoked by Arendt in order to shed light on citizenship's false, created aspect. Men-as-citizens, not natural men, should become apparent in public spaces. The paradox of citizenship refers to the idea that disclosing and hiding, or disclosure and closure, appear to be diametrically opposed but, upon closer examination, are two sides of the same coin. We demonstrate that the mask's function is not to conceal up social man, that is, membership in a social group, such as women or Jews, but natural man, that is, membership in the human species, by critically analyzing two feminist readings of Arendt's mask.

8 Public Invisibility, Private Visibility and Social In/Visibility

The diseases demand special attention because they demonstrate why public exposure and natural invisibility are key features of politics. Throughout her work, Arendt emphasizes that public inconspicuousness is the spot-on spitefulness of a number of undesirable political and social situations, such as poverty, slavery, displacement, and incarceration in concentration camps for it divests folks of the aptitude to live a noteworthy existence (Buckler, 2011, p. 26). These people are denied the ability to express themselves through actions and words, to be seen by others, and to be recognized as individuals with unique biographies. The disorders are linked, just as public exposure and private concealment are. Similarly, to how public transparency and private life protection promote participation, obscurity and exposure prevent involvement. As a result, both are politically unfavorable situations. Public invisibility is pathological because, without access to a public area, the natural man's private domain hiding becomes obscurity.

Natural visibility is just as harmful to political action and citizenship as artificial visibility. When one loses the ability to retreat behind invisibility and the mask of legal personhood, disclosure of who one is, whether a political actor or a citizen, gives way to disclosure of what one is to the public eye, natural man, who is no longer able to participate. To acquire recognition and participation, it is necessary to make a public display of who one is. Exposure, on the other hand, is passive and so non-participatory, and thus has little to do with public relations. Both disorders cause blindness, either as a result of too much light in the case of exposure or too little light in the case of obscurity. Obscurity and exposure are pathological modes of in/visibility because they are crippling and disempowering conditions that lead the paradox of citizenship, i.e., revelation and concealment, to break down.

The disclosure of who is replaced by the exposure of what people are in the absence of both the protection and security of the private sphere and legal personhood. The destiny of stateless people, for example, exemplifies this. Arendt's thoughts on stateless aliens in interwar Europe in the 1940s and early 1950s reveal that the stateless' dilemma involves the simultaneity of both diseases of political engagement and citizenship, namely, obscurity and exposure. As she is unable to participate in public space, the stateless refugee is the model non-citizen, the polar opposite of a citizen in every way. For starters, she has been stripped of her legal individuality as well as her ability to express herself in the realm of appearances through words and deeds, rendering her publicly invisible. Second, because she is vulnerable to naturalistic reduction, specifically, organic life reduction, she is destined to natural visibility. We believe that Arendt's critical deconstructions necessitate a reconsideration of the Enlightenment's human rights language, which is central to political involvement.

Exclusion, dominance, and exploitation of groups are frequently diagnosed in terms of social invisibility, and their solutions are typically formulated in terms of social visibility. The term "social invisibility" relates to social injustice and inequality along two axes: a socio-economic axis, which includes redistribution, and a socio-cultural axis, which includes acknowledgment. Identity politics, the demand of disadvantaged groups for acknowledgement of their distinctive group identity, the same ground on which recognition had previously been denied, rather than their inclusion in some universal common humanity, is the most well-known manifestation of the struggle for recognition. On these issues, we advocate for an alternate Arendtian viewpoint. We take inspiration for this alternate option from Arendt's council-model of political activity. Although Arendt recognizes that communal identities can be politically significant, she diagnoses exclusion as political invisibility rather than social invisibility (Arendt, 1970, p. 23). She then proposes a struggle for political rather than social exposure as a method for emancipation or empowerment, to be precise, for participation, political equality, empowerment, and freedom. We use four social movements and their related social conflicts, modes of social invisibility, and struggles to illustrate the issue of social, respectively political invisibility: poverty, the labor movement, and its contemporary twin, the alter-globalization movement (the 'social question') in the case of redistribution politics; and racism and the black civil rights movement (the 'race question') in the case of race politics.

Human dignity, according to Arendt, cannot be achieved alone through achieving social visibility and justice; it also necessitates the freedom to participate. Political freedom, according to Arendt, comprises the right to be seen and heard in the world, that is to say, access to the space of appearances. As a result, she sees the injustices that exist in the lives of the (very) poor, slaves, and other marginalized groups in political terms rather than socio-economic or socio-cultural grounds. This necessitates the use of a *Gestaltswitch* (Canovan, 1992, p. 25). A problem may have both a freedom and a justice dimension to it. The social and the political are best understood as two dimensions that are intricately intertwined in reality but are only intellectually distinct. We suggest that Arendt's divisive social-political difference is actually a phenomenological clarification that helps us to distinguish between social and political elements of the same problem, conflict, or event. Problems are neither social nor political in and of themselves, but they can appear to be either depending on one's perspective. The divide between the social and the political, as well as the ensuing struggle for political visibility, are crucial because, according to Arendt, the political itself, and hence political freedom, is at stake.

9 Conclusion

Having looked at Arendt's phenomenology of politics, it has been realized that the operations of this methodology could apply in so many realms of society and since politics is one such core sphere, it becomes incumbent upon philosophers to take centre-stage in making it efficacious. Arendt's contributions could not flourish as far as political philosophy is concerned were it not that she had utilised phenomenology in explicating her ideas in the realm herein referred. Consequently, phenomenology becomes a requisite tool in human political existence.

References

Arendt, H. (1959). Reflections on Little Rock. In *Responsibility and Judgement*. Schocken.
Arendt, H. (1960). Freedom and politics. *Chicago Review*, 14(1), 28–46.
Arendt, H. (1960). *Vita Activa*. Kohlhammer.
Arendt, H. (1961). What is Freedom? In *Between Past and Future*. Penguin Books.
Arendt, H. (1961). Freedom and Politics. In *Freedom and Serfdom*. Edited by Albert Hunold. D. Reidel & Co.
Arendt, H. (1968). *Between Past and Future: Eight Exercises in Political Thought*. Penguin.
Arendt, H. (1970). *Civil Disobedience*. Schocken.
Arendt, H. (1970). *On Violence*. A Harvest Book, Harcourt Brace Jovanovich, Publishers.
Arendt, H. (1972). *Crises of the Republic*. A Harvest Book, Harcourt Brace and Company.
Arendt, H. (1973). *Men in Dark Times*. Penguin.
Arendt, H. (1977). *Willing*. Harcourt.
Arendt, H. (1979). *The Origins of Totalitarianism*. Harcourt Brace & Co.
Arendt, H. (1979). *The Recovery of the Public World*. St Martin's.
Arendt, H. (1982). *The Life of the Mind*. Chicago University Press.
Arendt, H. (1992). *Karl Jaspers Correspondence 1926–1969*. Edited by Lotte Kohler and Hans Saner. Harcourt Brace & Company.
Arendt, H. (1992). *Lectures on Kant's Political Philosophy*. The University of Chicago Press.
Arendt, H. (1994). *The Nation*. Harcourt Bruce & Co.
Arendt, H. (1996). *Love and Saint Augustine*. Edited by Joanna Vecchiarelli Scott and Judith C. Stark. University of Chicago Press.
Arendt, H. (1998). *The Human Condition*. The University of Chicago Press.

Arendt, H. (2000). *The Portable Hannah Arendt*. Penguin Books.

Arendt, H. (1993). Personal Responsibility under Dictatorships. In *Responsibility and Judgement*. Schocken.

Arendt, H. (2003). Some Questions of Moral Philosophy. In *Responsibility and Judgment*. Schocken Books.

Arendt, H. (2003). *Elemente und Ursprunge Totaler Herrschaft Antisemitismus, Lmperialismus, Totale Herrschaft*. Piper.

Arendt, H. (2003). *Responsibility and Judgement*. Schocken Books.

Arendt, H. (2006). *On Revolution*. Penguin Books.

Arendt, H. (2010). *Thinking in Dark Times: Hannah Arendt on Ethics and Politics*. Fordham University Press.

Buckler, S. (2011). *Hannah Arendt and Political Theory: Challenging the Tradition*. Edinburgh University Press.

Canovan, M. (1992). *Hannah Arendt: a Reinterpretation of her Political thought*. Cambridge University Press.

Habermas, J. (1984). *The Theory of Communicative Action: Reason and the Rationalization of Society*, Vol. One. Trans. by Thomas McCarthy. Beacon Press.

Locke, J. (1690). *Two Treatises of Government*. Awnsham Churchill.

Rousseau, J.J. (1923). *The Social Contract*, Book IV, Ch. 14. J. M. Dent and Sons.

Sommerville, P. J. (1992). *Thomas Hobbes: Political Ideas in Historical context*. Red Globe Press.

Stangneth, B. (2014). *Eichmann before Jerusalem: the Unexamined Life of a Mass Murderer*. Knopf.

Index

accountability   13, 47, 147, 148
Aeta   215, 216, 217, 218, 219, 220, 221
African Union   192
Afro-pessimist methodology   100, 112, 114, 115, 116, 117, 118
agency   151, 186, 217, 219, 235, 240, 251, 272
ahistorical   13, 137
anti-blackness   11, 12, 19, 125, 126, 128
anti-colonialism   162
anti-oppression   136, 142–145, 152, 161
Arendt   272, 273, 275, 277, 278
Arendtian phenomenology   269
axiology   94

Bachelor of Social Work (BSW)   136
Baithak   149
bio-power   14
Black, chokehold   124
Black, death   125, 127
Black, epistemological death   127
Black, life   3, 127
Bridging gaps   264
Butler   15

Cathexis report   165, 166
civilian military cooperation (CIMIC)   203
climate change   204
colonial, violence   3, 30, 104
Community Action Research   76
Community Adversary Action Community (CAAC)   148
conceptualize   195, 228, 251
Constructivist Grounded Theory   24
Continental Early Warning System (CEWS)   193
critical reflexivity   28, 90, 257

Derrida   278
direct rule   101

economic implement   105
ethical dilemma   199
ethical framework   89

facticity   43

Floyd, George   122
Foucault   24

global emissions   12
grounded theory   24, 30, 247

hidden homelessness   258

indirect rule   101
industrialization   105
institutional ethnography   34, 37n

Kipande tag system   106
knowledge production   215, 222, 271
Komagata Maru   182

Lacanian mirroring   90
Levinas, Emanuel   90

marginalized   79
Marxist theorizing   57
Mbembe   104
methodological conception   127
miasma   11
Miller   72, 79
Ministry of Advanced Education and Skill Development (MAESP)   165
mixed methods   71

neo-colonial   147
newcomer   185
New Program Management (NPM)   163

objectification   11, 118

para-ethics   88
parrhesian   38, 39n
pathological misnomer   11
policy development   233, 237
profit-maxim   18, 130
pseudo   50
psychic amputation   179

radicalization   203
rainbow methodology   12

reciprocity   147
recursive loop   37–40
reflexivity   28, 34
Research Ethics Board (REB)   256
right giving   92
Rwanda genocide   196
Rwanda Patriotic Front (RPF)   200

saviour mentality   93–100
self-cannibalization   25, 98
slave labour   103
Smith, Dorothy   2
snowball sampling   166, 263
social, death   100
social, excess   25, 107, 114, 123
social, genocide   10, 24
social, policy   228
social, prisons   99
state sanctioned   10
Statistical Package for the Social Sciences (SPSS)   126
statistical surplus   11

status quo   162, 179, 180, 236
subterranean   1

tabula rasa   3, 98
theoretical analysis   57
thingification   1, 10
totalitarianism   270, 272, 275
traditional qualitative   74, 82
transcribing   262
Tuchman   44
Tuskegee experiment   11, 14

United Nations Security Council (UNSC)   191, 206

value gap   95
Van Der Mulen   75–76

Whitening   13
White supremacy   176, 178, 180
White truth   9

www.ingramcontent.com/pod-product-compliance
Lightning Source LLC
Chambersburg PA
CBHW070613030426
42337CB00020B/3776